T0333562

Braintenance

Brain tenance

A scientific guide to creating healthy habits and reaching your goals

Dr Julia Ravey

MACMILLAN

First published 2023 by Macmillan
an imprint of Pan Macmillan
The Smithson, 6 Briset Street, London EC1M 5NR
EU representative: Macmillan Publishers Ireland Ltd, 1st Floor,
The Liffey Trust Centre, 117–126 Sheriff Street Upper,
Dublin 1, D01 YC43
Associated companies throughout the world
www.panmacmillan.com

ISBN 978-1-5290-8005-6

1 3 5 7 9 8 6 4 2

A CIP catalogue record for this book is available from the British Library.

Illustrations by Julia Ravey

Typeset in Warnock by Jouve (UK), Milton Keynes
Printed and bound by CPI Group (UK) Ltd, Croydon, CR0 4YY

Visit **www.panmacmillan.com** to read more about all our books
and to buy them. You will also find features, author interviews and
news of any author events, and you can sign up for e-newsletters
so that you're always first to hear about our new releases.

CONTENTS

INTRODUCTION

Your brain likes to keep you safely in your comfort zone.

And that is what holds you back.

When it comes to thinking about our life-long ambitions, our biggest goals and wildest dreams, we have little trouble envisioning what we want. A house on the beach, a healthier lifestyle, a supportive partner, a creative career. If you close your eyes and think about achieving what you most desire, you may feel a lightness in your body and a tingle of excitement at your core. Your self-belief starts to rise and the motivation to make your goal a reality gathers pace. You start to think about how tomorrow, or Monday, or next month, or next year, you will take the action required – no matter how much hard work it takes – to achieve your mission. A game plan is agreed upon and an imaginary pact signed. With all the energy you feel in this moment, you believe this time is different. And nothing will stand in your way.

The problems all seem to appear when we stop thinking and start doing.

The first few days or weeks after pledging allegiance to your new life are great. You feel alive and on track, contentedly ticking off tasks that should make your dream situation materialize. But then, something changes. You begin to slow down. You get tired. You justify skipping one day because you have a lot on or you're just not in the mood. Besides, going off schedule once won't hurt your progress, right? Sadly, this is when one missed day can turn into two, three, four, until suddenly, the routine you had begun building has been replaced with the one that previously dominated your life. The heaviness and guilt associated with 'giving up' prevents you from giving it another go. Or maybe the lack of results from your new endeavours is what grinds your mission to a halt. Or maybe 'life happens' and you chastise yourself for thinking you could fit in time to devote to anything other than your current responsibilities. You pack your dreams back into a box in your head for a while, promising that when the time is right, you will let them out again.

The above situation is an exact replica of what happened to me over and over again when it came to trying to change elements of my routine. I would get overly excited at the prospect of making my goal happen but then mentally struggle when trying to actualize it. The sense of discomfort and effort – which I would always fail to include in my grand plans – would knock my confidence and drive until I gave in to the resistance and let life take the reins. It wasn't until I was trying to forge my career that I really thought about the repetitive nature of my goal-seeking-turned-goal-avoiding behaviours. I pictured myself working in a role that was completely different from the direction I was currently taking, which dredged up all sorts of internal pushback. But this time, I knew I had to weather the storms of change. And in order to face the obstacles ahead, I armed myself with the strongest skill I had: neuroscience.

I started studying the brain when I was nineteen years old, and now, many years later, having completed my PhD in neuroscience, I am still continually wowed by how this organ operates. As a scientist, my job was to tackle problems with curiosity to try to figure out how things happen. What makes brain cells die in Alzheimer's disease? How do our brains remember song lyrics but not information for exams? Why did that experiment fail again? When I awoke to my inability to persevere with a goal, I decided to apply this scientific way of thinking to my personal situation. Why is it that whenever I try to breach the boundaries of my comfort zone I crumble? What makes me hide when things don't go my way? What is this feeling of resistance that arises when I try to push forward with the things I really want?

By going through the basics of how we think the brain works and reviewing new neuroscience- and psychology-based research, I started to see potential reasons for my setbacks. And it was enlightening. Not only was science helping me get a grasp on these queries, but it presented me with ideas for how to keep on keeping on. Using what is currently understood about the brain and the way we behave, I came up with and adapted methods that should enable making achieving goals easier, which helped me make strides towards targets that felt unreachable before. And these methods are exactly what I am sharing with you in this book.

At present, you likely have contrasting ideas about your goals. On the one hand, there is that little voice in your head telling you how capable you are, and on the other, you sense a deep resistance to breaking the status quo you've settled in to. Like a constant tug of war between wanting to change versus your engrained routines and habitual behaviours. And nine times out of ten, those strong, deep-rooted defaults win. This manifests as ordering the pizza after promising to eat healthy food, snoozing the 7 a.m. alarm and skipping the gym after vowing to work out every morning, stopping content creation after making a pact to persist, or scrolling through social media when sat with loved ones despite claiming to give your full attention to those around you. It isn't that we don't want to change, it is just that the power of our brain's intention over how we spend our time is underestimated.

Every day, we are interpreting and assigning meaning to ongoing events in the world via our individually tailored brain networks. Shaped by our genetics and lived experiences, these networks provide us with options for how to respond and react to the situations we face. And altering our responses often requires conscious redirection.

How the brain is constructed means we rarely approach any situation with 'fresh eyes'. We pass new information through our bank of past knowledge to find an appropriate reaction or feeling that has served similar situations in the past. This can lead to repetitive behavioural patterns, thoughts and emotional responses as the brain attempts to use what it already has stored to solve the problems we are facing. Although we like to feel in complete control of how we act, rapid, automatic-like defaults can influence outcomes. And these strong yet near-silent instructions present a huge hindrance to our ability to change.

When it comes to change, our brains are hypocrites. Like that person who outwardly claims they haven't done any studying for an exam while beavering away behind closed doors, our brains may act like they hate change, but they are constantly evolving. Our brain's internal wiring is not fixed, and everyday experiences, events and interactions can alter its connections. However, when trying to make significant lifestyle or behaviour changes, the brain appears to resist; acting as if it is incapable of truly altering its ways. Persistence and passion can break through this facade, but only if we give them a proper shot.

A mistake many of us make in pursuit of our goals is too much too soon. When riding the highs of the motivation wave that can accompany the initial stage of our quest for change, we think we can do it all. We set our morning alarms two hours earlier, eat thirty types of fruit and veg in a week, work fifty hours on our side project, or give up our evenings to study. All at the same time. Trying to get the brain to deviate so much from its norm in one go is a challenge. If goal pursuit is like trying to make a toddler eat vegetables, many of us stick a huge plate of greens in front of the child, remove everything else they know from the menu and expect them to tuck in happily. How do you think a toddler would respond in this situation? Most likely, they would kick, scream, throw and cry until you have no choice but to feed them what they want. Lots of change all at once is a recipe for defeat.

Instead of giving our brain a plate piled high with unfamiliars and unknowns, a more effective means of getting it to eat up is a 'little and often' approach. If we want a toddler to eat more vegetables, a bit of trickery is in order. Start off small and increase their exposure to the taste over time. Adding a bit of chopped broccoli into their pasta sauce, softened carrots into their stew and a few peas mixed into their mashed potato. Over time, you can try adding small chunks of green to the side of their plate and eventually build up to the big portions that are so good for them. Increasing the toddler's tolerance slowly gets you to the desired result with far fewer tantrums. To reach our goals, our brain needs to be treated the same way – give it bitesize, digestible actions to promote drama-free behavioural change. This book will provide ways to break down any big goal, remove the histrionics and allow for a smoother transition to the change you want to see.

Goal pursuit is often glamorized, but it is a challenging process. Like an Instagram feed of a person travelling the world in a van, the amazing images of scenery and adventure is how we picture the journey towards our goals. But what we don't see – the behind-the-scenes of getting lost, fixing tyres and being exhausted (which occupies a good chunk of travel time) – is disregarded from our considerations. That can be why when we hit the road expecting a picture-perfect experience, it can be a shock to the system when we don't feel serene and relaxed with every mile travelled.

But the journey is actually what it is all about. The goal is what we aim for, the ideal end destination. When you eventually reach your target, how boring would it be to suddenly stop doing all the things that got you there? Don't just think about what you want to achieve, but the day-to-day routine of what you want to be doing with your life when you reach that goal. Would it be satisfying to just sit around and look at what you've accomplished? No! You want to be working on what you love. An athlete who wins a gold medal does not stop practising their sport after doing so. An actor who wins an Academy Award does not stop acting after achieving their accolade. A football team that wins the league does not stop playing because they have won the cup. It is an interesting mindset shift to think of your goal not as the achievement itself but in terms of the lifestyle changes the achievement requires.

In order to choose the changes you want to make in your life, it can be useful to think about what your ideal 'average' working day would be. If you have a clear idea of what that day consists of, from the time you'd wake up, to the work you'd do, to who you'd spend it with, you can start creating goals that will steer you in this fulfilling direction. While this serves as a useful exercise for goal-setting, it is also empowering. There will be aspects of this 'ideal day' that you are already doing or could quite easily introduce, meaning you can start to build routines that fit in with some of your goals right away. With new or unfamiliar actions, more effort needs to be invested and a solid plan laid. Using the exercises outlined in the pages of this book, you will develop a brain-backed blueprint for integrating these larger lifestyle alterations one small step at a time and feel confident about exactly how to implement these changes.

Before setting out on any journey, taking time to understand what to expect along the way will put you in better stead en route. Preparing for all eventualities so you can keep pushing forward is a key skill for thriving in the face of adversity. Before military operations, commanders put their troops through intense training exercises involving many different scenarios to enable them to think and react if any of these events were to arise on their mission. Mapping out potential problems and training hard gives people the best chance of success.

When it comes to setting ourselves a target, we may sometimes have a rough plan of action, and most of us stop there. We have the goal, we have the plan; all we have to do is execute it, right? In one sense, yes. But what many of us underestimate about the execution is the resistance the brain will throw up in the face of moving beyond our comfort zone. Being mentally unprepared for goal pursuit – no matter how water-tight the plan is – can threaten to sabotage the mission completely. What I propose is that understanding more about how we think the human brain operates, why we act the way we do, and how the brain changes, can provide some of this pre-match mental training. Breaking down the inner workings of our brains from a neuroscientific and psychological perspective can help us identify unhelpful patterns of behaviour which may be holding us back, allow us to question our defaults, and create new routines which will be essential to progress.

When it comes to changing our behaviours, having a thorough assessment of where we're currently at and where we would like to go can help assign the tools needed to get there. Like checking a car before a long journey, the person assessing the vehicle needs to know how the car works to identify any issues, before fixing it and keeping it running on the road. Following this theme, *Braintenance* is broken down into four sections: mechanics, mastery, methods and maintenance.

Mechanics describes some of our basic understandings about the nuts and bolts of the brain and how these components work together to generate our behaviours, our ability to change and why we strive for more. Mastery provides the ability to identify some beliefs and behaviours that may be preventing change, uncovering what it is you actually want, fine-tuning focus and establishing identity in your goal pursuit. Methods gives solutions for how to approach goal pursuit in order to alter processes, reward effort, plan ahead and foster self-belief. And finally, maintenance is all about keeping our vehicle functional on the road – with ways to stay on track in the face of procrastination, lack of motivation and pushback, while prioritizing rest. Together, these chapters aim to help you get to know your brain better, and that knowledge can be used to recognize what is going on under the hood when you hit a bump in the road. You will have a bank of techniques to deploy to keep you moving forward, one inch at a time.

Through use of analogies and stories mixed in with science explainers, the mechanics section enables the visualization of neuroscientific processes so you can get your brain bearings. For the mastery, methods and maintenance sections, all chapters are organized as 'Why–Sci–Apply' – **why** this topic is important; the **science** behind it; and some exercises based on what we know to **apply** to your life. You may be more keen on the why, fascinated by the sci, or here for the apply, so you can easily navigate to the aspects you most enjoy by following these subheadings throughout the book. The exercises are a mix of things to think about and actions to take with examples throughout. If writing is more your style, grab a notebook and pen to jot along as you read.

One thing I want to emphasize before we crack on is that this book is not about manifesting your dream life. It does not rely on you believing in a greater power to work its magic and make things happen for you. Whatever floats your boat on the belief front – be that religious, spiritual, humanist, atheist, agnostic or indifferent – the upcoming exercises will help your quest. My main aim is to empower you to strive towards your goals with the knowledge that you are capable of change and to help you fully believe in yourself by realizing this power. Sadly, societal systems mean some people have a steeper hill to climb when pursuing goals, and it is damaging to even suggest all responsibility lies with the individual. But this book should help with taking control of the little things you can and using them to move you in the direction of joy and fulfilment. At the end of the day, if you achieve a goal, big or small, you need to thank yourself. Because you did the work. And you need to give yourself the credit.

A final note. Neuroscience is by no means 'complete', and this book is definitely not an attempt to explain all the nuances of how the brain potentially works. There is so much about our brains we still do not understand and there are many gaps regarding its effect on our behaviour. What I will do is give you an overview of what we know about certain processes, some idea of how these concepts may connect and the exercises that I have found helpful for goal pursuit. No doubt in years to come, our knowledge will advance and we will be closer to the 'big' answers we crave. But for now, we can work with the advancements we have already made to make setting and getting goals more efficient. Also, some scientific studies have been touched on to illustrate how we think our brains work, and while some studies are stronger than others, it is important to recognize they all come with their caveats. Small sample sizes, self-assessed measurements, publication bias, cherry-picking data, test models, lack of diversity among recruited participants and neurotypical selection are some aspects that can weaken conclusions. Some of these issues are hinted at, and beyond this book, I will continue to share advancements in brain research as they are published.

Your brain is amazing, and by using our current understanding of neuroscience and psychology, we can craft real change in our lives.

Knowledge is power. Let's charge up.

Mechanics

CHAPTER 1

MEET YOUR MIND

Before jumping into why we behave the way we do, how we establish routines and resist changing them, a bit of demystifying about the human brain is in order.

We often think about our brains as an all-powerful, all-controlling master. We use our brain's outputs to define who we are: interpreting information, processing feelings and directing action. While these are incredibly important jobs, ultimately our brain is an organ, like a heart, or a lung, or a kidney. By framing these outcomes as a consequence of having a functioning brain instead of being 'who we are', we can gain perspective on our own behaviours. Like a heart pumping blood or a lung exchanging oxygen, our brains think. Holding a magnifying glass up to the brain and looking closely at how it works does two things: (1) it breaks down the facade of the brain being a magical master we are at the mercy of, and (2) it allows us to appreciate just how amazing this organ is.

These two objectives may appear contradictory, that the aim of unpicking the science behind how the brain works is to dismiss it as nothing special. That is definitely not the case. What we are trying to do is remove some of the emotional significance we assign to the outcomes of our brain's functioning while also being able to step back and admire its operations. If we take our heart, these two viewpoints exist simultaneously. Our heart beats without conscious direction to supply blood to our muscles and tissues, giving them power to work, while directing blood without oxygen back to the lungs for a fuel refill. Pretty awe-inspiring stuff. At the same time, we don't think about our heart as controlling; we don't judge it for doing what it is meant to, and we don't let its activity define our worth. This is the outlook we want when thinking about our brain: non-judging yet wowed by the jobs it does.

FIRST, LET'S MEET YOUR BRAIN . . .

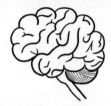

From the outside, it may not look like much. Just a wrinkly lump of tissue. But within these grooves, some of the most complex facets of humanity are constructed. World-changing ideas, dangerous ideologies, hallucinations, visualizations, the ability to feel love, the deep sadness of heartbreak and the awareness that we exist in this impermanent world yet act as if we have time to kill. It is incredible to think that potentially the most complex machinery to exist in the entire universe is sitting between your ears. By boiling down the brain to its smallest components and assessing how these work, we may be able to crack some of the biggest questions about the human species, including how we set and get goals.

NEUR-ON MY MIND

Mo Gawdat, the author of *Solve for Happy,* has described thinking as biological matter, the by-product of a working brain. And as a metaphor, this is pretty spot on. 'Thinking' is what our brain has been designed to do to help us survive – to solve problems, adapt to situations, avoid threats and plan for the future. Our thoughts are generated by chatter between brain cells called neurons, which exist in their billions in our heads. And their unique features allow them to speedily communicate with each other.

All the cells in our body come from an identical ball of cells which form after a sperm and egg fuse. When a cell becomes a neuron, it undergoes a dramatic transformation. The round, non-descript-looking cell sprouts branches at one end and a trunk at the other, like a tree. As time goes by, these branching networks can grow to become more and more complex, with tiny twigs and buds creating an intricate web of connections. The trunk, called an axon, also evolves, laying many roots which can spread far and wide. These branches and roots make up the connection points for a neuron, allowing it to contact others and pass on important messages.

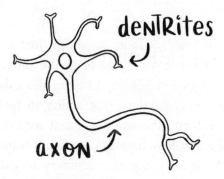

The branches of a neuron are called dendrites. These help to filter incoming information, ensuring only important messages get through. Like a busy CEO receiving a constant flood of demands, requests and questions, the dendrites act like a personal assistant to the neuron, only passing on messages that really matter.

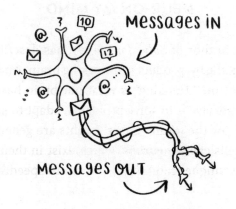

The messages that hit the 'importance threshold' trigger the neuron to relay this information to its networks. This is done using the cell's axon. The axon of a neuron can connect to thousands of others via its roots, forming junctions called synapses between a sending and receiving neuron. And we think our WhatsApp notifications can get too much.

Billions of neurons are generated within months following conception, and once made, they stay. Unlike the cells in our skin or our liver, neurons are not able to replace themselves, and there are thought to be only a few pockets of cells in the brain that can add new neurons to the mix over a person's lifetime. Our neurons are extremely precious.

ELECTRIC DREAMS

Unlike the instant messages packed with emojis and gifs we send to our contacts, neurons communicate in very different ways. If we think of the brain as a city, the cells are like buildings: packed together with distinct boundaries between them to protect their internal contents from the outdoors. To operate effectively, very specific internal conditions need to be maintained, like an optimal working temperature in an office.

Each building contains a thermostat to maintain its rooms at the optimal level of warmth. If the front door opened – letting precious

warm air escape – the internal temperature can be quickly readjusted back to its optimum by the thermostat, keeping the building functional. Neurons use thermostat-like methods to ensure the balance of different molecules and chemicals remain optimal within their walls. And the movement of these entities in and out of their boundaries is how they chat.

Neuron chatter is at the core of understanding how our brains operate and how they are able to change. Neurons talk in two main languages: electrical and chemical. Just like the electricity that gives power to our kettles and battery to our devices, the electrical signals in the human brain are produced by the movement of charged particles. In fact, it is estimated the amount of electricity our brains run on could power an LED bulb (we quite literally have 'light bulb' moments).

When one neuron receives an important signal from another, charge floods inside, like powering up your phone. If this surge of incoming charge is big enough, the neuron prods its axon to pass it on. The charge flows down the axon like a cable to spread the message in signals called action potentials, and when these hit the synapse, this message can be passed on.

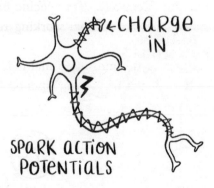

IT'S ALL IN THE CHEMICALS

A synapse between two neurons is a physical gap which uses a chemical 'lock-and-key' system to communicate. On the sending neuron's side of the synapse are bubbles packed with 'keys' called neurotransmitters.

And on the receiving neuron's side of the synapse sit 'locks' called receptors.

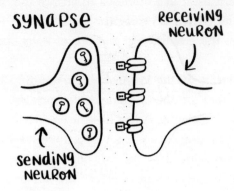

In order for a signalling neuron to pass on its message, it has to unlock the receiving neuron. Action potentials trigger the release of keys, with more signals in a row pushing more keys out towards the locks. Normally, the more action potentials, the more important a signal is, in a similar way to your phone continually ringing – this is usually a pretty good indicator somebody needs to tell you something ASAP.

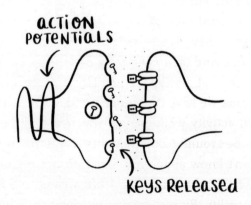

When the keys bind to the locks on the receiving cell, they open them up, creating little gateways into the cell to allow charge in. How much charge gets in depends on how many locks there are on the cell's boundary, and how many of them are open. The more open gateways, the bigger the incoming signal. Like ticket barriers at a train station – more open barriers allow higher numbers of people to get through to the platform at once.

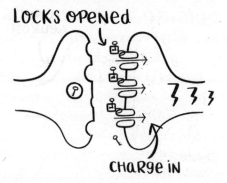

LOCKS OPENED

CHARGE IN

A large incoming signal can make the receiving neuron trigger action potentials in its own axon, and the entire process begins again – allowing signals to travel through the brain.

THINKING OUT LOUD

There are many different types of neuron in the human brain, which can be identified based on differences in their shape, the 'keys' they hold and the 'locks' they display, but their signalling methods are by-and-large the same. And their chattering underlies our thoughts.

It's still unclear what a 'thought' actually is in the brain, but it has been estimated that we have thousands per day. One study looking at changes in brain activity while people watched a film calculated this daily number to be around 6,000 thoughts – and that is only while we are awake![1] I don't know about you, but I do not register or remember thousands of thoughts each day. I often cling to a few and make them my entire reality. By recognizing we potentially have thousands of thoughts a day, we can see just how many of these go unnoticed or can be let go of. In this regard, thoughts can be defined as rapid responses that the brain generates to help us deal with situations and navigate the world. When put like that, our thoughts can seem much less consuming.

According to research, the most modern parts of our brain evolved a short 1.5–1.7 million years ago[2] and its latest hardware update was between 35,000 and 100,000 years ago.[3] In essence, that means we are living in the twenty-first century with a prehistoric machine processing our world. The brain exists in two halves, or hemispheres, splitting it into a right and a left side which talk to each other to coordinate each half of the body. These halves are almost mirror images, containing duplicates of many structures, but also possess some individual roles. Anatomy divides the large structures that make up the whole brain into three distinct parts: the brainstem, the cerebellum and the cerebral cortex.

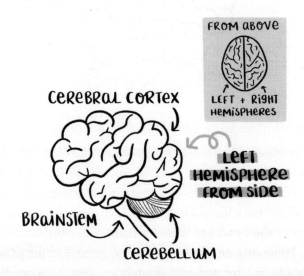

The brainstem is known to orchestrate our most essential functions automatically. This includes processes like breathing, heart rate and blood pressure control. Similar structures to our brainstem are found in creatures from the most complex mammals to the simplest insects, showing just how vital it is to life.

Then there's the cerebellum. This walnut-looking section of the brain has long been implicated in coordination of movement, as the cells within it provide updates between the brain and body, allowing tiny adjustments to muscle movements to keep us balanced. Although its role in motor commands stands strong, more recent work has indicated it may also influence how we think and feel.[4]

And finally, there is the cerebral cortex – the wrinkled 'hat' of the human brain. This section is thought to be the director of the functions that make us distinctly human. Due to its complexity and size, this part of the brain has been further split into four different lobes – mirrored on the right and left sides – based on some visible and some less visible boundaries, and roughly divided by function.

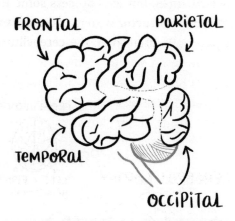

First up, there are the frontal lobes, which sit behind the forehead. These are the seat of some of our more complex behaviours, like planning for the future and decision-making, as well as directing voluntary movement of the muscles in our body. Next, the parietal lobes, found at the crown of the head, are where sensory information lands and is interpreted. Following on, the temporal lobes behind the ears contain structures important for processing what we hear, memory formation and emotional regulation. And finally, the occipital lobes right at the back of the head are, ironically, where we process what we see. All these brain regions are made up of neurons, and their activity coordinates this vast array of functions.

We have discovered which parts of the brain are responsible for various functions due to accidental damage, experimental tampering or observed activation in response to specific tasks. Damage to the prefrontal cortex – the area of the brain sitting right behind the eyes in the frontal cortex – resulted in reportedly temporary alterations to impulsiveness and inhibitory control in a man called Phineas Gage, after an iron bar penetrated his skull following an accidental explosion in 1848.[5] Additionally, people with certain types of dementia, where cells in this brain region are lost, can experience alterations to their personality. Surgical removal of brain tissue around the site of the hippocampus – a curved structure buried deep in the temporal lobes – from both sides of the brain of Henry Molaison, a person living with life-limiting epilepsy, prevented him forming new long-term memories.[6] And scaring participants during fear-inducing experimental set-ups consistently activates a brain region called the amygdala – an almond-shaped structure found next to the hippocampus.[7] Mapping functions based on how brain activity changes in response to an array of situations, and from how people or animal models behave without the full function of certain regions, has given us a better view of the 1,400 g wrinkled mass sitting in our skulls.

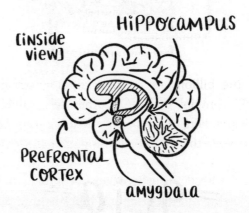

Mapping certain functions to specific brain regions has gone somewhat out of fashion, and instead, scientists now look at the brain more like a network of hubs that can interact with and influence each other. Although we can readily pinpoint locations in the brain associated with receiving information like what we see and what we hear, when we try to go beyond their receipt to their interpretation, many regions become involved. And when we start asking more complicated questions like 'what are memories?' and 'how do we make a choice?', the 'specific-regions-controlling-certain-functions' approach to neuroscience breaks down. Some brain areas – like the amygdala – are involved in multiple functions, and some functions – like making even a relatively simple decision – appear to involve multiple regions. While neurons within individual brain regions talk to each other, these cells can have connections that stretch beyond their home base to chat with cells in other regions, like tracks between train stations. These connections can vary in strength and be altered by experience, making networks in the human brain more dynamic than the staircases at Hogwarts.

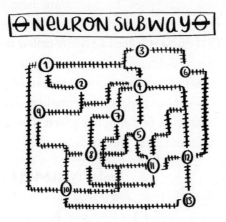

Aside from the billions of neurons zipping signals around our cortex, our brain contains billions of other cells called glia. Glia are considered the caretakers of the brain – helping to fight foreign bugs, getting good nutrients to cells and cleaning up neuron mess – and they

undoubtedly influence the hubbub of brain activity. Recognizing the brain as this complex, dynamic, interconnected web of cells is important when we picture our own brains and think about how we act on a day-to-day basis. Especially when we are trying to change how we behave. Nothing is ever a simple input/output situation. Everything passes through this complicated system which influences other thoughts, feelings and actions in ways that are sometimes obvious and sometimes more subtle (but just as important).

YOU MIGHT NEED SOME-BODY

As interconnected as the regions in our brains are to each other, the brain is also heavily influenced by another key connection: its one with the body. The brain is just one component in the suite of organs we need to keep us alive, and feedback from these other systems is important in telling the brain how we are doing as a whole. Like a head office wanting to know the state of the work on the ground, your brain receives signals from your body to let it know how everything is ticking along down there so it can adjust its strategy accordingly.

Knowing where your body is in reference to the space around you helps your brain prevent collisions with other objects or people. Protecting damaged areas after injury is ensured by your brain producing the sensation of pain. And deducing how you currently feel can be assessed by analysing feedback from internal signals like how quickly your heart is beating. Emotional states – which can heavily influence our ability to pursue a task in front of us – are a prime example of our brain–body connection.[8] Those anxious pre-presentation nerves, where we run through the 628 things that could go wrong in a ten-minute talk, can be felt in the body as stomach knots, sweaty palms and a racing pulse. Our interpretation of these sensations as 'WE ARE NERVOUS' can send our thinking into a tizz, which can lead us to become even more worried.

It is clear the state of our body influences our state of mind, but just how much continues to be investigated. We also know brain activity can even be influenced by non-human residents in our bodies, namely the trillions of microbes that inhabit our guts and help with jobs like digesting our food. The chemical messengers these organisms release can activate nerves around the gut to stimulate the brain, and the significance on how this activity can impact our brain's functioning is only just being recognized.[9]

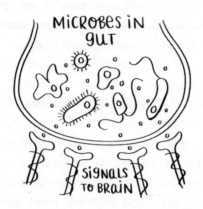

Seeing the brain as part of an entire system which can be influenced by how we treat the rest of our body provides us with an extended toolkit to gain some influence over how we feel. The connections between our bodily systems suggests that by looking after physical health and giving the body what it needs, we can impact our brain function, potentially helping us on our quest for change.

WHY'D YOU HAVE TO GO AND MAKE THINGS SO COMPLICATED?

When it comes to introducing the ins and outs of our brains, there is a lot we can say about how it operates. We have become really good at studying individual brain cells and their processes, which in turn allows us to understand how these cells may interact with others. However, the more we zoom out and try to answer big questions about how we function, the harder it is to say exactly how these individual units come together to make a living, feeling, complex human being. This is where it is useful to jump from the field of neuroscience, where we are concerned with unpicking the biological basis of the brain, across to psychology,

Psychology describes facets of human behaviour that we know exist, even if we don't exactly know the underpinnings of how they manifest. For example, phenomena in psychology like cognitive biases, which can lead us to make quick but poor decisions (we'd rather save £1 if something costs £5 over saving £5 when something costs £500), definitely exist, but the mechanics of how are still unclear. By using a combination of neuroscience- and psychology-based research, we can get a broader understanding of the human brain and our behaviour.

The gap between what we understand about the brain and know about our behaviour continues to persist as the brain's complexity may be too much for us to currently comprehend. We often compare our brains to computers, the most complex form of technology to ever exist, and still, this comparison doesn't stand. Unlike a computer, any information that enters the brain has the capacity to change its connections (more on this in Chapter 3), and due to the flexible, network-based way our brains are set up, we can never process information independently. Whereas a computer can objectively analyse and sort data, everything we interact with is passed through our unique filtering systems, leaving us with ideas which can feel right even if they may be completely wrong. The limitation of our own definition of 'advanced' is likely a critical barrier in truly understanding how our brains operate. This means that when considering processes we think may be involved with helping set and get goals, there will inevitably be some unknowns. And this can be frustrating. We crave clear, concise explanations – they appeal to our desire for order in a world of chaos. When it comes to neuroscience, we don't have all the perfect answers we seek. But what we do know so far can be used to more effectively pursue our goals.

WRAP UP

With its billions of neurons and their trillions of connections, operating in close-knit 'hubs' as well as communicating with cells in distant regions, we are just scratching the surface of how our brains truly work.

Seeing our brain as a complex network of chattering cells that generates our thoughts, emotions, interpretations and actions can be useful as we contextualize the events going on around us. Our brains make a lot of noise, and recognizing that this is normal can remove some of the significance we attach to our interpretations.

CHAPTER 2

ROOTS OF BEHAVIOUR

PUT YOUR BRAIN INTO A
WORLD OF UNKNOWNS . . .

If your brain was dropped onto an alien planet, what do you think it would need to survive? Of course, all the basics like water, food and shelter. But it would need another function, something a little bit less obvious but crucial to survival: to learn how the world it is living in operates.

Think of the human brain starting out as an unruly, wild hedge. All hedges have the same components but differ slightly in terms of shape, leaf type and branching structure. These fundamental foundations of our brain are laid down due to instructions in our genes, meaning the millions of years of human evolution plus specific traits from parents influence how we operate.

Once our brain is out in the world, the hedge trimmers start hacking. Depending on what influences the cutting, that hedge can be chopped and pruned into a variety of shapes. Our initial experiences and early life lessons are the strongest trimmers, allowing us to absorb what is going on around us and amend our connections to keep us safe. As adults, we go about our daily lives with our bear-, or dragon-, or swan-shaped hedges in our heads, acting under their direction. And although these hedges can change and adapt in adulthood, those early chops and cuts leave a lasting imprint.

WHAT DO YOU MEAN?

Like an interpreter, the brain detects signals – what we see, hear, smell – from our surroundings and assigns them meaning. These signals enter the brain through our sensing organs, like eyes and ears, in varying forms, like light and sound waves. Incoming signals are converted into our brain's language – electrical impulses – so we can process and interpret them.

How different signals are detected by the brain can be visualized by imagining a grand piano. Each incoming signal presses a different combination of keys to make a unique sound (or pattern). When these specific patterns are played, our brain's store of acquired knowledge and past experience linked to these combinations is activated, giving us a rough picture of what is going on and influencing how we act. If we see an apple, the combination of keys coding for this fruit may trigger associations such as 'food', 'sweet' and 'healthy', while also activating memories of your friend's infamous apple pie. And if you are feeling peckish, these signals may compel you to take a bite.

If the human brain applied for the job of 'main interpreter' to help us navigate our high-tech, structured, twenty-first-century world, it would have a tough time getting past the interview (more on this shortly). But tens of thousands of years ago, it excelled at this role. So much so that we became one of the most dominant species on the planet.

Up close, the human brain is very similar to those of other animals. Our cells operate in the same way – using electrical and chemical signals – and certain brain structures like the amygdala and hippocampus exist across multiple species. This means some of the processes that drive our behaviours exist in animals that don't have anywhere near our level of (as we define it) 'intellect'.

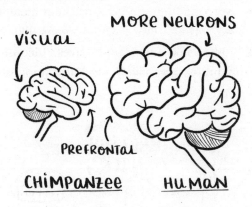

A key difference between the human brain and those of our closest living ancestors, like chimpanzees and bonobos, is thought to lie in our internal wiring. Certain regions of our brain like the prefrontal cortex and visual cortex are much larger compared to those of our ancestral cousins as the human areas contain more neurons. More neurons means more connections, massively increasing the number of keys on the grand piano keyboard, allowing for more advanced information processing because there are more brain patterns available.

You can also think of the brain like a railway network: each neuron is a station, with tracks coming in and out of a platform. If you have a rail network with only a few stations, the possible routes you can take between stops are limited. If you wanted to get from station A to station B, there are only a handful of ways to make that journey. By adding more stations and tracks to the network, the routes all of a sudden become much more complex, increasing the number of options to reach station B from station A. This heightened level of connectivity generates a more efficient system for processing passengers, and in the brain, this translates to being more efficient at processing information.

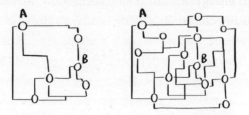

FEWER CONNECTIONS = FEWER ROUTES

The human brain has billions of stations, and many of these have thousands of connection points, quickly allowing the transmission of signals and facilitating new routes for connecting and interpreting information.

PREHISTORIC DRIVERS

Our brains evolved over millions of years, before humans as we know them today even existed. Evolution is often an extremely slow process. It relies on passing on changes to genes in our DNA code – the recipe book for how to make a human – to our offspring.

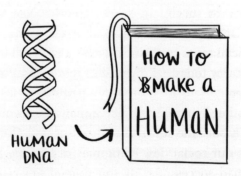

HUMAN
DNA

HOW TO
&MAKE a
HUMAN

This slow transfer of information means it can take years for traits which aren't useful to die out of a population and for those which are advantageous to spread. Like if one individual in a population randomly had a gene change – or mutation – which gave them Hercules-esque strength. This person might be better at hunting for food as they can more easily take down animals. Having more food could mean having more sex (both energy-wise and attracting more mates), which results in producing more children carrying the same Hercules gene mutation.

With each generation, these super-strong individuals will continue to succeed, having more and more kids until, over many generations, every person in the current tribe has superhero-like strength. This somewhat far-fetched example of evolution illustrates how individuals better suited to survive in an environment can take the limited resources available, making them more likely to reproduce and pass on their beneficial traits to the next generation. And many of the gene variations we carry today are a result of this painstakingly slow hand-me-down system.

Like most other living organisms, humans are motivated to pass on their genes to ensure the survival of their species. One of our survival mechanisms is our social ties. Being part of a group has been fundamental to human success. Living together meant safety in numbers, being able to gather more food, and share the load. Solo hunters will have likely been outcompeted by groups who shared what they had, allowing for more to survive and reproduce. Therefore, our genes today come from pools of people who cooperated with each other, and our brains continue to motivate us to be members of a group. It will celebrate when we are 'accepted', and many of our strongest emotions, like compassion, empathy, jealousy and rejection, only exist in relation to other people.

Another advantage we have sustained through evolution is our intelligence. Our ability to acquire extensive levels of knowledge and use it to make weird and wonderful connections between different events continually allows us to push the boundaries of what we know. Our intelligence also gave birth to a uniquely human trait: our imagination. We can think of things that have never happened before, using our past experiences and new information to make predictions about the future. These predictions have given us a survival advantage, as we can assess what might happen when faced with a certain situation, allowing us to forecast potential outcomes beforehand. Our overactive imagination may help us plan the steps we need to take to achieve a goal, but can also lead to overthinking, a mental state which can be debilitating for progress.

social   imagine   stories

Telling ourselves stories is a key mechanism that aided our advancement and continues to influence how we operate today. The way humans communicate is one of the starkest differences separating us from the rest of the animal kingdom. Complex language gave us the means to tell others about where food was or what danger lay ahead, build ties with other groups, and opened up our ability to construct narratives. Storytelling is still the most captivating way to receive information, with some of the most successful memory techniques having stories at their heart.[1] Ascribing words to objects and compiling information into sharable stories made it much easier to survive and thrive in a group. Also, crafting narratives about ourselves, our place in the world (mostly at the centre of everything) and our relationships to others through beliefs and biases is a key way we navigate our daily lives.

It's clear these ancient priorities still impact how we act, but the technicalities of how these skills came to be remains vague. Many tiny changes to our genetic codes over time may have made these behaviours slightly more likely to manifest, potentially by influencing brain structure and function. In any case, the drive to be accepted by others, our propensity to overthink in the face of a problem and feeling like we are the main character of our own story all seem to be by-products from our world domination.

SHAP(ING) OF YOU

We are constantly bombarded with information, and these signals are used to determine if an environment is safe, predict what might happen next and direct how we should act. When new signals are detected, they can be associated with previously acquired information to update our 'models' of how the world works, allowing us to carry on going about our business.

However, our brains are not born with these models set in stone. Rather, they are shaped through our experience, particularly during early years, childhood and adolescence. The human brain is not thought to be done with its development until age twenty-five. AGE TWENTY-FIVE!! Which is why, if you are beyond this age, you can look back and see a pretty stark difference in the way you acted at age eighteen – when we are legally classed as 'adults'– versus your mid-twenties (I *definitely* can). And if you are under twenty-five, it is good to keep in mind your brain may still be under construction (giving you the *best* excuse of 'my brain is still developing' to get out of doing something you don't think

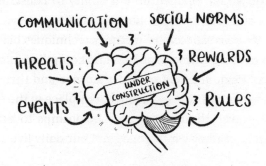

will benefit you). It's thought this extended developmental period has benefited us as a species because we are able to learn more about our environment – with all its threats and promises – and increase our chances of survival.

Before we are born, our brain's initial development is largely orchestrated by our genes, which provide the instructions for making every protein in the human body. In the earliest days of brain development, switching different genes on and off allows different proteins to mould the brain by generating neurons and guiding their movement. Initially, the brain contains an abundance of cells – spares if you like – to ensure the developing brain has everything it needs. But it undergoes a drastic trim down before we are born to produce a brain with roughly the same number of neurons (approximately 60–86 billion[2]) as we have today. Like building a house, this process is equivalent to laying strong and stable foundations.

Even though we are born with most of the neurons our adult brain contains, a baby's brain weighs about a quarter of one that is fully formed. This drastic increase in weight is thought to come from the expansion of neurons present at birth. Like saplings that grow into complex trees, these neurons extend their branches to connect with other neurons in local and far-reaching areas of the brain. This process is influenced by our experiences, with some dramatic changes happening in the brain all the way into young adulthood.

Firstly, there are changes in the number of synapses in the brain. These numbers peak in babies and gradually decline as connections are pruned away, like transforming an overgrown patch of plants into a neat garden. Experience helps the brain decide whether connections should be pruned or not. Connections that are used a lot get the green light, while the less-frequently-used ones are weeded out. Different brain areas are pruned at different times throughout this period, with the prefrontal cortex – housing complex functions like decision-making and inhibition – saved until last. This allows us to learn social cues from our peers and continue to shape our behaviours through experience in our teen years. It also explains why we can do some pretty wild things as teenagers which we wouldn't dream of doing now (thank you, disinhibition).

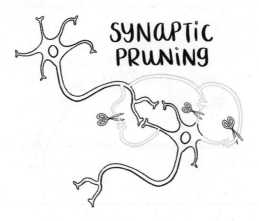

SYNAPTIC PRUNING

Another process that influences how neurons communicate is how quickly signals can be passed between them. Pathways that are important get a special 'wrapping' around their branches to speed up their signalling, and these speed limits are still being assigned far into early adulthood based on how often they are used. As well as structural changes, brain activity also shifts as we age. Early childhood activity is dominated by slow brain waves associated with deep learning,[3] allowing what is going on around us to be readily taken in and stored as 'this is how the world is'.

Our prolonged period of brain development is both a blessing and a curse. On the one hand, it means we can more finely tune our behaviours to adapt to the environment we live in, but on the other, it means early experiences can generate behaviours down the line which are no longer useful. That doesn't mean to say experiences after this developmental phase don't affect us (the amazing ability of the human brain to change irrespective of age is covered in the next chapter); it is more that during the shaping and modelling of the brain, we may be more susceptible to these influences and can continue with these no-longer-helpful default responses later in life. Early events or experiences like trauma, stress and play have been proposed to influence some of the ways we behave as adults. From an outside perspective, you can imagine what each of these situations is teaching the brain about how to survive in the world it perceives itself to be living in.

All of us have experiences early on in life that may continue to impact how we behave today, be that people-pleasing, perfectionism, a quick temper or pushing loved ones away. It is hard to measure how unhelpful behaviours come about with research due to the unique upbringing we each experience. But because of how the brain develops, it's likely early experiences have a lasting imprint on our neural networks. Shining a light on early experiences – the good, and the maybe not so good – and recognizing their potential long-lasting impacts on behaviour is a method often used in therapy and can represent a powerful step in understanding why we act the way we do. This can help us to stop defaulting to these reactions and begin challenging them. If your past experiences are negatively impacting your life or you are struggling, reaching out to a professional for confidential advice and support can be hugely beneficial.

GENE-IE IN A BOTTLE

While the human brain is designed to be moulded by experience to optimize survival in a given environment, some of our tendencies may be written in our genes. You have probably experienced the random uncle you see once a year at Christmas saying, 'You are so similar to your great-grandma'. I get it all the time from my grandad saying the way I act is uncannily like my mum when she was my age (and, to be fair, I get it. Looking at my mum now is like staring thirty years into my future. I am happy to report the chaotic energy is still going strong). While we obviously inherit physical features from our parents, the whole nature vs nurture debate on behaviour still rears its head. Are our traits shaped by experiences? Or is our destiny declared in our DNA? The consensus from this argument is: a mixture of both.

Thinking again about the initial period of brain development as laying foundations, our genes provide the instructions for making the materials required for this process. We all have similar starting components: like bricks, concrete, steel and wood. But tiny changes in our genetic code, which make us all unique, can slightly alter the properties of these resources. Some bricks may be slightly denser than others, some concrete more solid, some wood more brittle. These small changes don't alter the ability to build the structure or its overall appearance, but they influence the underlying properties of the building and how it functions. These genetic differences could impact our brain circuitry or how individual cells function, giving us all slightly distinct structures in which our behaviours arise.

An area of research that has investigated the genetic influence over behaviour is the study of personality. The most well-used model to study personality is the 'Big Five', assessing openness (how much you're up for trying new things), neuroticism (how anxious you get in the face of stress), extrovertism (how energized you are being around others), agreeableness (how much you like to help others) and conscientiousness (how organized and structured you are). You may have done one of these tests online with your friends and been given a printout of 'who

THE BIG FIVE QUIZ!

Openness
Neuroticism
Extrovertism
Agreeableness
Conscientiousness

you're a 'K Type!'

you are' based on your answers (although the validity of these non-research-based questionnaires is questionable).[4]

It is unclear exactly what genetic changes may contribute to certain traits, but it does appear elements of our natures are determined by DNA. Identical twins, who have nearly 100 per cent-matching genetic codes, share more personality traits than non-identical twins,[5] indicating some mechanism of inheritance is involved when it comes to how we act. Another study identified 700 genes – many of which coded for proteins influencing processes in the brain – thought to contribute to personality traits. Certain mutations were found more often in people with similar personality types than others,[6] giving more evidence that our genetic instruction manual may have sway over how we behave day-to-day.

Now, it is obvious that not all our 'core' ways of acting come from our genes (if you have ever met identical twins, you will know they are in no way identical in their personalities). But the role genes play in constructing our personality is an important consideration in the pursuit of goals. Many of us dream about our aspirations and think 'If only I had this trait, then I could achieve that' or 'If I was more like so-and-so, this would be easy'. While we may hope to change core elements of how we act, science is yet to deliver an evidence-based technique for personality change – even though some think this may be possible with a lot of effort and the right timing.[7] Focusing on what we feel we lack and spending time pining to be less like ourselves is probably a fruitless endeavour when trying to work towards a goal. Instead, thinking about the ways of working that suit you and how you can use these to your advantage will help propel you towards where you want to be.

INHERITING EXPERIENCE?

Our genetics and our experiences collectively impact our behaviours, as they heavily interact. For example, the activity our brain experiences based on external events causes different genes to switch on and off, guiding which connections should stay and which should go. This dynamic regulation of which genes are turned on and off is called epigenetics. Unlike our genetic code, which is relatively stable through-out our lives, epigenetics involves modifications to our DNA which can be reversed. If our DNA is like a long list of words, then epigenetics is typographical emphasis; guiding which words should be **emphasized** and which should be ~~missed out altogether~~. Experiences such as stress, smoking and diet are all thought to alter switching genes on or off via epigenetics, and these gene-environment interactions are now heavily studied in diseases like cancer.

A recently popularized yet controversial notion in neuroscience is that epigenetics may have the potential to pass on the experiences of the parent to their offspring. That is, if a parent experiences something traumatic, the child of that parent will also show the same behavioural response when faced with the traumatic stimulus because of altered gene expression. If a parent or group has faced trauma, future genera-tions can be impacted by this during their upbringing, learning from the behaviours and actions of those around them. But in an epigenetic model of inheritance, this response would occur independent of per-sonal experience. So far, this work has only been shown in mice, where parents who fear a certain smell due to receiving a mild shock in its presence give birth to children and grandchildren who show, on aver-age, a greater aversion to the same odour, despite never receiving the initial shock.[8] It is uncertain whether this phenomenon takes place in humans, and much more research is needed to pin down how exactly this mechanism might work before jumping to conclusions that your actions today might impact the behaviours of your future grandchildren (I mean, they might, but maybe not in a modification-of-their-genes type of way). As the field of epigenetics research expands beyond its role in disease to discovering how lifestyle factors alter our gene expres-sion, it will be interesting to see if there's any way a parent's experience can affect their child's behaviour purely via genetics.

WRAP UP

Understanding the origins of why we behave the way we do will always present a challenge to scientists. Studying human beings is messy – we cannot control our environment like we can in a lab – and many inter-playing factors, like experience, interactions and genetics, influence the results observed. Plus, we all experience unique life events, making it hard to deduce 'interaction A leads to behaviour B'. It is unlikely we will ever get to that precise input/output situation. That being said, it can still be useful to consider the roots of your own behaviour when working on your quest for change and come to terms with the idea that some of our modes of being may take work or be beyond our current influence to completely transform.

Personally, seeing how my desire to be accepted and 'liked' as a part of human nature which gave our ancestors an evolutionary advantage creates space for self-compassion. Reflecting on my own experiences during those first twenty-five years of my life when my brain was developing has let me pinpoint some roots of why I act the way I do in certain situations. This has helped me detach from these behaviours defining who I am to them being something my brain learnt once upon a time to protect me. And by considering that parts of my personality may be orchestrated by my genetic code has given me grace to release the 'this is all on me to change' mindset, helping remove some guilt I have felt when struggling to alter certain elements of my behaviour (like oversharing my life details with strangers when on an extroversion high at a party). In terms of getting a goal, considering all the roots of why we act the way we do is fundamental in seeing what behaviours may be helping or hindering us, and we'll be covering how to do this with your goal in mind in Chapter 6. But before that, it is important to understand how your brain can change certain patterns of behaviour – regardless of age – to allow us to learn new ways of being.

CHAPTER 3

YOUR BRAIN ON CHANGE

YOUR BRAIN MUST STORE RESPONSES TO FUNCTION EFFECTIVELY . . .

Our brain has taken in information from its environment to learn how to survive and navigate the circumstances it is facing. What would be even more useful is if the brain could store some of these reactions, like a guidebook for what to do when encountering the same situation repeatedly. It would be really annoying if every time it went to tie its shoelaces, it had to actively think about the steps involved. Instead, its hands just move, and a bow is formed.

Habits are our brain's stored responses to situations. They are mechanisms which allow us to save our mental resources for dealing with new challenges and problems by defaulting to a routine in familiar circumstances. However, it isn't always what benefits us in the long-run that becomes our default. Normally, we feel compelled to repeat instantly rewarding or pain-avoiding actions. Repeating these actions strengthens connections between the brain cells involved, and these strong pathways are what forms the compulsion to carry out an action even when we know it isn't doing us any favours.

LIFE IS PLASTIC

Imagine you are walking through open countryside and reach a field of tall grass. You need to reach the other side, but there is no existing path through. So, you walk forward unknowingly, flattening blades as you go.

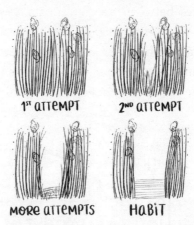

1st attempt   2nd attempt

more attempts   Habit

You reach the other side safely and carry on with your journey. The next day, you head out on the same walk and once again approach the field. But this time, you can see a weakly imprinted trail from where you walked the day before. You know that route got you out of the field unharmed, so you tread it again. Each day, when you reach the field and walk along the path you initially established, its boundaries become more and more defined until this once non-existent route becomes the obvious way through the field. The thought of making a new route through the long grass isn't even a question – why bother doing that when the path you have carved gets you through safely and it is easy to follow?

This is like how we think our brains form habits.

The human brain contains billions of connections between neurons, forming paths that allow these cells to chat to one another in different groups. Some of these conversations are more important than others, and these are differentiated by altering the strength of the synapses connecting them.

Again, thinking of our brains like a rail network, it is like looking at an app which gives you the best route possible from one station to another. The route of choice is highlighted, standing out above the other tracks, making it obvious exactly which way you will be going. And the more times a route is taken, or the more emotional significance the route has, the more likely it is to become the default way from A to B. Altering the strength of synaptic connections makes similar strong routes between neurons in the brain, meaning when one cell in the loop receives a message, it will more easily pass it on to the others. In the case of habits, it is thought situations – like waking up to your alarm in the morning – that trigger behaviours such as stretching your arm out, hitting snooze and turning back over, do so via such loops.

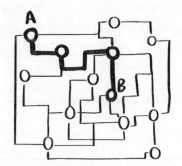

RECOMMENDED ROUTE

How strong a connection is between two cells is determined largely by how often that connection is used, allowing routes that are commonly relied upon to be triggered quickly. When two brain cells are in constant communication or are activated in conjunction with strong emotions like fear, physical changes occur at the synapse connecting them, making it easier to pass signals on.

In the 'lock and key' signalling method of neuron chat, these numbers can be altered to produce stronger signals by adding more locks or more keys at specific connection points. Having more keys to release in response to a signal means it is more likely the receiving neuron will be unlocked and pass the signal on, and having more locks means that when opened, more charge can get inside the receiving neuron. Both these physical changes more readily allow the communication of fainter signals, as the connection is easier to activate.

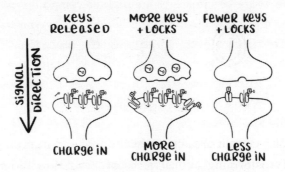

Synaptic connections can strengthen or weaken over time. These changes in synapse strength – or synaptic plasticity – are a form of neuroplasticity: mechanisms which allow the brain to change and adapt to new situations throughout life. It would be pretty detrimental if after age twenty-five you couldn't learn anything new. The various forms of neuroplasticity mean we can keep mentally growing and flexibly alter how we act when faced with new challenges.

AUTOPILOT

Synaptic plasticity is key in habit formation. If we can increase the strength of the connections between a specific reaction (like waking up) to a stimulus (like the sound of an alarm), we will more likely follow through with that action; moving it from a consciously directed notion to a learnt, almost-automatic sequence. In research set-ups, scientists classify habitual behaviours as ones that are carried out with little hesitation following training, even in the face of no reward. And outside the lab, we see this definition play out. How often do you scroll through your phone for hours even if you know it is detrimental to you getting a good night's sleep? And if a behaviour is continually carried out in the face of receiving a punishment, this is the sign of an addiction or compulsion; a habit that not only doesn't serve you but is potentially harmful to you and others.

STiMULUS

ReSPoNSeS

In the brain, certain areas have been indicated in prompting habit formation. Transforming a consciously driven action into a more rote response is thought to involve chatter between the frontal brain regions involved in decision-making and directing action, emotional control elements of the brain like the amygdala, and another deeply buried area involved in reward and initiating movement called the striatum. The striatum is also key in goal-directed behaviour (more on this in Chapter 4) and it is thought the switch from an action being reward-seeking to automated could happen here.

Like wearing a pair of headphones with different audio coming through each earbud, different parts of the striatum receive messages from different brain regions. One side is hearing messages that prompt goal-directed behaviour, communicating the value of certain actions and sending reminders of why this action is important to you, whereas the other side gets direct information about how the body is moving and sensing in response to a situation. When an action is repeated, the goal-directed side of the striatum quietens down and the more auto- mated side pipes up, essentially encoding 'this is the movement we do and how we feel in this situation'. In the lab, losing contact with the automated side of the striatum prevents habits being formed, as seen in rats with this area switched off.[1] Despite going over and over the same situation, these rats fail to automate the behaviour, hesitating and still being swayed by the value of performing the action.

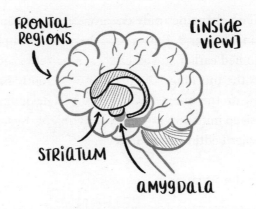

FRONTAL REGIONS

[INSIDE VIEW]

STRIATUM

AMYGDALA

Most research on habits has been conducted in animals, meaning we can only speculate how these mechanisms may work in humans. Also, while we know a fair bit about plasticity between the synapses of two cells (helped by work using computer models) and that certain behaviours can become habitual, how these link together to produce habits is still not clear. We know it is not as simple as 'repeat this action twenty times to strengthen these specific synapses and it will become habit' or 'stop doing that thing for two years and you'll never do it again as the connections will have weakened'. However, we can apply our knowledge on the roles of reward and repetition in the formation of habitual responses to start to lay new paths in that field of tall grass.

CHAIN REACTION

When it comes to actively changing behaviours or incorporating helpful responses into our daily lives, we can look to the components of habitual responses. Following the notion that certain behaviours can be tied to particular situations, there are several ways we can start trying to induce change to our auto-pilot responses based on this call-and-response model.

HABIT THEORY

SITUATION = BEHAVIOUR
[CUE]   [RESPONSE]

More detail on changing these components in relation to your goal is coming up in Chapter 9. But as an illustrative example, say you are trying to get to bed earlier so you can wake up refreshed to work on a side project in the morning. The habit you currently have is 'get into bed' (situation, or the cue) = 'watch TV' (behaviour, or response), pushing your sleep initiation to well past midnight. In attempts to shift towards an earlier bedtime, we can try to:

1. **Change the situation**

   Tough one: we can't exactly change 'going to bed'. And even if we could, this scenario wouldn't actively alter the habit. As soon as you are faced with the same situation, the habitual response is waiting to kick in again.

   $$\cancel{\text{Situation}} = \text{BeHaviour}$$
   $$\cancel{\text{[cue]}} \quad \text{[Response]}$$

2. **Prevent the behaviour**

   This is more feasible: we could move the device we watch TV on from the bedroom to prevent a Netflix marathon. However, this situation is still not the most efficient at changing the overall habit. Even though over a prolonged period of time, prevention can weaken association, if you stay in a hotel room with a TV on the wall, you may find yourself having to fight the urge. Plus, going cold turkey doesn't quite scratch the craving itch we get when faced with the cue.

   $$\text{Situation} = \cancel{\text{BeHaviour}}$$
   $$\text{[cue]} \quad \cancel{\text{[Response]}}$$

3. **Replace the response**

   The best option: instead of sticking on a six-part series once under the covers, you could read a book. And repeating this new activity night after night will start to alter the habit, building a new response which serves you. The craving to watch TV in bed will fade until, eventually, it will be rare you even think about reaching for the remote.

How long it takes to replace engrained habitual behaviours with new ones is a challenge to calculate. One research study found reaching automaticity with a single behaviour spanned from weeks to months and varied hugely from person to person.[2] How familiar the new behaviour is to you, how easy or challenging it is, how much you enjoy it, the reward it provides, your emotional state and the thoughts of others can all impact the implementation of these long-lasting changes, and old reactions still rear their heads from time to time. But persistence is a key ingredient in prompting long-term change. Just like with neurons whose synaptic connections are strengthened by repetition, the more consistent we are with performing an action, the higher the chance it will stick.

WELCOME RESISTANCE

A common feeling that comes with change is resistance: the mental pushback that crops up when trying to engage in a new behaviour or the pull to old, familiar routines because of their apparent ease. Resistance exists in many forms, including excuses (being too tired), get-outs ('missing this one won't hurt') and statements of defeat ('this isn't going to work anyway so what's the point?'). The urge not to perform new actions that you know will be beneficial is the ultimate frustration when it comes to making change. But this resistance is a natural response to the new and unknown, and by recognizing it as normal, we can start to tackle it head on.

Familiarity

Firstly, resistance arises when trying to consistently pursue something new because change means moving away from the familiar. Familiarity is like the worn-out old jumper in the back of your wardrobe which is beyond repair, but you just can't bring yourself to throw it out. It no longer serves a purpose or does the job it is meant to do, yet we cling to it, even if it takes up vital space. The human brain seeks the familiar as familiarity is safe. And protecting us is what the brain is designed to do.

In its efforts to make sense of the world around us and keep us out of harm's way, our brain is susceptible to making pretty poor decisions. These sub-optimal, sometimes illogical processes are described as cognitive biases. In psychology, these biases describe flaws within the brain's processing of information to give quick yet inadequate solutions. And it is potentially impossible to stop them happening (but with awareness, it is possible to stop acting on them).

The neuroscience underlying why we make such rash and sometimes unjust conclusions is still under investigation, but a recent theory suggests this thinking evolved when our brains' main concern was to perceive what was happening in the world, assign each situation to a category like 'safe' or 'unsafe', and react accordingly.[3] This method of rapidly processing and categorizing is facilitated by how our brain cells form connections; with incoming information filtered through networks built from previous experiences to associate the situation at hand with those we've gone through before. This means familiar situations are repeatedly activated in the brain, making them even more familiar.

Connecting pieces of similar information in the brain might explain why we tend to gravitate towards the familiar while repelling the unknown. We have a preference for information we have processed and come across before. The 'mere-exposure effect' describes a cognitive bias where the simple case of experiencing something multiple times makes us more likely to like that thing purely because it is familiar. For example, if you are in a restaurant that serves a cuisine you have never tried before and notice they have burgers on the menu, you might be tempted to go for the burger purely because you've had burgers before, even though there might be other delicacies on the menu you would enjoy more.

Another observed cognitive bias associated with familiarity is 'cognitive ease'. This describes the phenomena that we feel information is right when we can handle and process it easily – normally because we have experienced a similar situation before. The feeling of processing unfamiliar information as 'hard work' further pushes us away from making dramatic changes to our current situation. When trying to shift familiar behaviours into new actions, it is inevitable we will face novel circumstances, which requires us to process information in an alien way. And because of our brain's preference for known information, this can make it harder to persevere with new ventures.

Familiarity makes things feel easy, even if those things are not good for us. It feels easy to let the next episode of a TV series play instead of getting an early night if that is the usual routine you follow. Familiarity also means predictability. It is a way to keep us safe. If we are approaching new situations, the brain is unsure how it will pan out. Familiarity protects the brain from one of the most stressful states it can be in: uncertainty.

Uncertainty

If you can guarantee one thing about life, it's that uncertainty will be part of it. Yet the human brain strives to mitigate this state at all costs. We like to know that the job we are in will be safe and secure, that the fitness plan we are doing will make us as strong as we want to be, and that the person we are dating will be the one. If a future outcome cannot be predicted, that is when uncertainty can really wreak havoc with our mental and physical state. And that is where many of us find ourselves when on the quest for change.

Through research, it has been reported that we and other mammals prefer to know the outcome of a situation, even if it is a hard one to deal with, rather than be in a state of uncertainty. In fact, it has been proposed that chronic uncertainty is a major contributor to anxiety. We get anxious when we fixate on potential future scenarios which may be difficult or not what we want to happen, and for individuals living with anxiety disorders, this state can be persistent. A big problem with pursuing the unknown is that anxiety triggers avoidance behaviours. In experimental set-ups when having to pick between predictable and unpredictable shocks, most animal and human subjects go for the environment where the shocks can be predicted, avoiding the uncertain condition.[4] Unlike fear, which triggers a short-lived, energizing 'fight-or-flight' stress response to tackle a perceived threat head on, anxiety is sustained in response to less obvious threats which *could* happen, and is normally only resolved once the outcome of the situation is known. Avoidance behaviours kick in because our brain rationalizes that it's better to not approach a situation until we are sure we will remain safe (and instead, spends its time worrying about the 200 different possible outcomes).

When it comes to changing our behaviours in pursuit of some-thing new, experiencing a state of uncertainty is inevitable. If you have worked towards a goal before, you have probably asked yourself: 'If I try this new thing, what if it doesn't work out?' Or even if you think of the best-case scenario, you may still find yourself questioning: 'How will my life change? I don't want to lose those closest to me.'

These questions, or worrying about potential outcomes, stop us from taking action. And this then keeps us stuck in the state of wanting to change but never getting there. An element of our brain would like to see us repeat the same behaviours day in, day out because it can predict how each moment will go. But even when sticking firmly in the comfort zone of familiarity, things can happen (like a global pandemic) that rip the mask of 'certainty' from our eyes and show that not much is truly predictable. Thinking this way, uncertainty can be seen not as something to avoid, but something to expect. And one of the ways to resolve anxiety is action. When a situation is faced, the brain can process the real outcome and discard some of the more extreme endings it has crafted, allowing you to break out of the 'what if' headspace.

Putting a plan in place and giving it a go is worthwhile because, while it may not be clear exactly where it will lead, taking action will result in much greater progress and teach lessons. 'Doing' is far more beneficial than staying in the same old routines under the fiction that they are safer. The only thing this way of acting protects you from is opportunity.

Effort

A given with true change is that effort is required to move from your current state. If you are trying to motivate yourself to go to the gym after work, the resistance you feel when thinking about leaving the couch can be imagined as the energy required to forge a new path in the field of tall grass. There are ways of lowering the energy required to take action (more on this later), but on the whole, change is a long process which requires input.

Effort is required when changing because decision-making and attention processes in the brain need to be engaged to divert you down a new path. The brain has a constant fuel supply, using about 20 per cent of the body's energy to keep business ticking over.[5] When certain regions of the brain are activated, this energy supply is thought to be directed to those regions at the detriment of others, like splitting a bag of sweets and giving more to areas that need a boost. The prefrontal cortex, where the decision-making and attention processes are directed from, is a recipient of this candy fix when acting in new ways. But this area is thought to be subject to fatigue due to the way the brain cells in it are organized,[6] meaning there are a limited number of hands available to do the work. This constraint limits how many tasks the prefrontal cortex can perform at any one time. So, depending on the circumstances, if a default behaviour already exists for a situation, you may find yourself down that path with what feels like little choice.

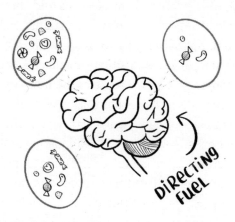

DIRECTING FUEL

These mechanisms are tricky to study in humans, but you can imagine if strong connections already exist between neurons, like a loop associating 'after work = sit on the couch and watch TV', this response is more likely to be triggered in the face of a stimulus. Once the train leaves the 'after work' station, the established route for it to take is via 'grab the remote', 'pour a drink' and 'put your feet up'. To change this response to 'go to the gym', it requires not only energy to execute the new behaviour (and over time, form a new path), but also effort to stave off the pull towards default behaviours. Like driving to work and trying to take a different route; if you are not focusing on driving in a new direction, you will find you end up back on the old route even if you didn't mean to be there. Without putting in effort, your brain will steer you back to the default.

Having this in mind when trying to move from one response to another – that you are both trying to make a new behaviour while breaking an old one – helps us to see resistance as an obvious part of the process. And in the face of resistance, what is required is consistency. Like paths in the field of tall grass, the more you walk down a new route, the clearer it becomes, and the less you tread the established path, the blurrier its borders seem. As certain connections strengthen while others weaken in the brain, resistance will be there. And going into a venture knowing it will take consistent effort over time helps prepare you for the inevitable mental pushback you will face.

BRAINTENANCE: REASON FOR RESISTANCE

When you feel resistance in the face of trying to perform a new behaviour, even though you are rested and well, ask yourself these questions and try answering honestly, or say the written answers below to yourself.

Reason for resistance	Not wanting to act	Repeating unhelpful behaviours	Answers
FAMILIARITY	'Am I pulling away from doing this because it is unfamiliar?'	'Am I only doing this because it is what I know? Does it actually serve me or is it just familiar?'	My brain likes what it knows because it is made up of connections based on past experiences and actions. Just because something is familiar and feels easy doesn't mean it is best for me. Anything new will feel unfamiliar and I have to show my brain through new experience and action that it is okay.

UNCERTAINTY	'Is me not wanting to do this because I am uncertain of the outcome?'	'Is the reason I keep repeating this routine because it is predictable, and I know what to expect?'	Uncertainty is one of the states my brain will naturally try to avoid. It wants to know how things will play out for me. But not knowing the outcome is no reason to not act. Not much in life is certain, and as soon as I become more practised at this action, the uncertainty will resolve itself.
EFFORT	'Does acting in a different way in this situation feel difficult because I need to put in effort to change my default?'	'Does this unhelpful action come easily to me because it is my default?'	Change always takes time and effort. It is a long game, and it is easier in the moment to repeat what I have done time and time again in the past as the connections triggering those behaviours are already established. The more consistent I am with my actions now, the less effort I will need down the line as I am defining a new path and training my brain to react in a new way to this situation.

WRAP UP

Our brains are designed to change. Plasticity allows us to adapt to new situations and forget unimportant information. But just because the brain is designed to change doesn't mean it will be straightforward. The key to crafting change is being consistent, exposing the brain cells involved in the behaviour to repeated activity to strengthen their connections. You will face resistance, but instead of seeing it as a signal you shouldn't push forward, face it head on. Expect it. Welcome it. Work with it. View resistance as a sign you are doing exactly what you should be doing: moving in a new direction. And the more you stand up in its presence, the more likely it is that you'll move your default from one behaviour to another.

CHAPTER 4

STRIVING FOR MORE

YOUR BRAIN WANTS TO GROW . . .

As much as our brain may want to stay in our zone of 'knowns', part of us wants something more. Having a flexible brain which can be driven by our desires and beneficial actions has allowed human beings to push the boundaries of our mental and physical capabilities: acquiring new knowledge, adapting to new environments, and understanding that we can make changes that can create a real difference to ourselves, our group and the planet.

(UNDER)SCORING GOALS

Before we even have the capacity to fully remember events, our progress is assessed using goals. Healthy weight, percentile for length, age at first word – we are constantly compared against milestones as we develop. And it doesn't stop with talking and crawling. Throughout life, we are measured up against societal benchmarks. We live in a goal-obsessed world, where we always seem to be working towards something. Although the societal and cultural checkpoints we are pitted against have evolved over time, our desire to pursue goals has been within us since before the days of humanity. And that is because chasing something new can bring an array of benefits to not only humans but any species.

Many animals, including our ancestral cousins the great apes, display goal-oriented behaviour when it comes to sourcing food or pursuing a mate for reproduction, obtaining reward via effort-fuelled actions. If you've ever watched a nature documentary, you will have witnessed some of the extreme lengths creatures will go to to achieve their goals: trekking for miles across frozen terrain for food, scaling rock faces to find the ideal egg-laying spot or sacrificing a mate to create the next generation. Some animals will literally put their lives at risk for the chance of crossing the finish line.

While the feat of these events may make our own quests for change seem somewhat insignificant, it is thought humans have a unique ability when it comes to achieving goals: we can turn imagination into reality. We can picture ourselves years in the future and bring these visions to life by sticking to a plan of action. Our future-orientated minds can intervene now to encourage new ways of acting to bring us closer to the person we envision being, even if the action being taken feels like a huge effort with no immediate pay-off. We are able to choose the less appealing path for the sake of our future self, knowing it is bringing that vision ever closer to reality.

We make many choices every day. Some seem small, like deciding what shirt to wear for work, whereas others feel huge, like contemplating whether to send that email to the person you would love to work for. In a 24-hour period, a lot of the decisions we make are decided by our established habits: what time we wake up, when we brush our teeth and what we eat at night. But there are moments of purpose-fuelled intervention, where the choice you make goes against what you may normally do or when you are faced with a new situation. This effort-filled, conscious mode of picking what to do is called goal-directed behaviour.

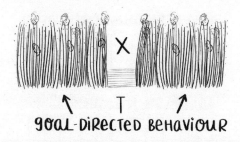

GOAL-DIRECTED BEHAVIOUR

Goal-directed behaviour is almost the antithesis of our habitual responses. It is like facing the field of tall grass, disregarding the established path and thinking 'which way is best for me to go right now'. This requires conscious decision-making processes to weigh up options about which route is going to be the most optimal. This process is also sensitive to reward, meaning each action is assessed against whether it will bring about the desired outcome we are looking for. And while thinking about what action will be best for you to take, the brain must also suppress the urge to act in a more default way. These processes are mostly under the control of circuits between the frontal and parietal lobes of the brain, plus the striatum, with the different elements of goal-directed behaviour having distinct activity. These elements can be described as:

Switching

Switching, or flexibility, is our ability to move from one task to another, discarding our current way of thinking and loading up a new set of rules to abide by. When pursuing a goal in a constantly changing environment (hello, planet Earth), the ability to load in a new mode of acting is essential in making progress. In experiments, switching is often measured using card games where one goal (match cards by colour) is replaced with another (match cards by symbol). Like changing a game in an old school PlayStation, you have to physically eject one disc with all its characters, quests and baddies in order to insert a new game, loading up a different virtual world with its own unique rulebook.

In the brain, this switching is thought to be mediated by a brain circuit described as the executive control network, a group of regions in the frontal and parietal lobes that talk to each other to exert influence

RULE BY SYMBOL...

| 1 ♡ | 2 ♡ | 3 ♡ | 4 ♡ |

RULE BY NUMBER...

| 1 ♡ | 1 ☆ | 1 O | 1 △ |

over our course of action, and another circuit called the salience network, which is involved in coordinating the body and brain to direct our limited pool of attention to events which are deemed important. Animals with disruptions to the back of their prefrontal cortex are unable to effectively switch tasks, and in neurotypical humans, it has been noted that individuals with higher scores in task-switching card games experience more changes in brain activity patterns. From person to person, how these networks function varies, indicating we all have differences in the ability to jump from one task to another.

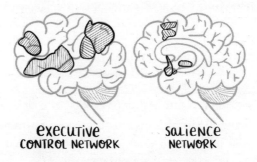

executive
CONTROL NETWORK

salience
NETWORK

Monitoring

When you do any project, you want to get an idea of how it is going to ensure you are on track towards the desired result. And our brains are no different. While we may use activity trackers and metrics to assess our own progress, our brains are constantly weighing up the cost of performing an action versus the reward it will eventually reap. If the reward is immediate and obvious, we will likely do it (eating ice-cream, having sex, sipping wine). However, with most goals, the actions needed to make progress aren't going to result in a quick buzz. It is thought the human brain can also hold the abstract idea of 'the goal' in mind and assess whether the current action will help or hinder moving towards it.

Exactly how the brain can do this is still being investigated, but it is thought to involve holding information about what you want for the future in the attention-dependent working memory, a temporary store of information where information can be manipulated, while the current action is weighed up in terms of how useful it will be with respect to this overall goal. These operations largely depend on processing-limited frontal brain regions like the orbitofrontal cortex and the anterior cingulate cortex, whose activity can be thwarted if other 'more important' energy-requiring states (tiredness, hunger, stress) are occurring. And if we do something that results in a negative outcome with respect to our desired results, the brain registers this feedback as an error. This allows us to, hypothetically, learn from our mistakes and dissuade us from engaging in unhelpful behaviours in future.

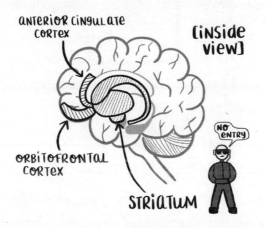

The image we hold in our working memory about our wants can also be updated to represent changes in our goals, and this is thought to be coordinated by chat between our good friends the striatum and the prefrontal cortex. One of the ways they interact together is to prevent new information from other brain areas coming in and muddying the focus of the goal in our working memory. Like a bouncer when a club is at capacity and people in the queue are pushing to enter, the striatum holds back other signals from flooding in. When updating a goal, the bouncer striatum relaxes its stance, allowing information from other areas of the brain to enter our working memory and edit the aim.

Inhibition

The final element of goal-directed behaviour, and one we tend to forget about when advancing towards an aim, is inhibition. In most scenarios, working towards a goal requires performing new behaviours or existing ones in a more consistent way. However, our old 'ways' will continue to exist and still activate when trying to craft change. In order to stop habitual responses interfering, our brain has to actively suppress these unwanted impulses, giving us the chance to perform beneficial behaviours that are currently weak or non-existent options.

This inhibition is thought to involve brain areas within the prefrontal cortex, as when this area suffers damage, individuals are more likely to rely on default behaviours. Prefrontal cortex activity in this instance is like the class teacher saying 'let's give another person a chance to talk' when that one kid with the loud voice who answers every question pipes up again. Holding the floor for quieter voices to express their views is a key component of pursuing a goal because without this suppression, the loudest voice would get there first and no change could take place.

If the thought of juggling all these elements of working towards a goal feels exhausting, that is because it is. Goal-directed behaviour requires actively choosing a weaker, less obvious path in the face of other more strongly established options over and over again. The more this less favoured path is chosen, the stronger it will become, which is why sticking with goals in the initial stages of building new behavioural responses is essential. This should transform your default behaviours to ones that help you towards your goal and will require much less effort to perform. But even if these more beneficial behaviours become habitual, goal-directed behaviour is still needed throughout goal pursuit. What if the environment changes? Or you plateau? This is when we need that flexible thinking, the ability to monitor a situation and change tack to keep moving towards your desired result, which is covered in later chapters.

HOW DO I KNOW (WHICH WAY TO GO)

Generally, visualizing what you want for your future self can be relatively straightforward, but figuring out how to make that happen can be much less clear. Being unsure of how to select the 'right' goal holds many of us back from getting started. Or picking a goal and deciding part way through it isn't working out can make us feel defeated. There are certain methods which are deployed to effectively set goals. For example, you could set SMART (specific, measurable, achievable, relevant and time-bound) goals, a popular technique used in work environments to measure progress. Or you could go for an overshooting goal, a method used by self-help experts to push you beyond your believed capabilities by setting a target you consider out of reach. According to an analysis of over 100 behavioural change studies, the most effective goal-setting methods were to make goals difficult but achievable in terms of challenge level, and to set goals publicly, face to face or in a group (although these results are caveated by the fact the studies contain a mixed bag of methods and measures).[1] Also considering effort level during the goal-selection process could help with achievement, as our choices are often guided by reward rather than reality.[2]

While you may find some of these tips useful when setting goals, some might not be as helpful. If these methods have been tested, they will have been trialled in populations of people, meaning any beneficial effect they show is an average. That is why it is really important to take 'scientifically proven' or popular methods and try them for yourself. Experiment and see what works for you. I walk through my personal goal-setting exercise at the end of this chapter, which contains an amalgamation of different elements I have found to be most useful for choosing my goals.

NEVER ENOUGH

When pursuing a goal, we normally have an idea in our head about how amazing we will feel when we achieve it. We believe reaching this benchmark will make us happy, that our lives will be vastly improved, and that we will want for nothing again. But we all know this is very rarely the case. If you look at yourself right now, you are the product of achieved goals. Whether academic, relationship, career, health, financial or general life goals, you have achieved a lot up to this point. However, the sense of achievement is fleeting. As soon as we get to where we wanted to be, we are looking to the next goalpost up ahead. Like a kid at Christmas who receives a pile of presents, no sooner is the wrapping paper off one gift before they are looking towards the next. There are thought to be biological reasons behind why we quickly move on to the next goal, but there are some ways to savour that feeling of joy when we see progress.

It is a sad fact of life, but we are not designed to be completely elated all the time. Total joy is a goal many strive for, but in reality, this is a state of arousal, a fleeting emotion, a response to tell our bodies that whatever just happened was (usually) good for us. Just like extreme sadness, all-encompassing happiness for prolonged periods of time is not beneficial, and can even be dangerous. Imagine our ancestors thousands of years ago, living in a world of scary unknowns and exposed to the elements. If they felt super upbeat all the time, what do you think would happen? While they might be buzzing in the safety of the tribe, as soon as they were threatened by predators, happiness would not be the state they would want to be in.

As much as we try to avoid negative states like anxiety, distress, sadness and anger, we need them (in moderation) in order to survive. These states allow us to predict and plan, keep us safe and warn others. However, an excess of these states can cause debilitating conditions like major depressive or anxiety disorders. What is ideal for human survival is to have an emotional baseline that can permit us to jump to the highs of exhilarating joy and the lows of melancholic sadness, then eventually resume to some sort of normality. This baseline has been described in psychology as the hedonic treadmill. Like pacing on a running machine, no matter how fast or slow you go, you remain in the same place; the baseline emotional stance we repeatedly return to. On the bright side, our baseline is thought to rest in a more positive state, with the level determined by factors like genetics, thoughts, feelings, actions and external circumstances.

When we experience a high in life, like securing our dream job, or a low, like losing our cat, these emotional states peak before moving back towards the baseline in a process called adaptation. The time it takes for adaptation to happen can vary from person to person and be influenced by the event that caused them, and failure to adapt could lead to persisting extreme states. After the high of an achievement, emotions fall back down to our baseline, meaning we are then looking for the next thing that will bring us that level of elation again.

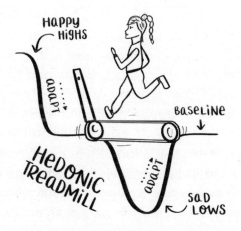

However, there have been some proposed mechanisms to slow down adaptation to feel that warm glow of joy for longer. One of these techniques is to continually express gratitude for the things you have gone through, made happen, and/or survived. For example, if you are in a contented relationship, but have a big project at work which is taking up all your resources, chances are you are not fully appreciating your partner. But think back to when the two of you got together and remember the absolute buzz you would get when you saw them. The joy of being with that person was all you needed and you felt like the luckiest person in the world. By reflecting on those thoughts you bring that joy back to the forefront of your mind. Gratitude practices vary from the written word to sitting and thinking about what you are grateful for. While the research-backed jury is still out on whether these are truly effective at improving well-being, being grateful for what you have, from past or current experiences, will help you stay with that feeling of joy for longer.

Other methods to slow adaptation include monitoring your aspirations. Once we achieve something like a pay rise, we are quickly looking for the next bump up in salary. In most jobs, an expansion in pay packet is normally months or years away, so immediately seeking the next step up shunts our happiness from our most recent well-earnt promotion. That's not to say don't have aspirations (I wouldn't be writing this book otherwise), but keeping future aspirations on the shelf for a little bit longer, until they are ready to be worked towards, could allow you to more fully appreciate the feat you have just achieved. Also, adding a bit of variety and surprise into events which bring you joy can help stop them becoming predictable. Even though the brain loves predictability, it can make occasions lose their excitement and increases the ease of adaptability. If you are wanting to appreciate your partner more, you could plan a surprise date night or cook their favourite meal when they are not expecting it, keeping the glow of appreciation burning for longer.

The regulation of emotion is most likely a component of why, after we achieve a goal, we go back into seeking mode and look towards the next accolade on the agenda. Another potential reason for this normalization is simply the way our brains work. Our brains are prediction machines. When you achieve a goal, whether that is lifting a certain weight or hitting a certain revenue, the brain will integrate this success into its model of what it expects of you. You are modelled within your own brain. And rightly so – imagine if there was no update on your abilities? It would be impossible to judge what situations you can take on and which you should potentially avoid. The human brain normalizes achievements to help you better predict how you can act in the future. This makes these milestones blend into the background noise of life to help you identify novel opportunities and threats, rather than being distracted by what you have already 'solved'.

The problem with these inner expectations is that they prevent us from recognizing our past achievements and can also erroneously predict how things should go. For example, say one of your social media posts goes viral. You receive thousands of likes, hundreds of followers and a bunch of comments. This one-off event can alter the internal model of how you think your posts go down on the 'gram. When your next post doesn't take off, there is a conflict between your internal expectation and outward 'reward', making you feel disappointed and questioning what you did wrong (the answer to that is nothing; more on this in Chapter 12). While the models of ourselves are beneficial they can leave us with this sense of not having enough.

You are enough. If no one has said this to you, or you have not heard them, hear me now. You, as you are, in your current state of being, reading this page, are enough. While it is great to have goals, to want to make changes in life which will bring benefits to yourself, others and your community, it is also important to celebrate yourself as you are. Achievements, accolades and progress are all nice, but they are a bonus. They do not summate your worth, although it is easy to feel like they do. We are praised throughout our lives for what we achieve. From exam results to match scores, follower counts to job promotions, our efforts are normally recognized by others, society and even ourselves only once the prize is secured. Our brains learn from going through the school system that while effort is nice, results are what counts. This prevents us from feeling the true enjoyment of working towards a goal, and stops us appreciating ourselves for just being. The millions of years of evolution that have led to us existing is a marvel in itself. Put on top of that our relationships, moments of laughter, the little things we enjoy, and we can start to see how incredible it is to just be here. Constantly striving for the next win and feeling incomplete or unworthy until it is met is a recipe for never enjoying the moment. Look at the day, the hour, the minute ahead and be grateful to yourself for being there to experience it. The tiny things you do on a daily basis which may seem insignificant can be the most powerful in bringing you that sense of calm, joy and happiness.

You have a world of possibility in front of you, but you also have a world of things to be grateful for right now. And no pursuit can take that away.

BRAINTENANCE: YOUR IDEAL DAY

On the same theme of appreciating the small things in life, my favourite exercise for selecting goals that align with feeling content is to describe **my ideal average working day**. 'Working' here doesn't necessarily mean work – you might be in a support role or not working in the traditional sense. It is a way to describe an average day that isn't a holiday or special occasion.

I think about this ideal day **a year or two down the line** to find what my current self wants to get out of each twenty-four hours, but if you have a pretty sure idea of a big overall goal five, ten or fifteen years away, feel free to use these time frames too. This exercise not only helps you set goals which will bring you closer to these future desires but also see the small things in your day that you can easily incorporate or are already doing. So take some time out, grab a cuppa, light a candle, play your favourite music and enjoy . . .

On my ideal average working day, I would . . .

Wake up around *6 a. m.*	And then I would . . . *get out of bed, make a tea, chat to my partner and watch the sunrise over water.*
Before work, between the hours of *6:15 and 9 a.m.*	I'd . . . *work out – either going for a run or to the gym, shower, spend an hour doing something creative, like writing, and meditate for ten minutes.*
I'd begin work at *9 a.m.*	And I would be . . . *in a creative role where I am in control of my own schedule. I'd be working on media projects and the morning would be when I'd work on writing scripts for videos.*
I'd take at least four short breaks throughout the working day	And on my breaks I'd . . . *take my dog for a walk, catch up with a friend, read some more of my book, have a really good coffee, do a task to keep the house tidy.*
I'd stop for lunch at *12:30*	And during my lunch, I'd . . . *eat fresh food, read my book, move my body, have a break from screens.*

During the afternoon hours of 1:30 and 5:30 p.m.	I'd . . . *schedule collaborative work – like meetings, idea-generation sessions, group coffees – and tackle organizational tasks like emails, planning and gathering sources for projects.*
I'd finish work at 5:30 p.m.	And immediately, I would . . . *shut down my emails and begin preparing dinner.*
In the evening, between 6 and 9 p.m.	I would be . . . *cooking dinner to have with my partner at home, sitting to enjoy our meal and share about our days, and watch an episode of our current favourite TV show in our cosy living room. Or go to meet friends or family for dinner.*
I would start to wind down at 9 p.m.	By . . . *putting on a podcast, slowly organizing items for the next day (like packing my gym bag) and tidying clothes/ washing up, putting face cream on and brushing teeth, then sliding into bed with a book.*
My lights would be switched out at 10 p.m.	And I'd . . . *get eight hours of sleep/time in bed.*

Looking at your ideal average working day plan . . .

Which of these activities are you already doing?
(e.g.) Getting up at 6 a.m., working in a creative job, eating a healthy lunch.

Which activities could you easily slot into your day now?
(e.g.) watching the sunrise, taking a walking break, winding down at 9 p.m.

Which one of these activities do you want to work towards as your current goal?
(e.g.) incorporating a morning workout.

Taking this goal, what do you want from it? What output are you after?
(e.g.) to get stronger.

Compared to where you are now, what would be a practical sign within your control* that you have achieved or are on your way to achieving this output?

(e.g.) *being able to squat 80 kg.*

(*try to avoid measures that rely on other people for this overall goal: follower count, subscriber numbers, winning an award. These can be used as milestones on the way (more in Chapter 7) but not as the overall aim. Instead choose a measure that can be achieved by you alone: draw ten pieces of art, make twenty videos, study for sixty hours).

You now have a tangible target to work towards which will aid you in crafting an element of your ideal average working day, and throughout the rest of the book, there are exercises on how to put this plan into action.

Overall, the aim of this exercise is to identify what you truly want from your days and to use these aspects to set specific goals. I normally work on one goal at a time if something is brand new – allowing it to be my focus. I like to do this exercise at least once a year to update where my current version of 'ideal' is. It is also nice to redo if you change jobs, move cities or start a family to help incorporate these big life adjustments into your vision.

WRAP UP

As living beings, we are built to strive for more and having goals is a solid way to steer the direction we are heading in. Exactly what those goals are can shape whether we find fulfilment day to day, or chase aims we actually don't truly desire. But with any achievement, be prepared for it to be normalized, and know that outside the accolades and acclaim, you are enough.

Mastery

CHAPTER 5

FIND YOUR WHY

With a goal in mind, you may be ready to jump straight into action. When we've figured out the final destination, we want to throw ourselves into the car, put our foot down and zoom towards the end point, full steam ahead. We know where we want to go and think the sooner we get started, the sooner our dreams will be realized.

This is often a mistake.

Before turning on the ignition, it is vital to put real thought into where you are heading. Why is that my destination of choice? Is that really where I want to go? So often we pick goals without considering whether the result of our aim will bring us a real sense of fulfilment, and we fail to recognize our true motivations behind chasing it. One of the best ways to assess whether this is the goal for you is to understand what you truly value in life and craft an overall purpose informed by that.

You might know why you want to achieve a certain goal. You want to be stronger, or richer, or have a better quality of life, or find a person to spend your time with. But our reasoning can be heavily influenced by expectations from others or societies' version of 'desirable', and we often don't realize it. A personal goal can be based on what your friend has achieved, or something you've seen online, or come from pressure of not fitting the mould. It could be a goal your parents have for you, your partner has for you, or society has for you. It could be that the end destination would see you admired by others, and it is that admiration, rather that the goal, that is being chased.

Our brains can be influenced and swayed in subtle ways we barely notice to follow the norms of the pack and fit in. Like fashion trends. You can look back at photos from even a few years ago and cringe at what would be wardrobe faux pas today (heavy under-eye pencil, I'm looking at you). The subtle shifts in taste make certain products – which we would have never dreamt of spending money on – *the* items of season, due to our brain normalizing garments from frequent exposure and them being worn by influential people. Our own aspirations and desires can also fall prey to trends and current issues, which can be beneficial (saving the turtles ♥) or detrimental (virality on social media) to what we genuinely want to do.

Each one of us is an individual. We all have different things in life which are important to us. By defining what these are and keeping them in mind when we are setting and working towards goals, we can push through hard times and fend off external influence. Getting to know what you truly value and living by those core themes will not only create a more fulfilling existence for you but will have a huge knock-on impact on those around you too.

WHY

You may hear the word 'purpose' and want to run for the hills. Purpose feels big, it feels scary, it feels mysterious, it feels out of reach. The word normally leaves us in an internal scramble.

'What is my purpose?! How do I find it?! How will I know if this is it?!'

Purpose is not something you find, but something you define. It is unlikely to hit you in a sudden flash of wonder. Instead, it is the small moments, the inclines of joy, the bouts of awe, the warmth of connecting with certain people, animals or nature that can give you an insight into what your purpose could be. Purpose is different from having a goal; it cannot be ticked off a list. Instead, purpose acts as a fertile ground from which your goals can grow. Having an overall mission and selecting goals whose outcomes complement your ultimate aim will provide you with a powerful force to push on and make a real change.

When defining and moulding your purpose, this quest often turns into a search for 'meaning'. For some groups and organizations, life's meaning is set in stone – like religions that define their purpose as serving a higher power (and this clarity can definitely be an appeal for practising members). On the other hand, you have individuals who conclude life has no meaning, that we are all just survival machines who roam Earth for a snapshot of time to pass on our genes to the next generation. But individually, meaning is a personal conclusion that can be used to inspire action. Whether that is derived from an organized collective, individual desire, or creating a positive difference, these reasons provide a foundation from which you can act to find real fulfilment in everyday life.

Purpose is not this grand, unmoveable, permanent plan. Shaking off the association of 'forever' from the mission you align yourself with takes away some of the pressure. You have lived with purpose for most of your life, even if you were unaware of what it was. Our purpose shapes our actions and goals for periods of time. For me, as a teenager, my purpose was to go out, have fun, experiment and make my friends laugh. As a young adult starting university, my purpose was to make my family proud by getting my degree. And during my PhD, my purpose was to contribute towards the field of Alzheimer's disease research in memory of my nan. Our purpose has permission to change because *we* change.

Purpose is often derived from our core values: tough-to-shift beliefs ingrained as part of 'who we are'. But even these ideals can alter. This is currently being exemplified by many of us trying to save our planet. Ethical choices in terms of what we eat, what we buy, how we travel and how we recycle have become top of many of our agendas, whereas not so long ago, we'd use a plastic straw without a second thought. The core value of 'living ethically' has become central in thousands of people's lives and, with it, completely changed their purpose.

In the past, I have struggled with defining my purpose and had a really hard time unpicking which of my goals I'd absorbed from others' expectations of me and what I actually wanted to achieve in my life. During my PhD, I started a social media profile to talk about the brain and make some of the cool neuroscience being published understandable, fun and applicable. I noticed that posts about myself – my achievements, my downfalls, my advice – got the most engagement. Without consciously realizing, my goal switched from 'making fun and accessible neuroscience content' to 'let's please my audience'. I began obsessing over ridiculous things like how often I should post, what time that should be at, and what tags I should use. I would be buzzing when I had achieved something – an experiment working, a new job opportunity, a passed exam – not because I was proud of myself, but because I knew it would make a good post. I crashed so hard into the 'followers + likes = self-worth' equation of our digital society that I decided to step away. Did I want my mood ruled by how well a post did on social media? Did I want to worry on every trip I took about when I could get the 'right' photo? Did I want to spend five hours a day scrolling on my phone so I could keep up with trends? And the answer to all these was **absolutely not**. I took stock and thought about my original goal – bringing brain science out of academic journals and into the mainstream – and came back to the conclusion that that was how I wanted to use these platforms. I had to reorient myself using my purpose to educate and inspire, and not rely on trends to tell me what to create.

SCI

Purpose and meaning in life are not readily defined with regards to chemicals, processes and experiments. But when considering why we might ascribe meaning to our lives, our brain's desire for order and control likely plays a part. Day in, day out, random things happen to us. Some of these events can be labelled as 'good'. Maybe you bumped into an old friend who has an exciting job opportunity to tell you about, or you walk through your favourite neighbourhood and notice a 'for sale' sign on your dream house. Or you study the exact three topics that come up in your final exam for a tough course. Alternatively, events can also be deemed bad: spilling coffee over your white trousers, missing the train into work, or losing your job.

No matter what label an incident receives, we are attempting to make sense of events in the context of our individual life story. Like going through a hard break-up or missing out on a place at the university of your choice. Your friends and family will continually tell you 'It wasn't meant to be' and 'You'll see why it didn't work out'. At the time, it can be hard to respond to these statements with anything but welling up or an outburst of frustration, whereas later we can often reflect and slot this event into our story. For people in religious groups, tough times can be a challenge from their god. For climate activists, a bump in the road is (probably the worst word to use here) fuel for the next rally or protest. Rough patches or things not working out as we hoped become springboards for new opportunities. In my own life, if I had been accepted into Oxford University at age eighteen, I would never have met my partner or all my wonderful friends. It is unfathomable to think of my life without those people or experiences, making me grateful for the Oxford rejection.

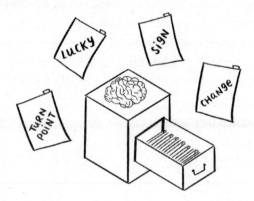

Even if meaning were to be boiled down to a simple mechanism to help our brains make sense of situations, it is still extremely powerful. Meaning is one of the major driving forces behind getting over, moving on, accepting challenges and handling defeat – all processes critical for making change. And having a purpose, or a meaningful mission to live by, can help us to get through testing times – whether we push, crawl or muddle.

When defining a meaningful purpose for ourselves, we are heavily influenced by our core values. Core values are internal constructs which give us a sense of 'who we are', guiding our decisions and behaviour. Say you were told to give feedback to someone in your work team or project group for not pulling their weight. How would you deliver it? You may think it is most important that your peer gives you and other members of the team respect, so your approach could be to outline where they have let you down. Or you could navigate the conversation with compassion, considering what this person might be going through outside work which has led to their disengagement. These approaches show how different core values – self-respect and compassion – drastically alter a person's response to the same situation.

In neuroscience, value has largely been defined in an economic sense regarding decision-making. How much value 'choice A' has over 'choice B' impacts which of the two options we decide to go for. But some investigations into core values have shown they have real sway in influencing action. According to social psychology from the early 1990s, there are ten core values that can be classed into four domains:[1] conservation (keeping things as they are), openness to change (changing things), self-enhancement (helping yourself) and self-transcendence (helping others). If someone is more conservative, they will prefer upholding traditions, whereas a person more open to change will seek novelty. Self-enhancing individuals prioritize power and achievement, whereas those who are self-transcending put focus on the greater collective good.

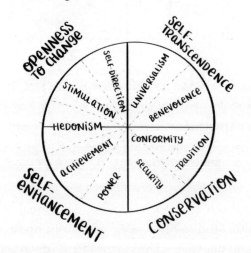

An individual can house a mixture of traits from all four domains. You may love your holiday traditions but vote liberal; you may focus on passing your finals to achieve your degree but volunteer at your local food bank. When you search 'core values' online, extensive lists pop up with tens of words to choose from. But research exploring how people's core values impact how they behave in specific situations has focused on these four categories. Most of these assessments have been done in the context of keeping or giving away money, meaning results should be approached with caution. Money means different things to different people. If you have had very little all your life and make a choice to keep the money rather than give it away, that might not necessarily reflect the value of that gift or your belief system. But a small study reported that individuals who tended towards giving the money they received away to a charitable organization (denoted as self-transcendence) had increased brain activity in regions associated with considering others (like the dorsomedial prefrontal cortex). This contrasts to individuals who kept more of the monetary gift for themselves, who had higher activity in certain areas associated with valuation and reward upon receiving the cash.[2] This area of research still has a long way to go in terms of exploring other core values outside the realm of financial rewards, but studies like this are beginning to provide data for how our core values – whether we recognize what they are or not – impact the choices we make.

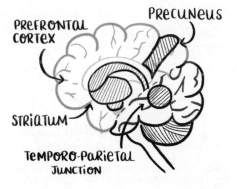

Identifying and acting in accordance with personal core values may also impact health. Studies have linked these with boosted well-being,[3] reduced levels of negative emotional states,[4] decreased depressive symptoms,[5] and even improved the richness of memory content.[6] One study that followed an ageing population over many years found those with a greater sense of purpose in life had better cognitive abilities and fewer brain changes associated with Alzheimer's disease.[7] However, caution must be exercised when interpreting these results, as associations alone do not prove causation. Understanding the biological impact of living by values and purpose may help validate these effects. Does a sense of purpose increase connections between neurons and help build a more 'resilient' brain? Or lower overall stress by being able to handle negative events better? Or is it just that people with a sense of purpose are more health conscious so seek medical help early? There are still a lot of questions to answer regarding the true impact of purpose on our health. But still, having a purpose in life potentially provides benefits beyond goal-seeking.

Another way to define a purpose is to think about how your work can impact other people. Altruism – helping others without an agenda – has been shown to be incredibly rewarding for the person helping others (cue the debate on whether altruism is actually altruistic). For example, a study looking at the impact of purpose in life on happiness in South Korea found individuals whose values prioritized self-transcendent values, like spirituality and social relationships, tended to rate themselves as happier than individuals who prioritized self-enhancing values, like striving for more power, achievement and money.[8] Linking others into a purpose, whether directly – by trying to help a certain group of individuals, like sharing knowledge on a certain subject area to help people learn – or indirectly – by knowing this change will ultimately lead to others being happier, like getting healthy to improve interactions within relationships – can make a mission more meaningful and rewarding.

APPLY

To define your current purpose, it is important to recognize what purposes you have lived by in the past, your current core values, where you find meaning in life and how you can beneficially impact others.

BRAINTENANCE: PAST PURPOSES

By looking at your behaviour, or the goals you had at certain times in your life, you can normally whittle down what your overall purpose was. Sometimes these purposes may feel like they align with your values, and your goals at the time were in keeping with how you want to be. Other times, you may not like the purpose you uncover. These could be out of alignment or driven by external validation. There will also be instances where it is hard to pin down what your purpose was – normally observed as a period without many goals or lower life satisfaction. And on other occasions, you may feel like you had multiple purposes, with goals all over the shop. I have definitely had windows like this and I can normally find one purpose that dominated, or a common theme that tied them together. Seeing how purposes have guided you in the past makes a case for setting them with intention moving forward.

Consider four points in your life and try to figure out what your purpose was at the time.

Time ago	Age	What was most important to you?	What actions were you taking? What were you working towards?	Purpose
10 years	20	Getting into university	Reading neuroscience books, visiting universities	To realize my potential and go to a top university
5 years	25	Being in athletic shape	Gym 4 times a week, 15,000 steps a day, eating high protein diet	To improve my health so others would look up to me
2 years	. . .	. . .	. . .	. . .
1 year	. . .	. . .	. . .	. . .

BRAINTENANCE: VALUE VANTAGE

Defining your current purpose involves understanding what is important to you and the principles you want to live by. For some, looking through a list of values and picking their top two, five or ten can bring focus and insight. Personally, I find these lists overwhelming. I scroll through them thinking 'yep I want that one, and that one, and that one' until 90 per cent of the values are in my basket like it is a Black Friday sale. The method that works for me is reflecting on moments in my life where I have felt most myself, most at peace, most joyful and most proud. It helps me focus on what is truly important to me. Referring back to these answers has helped me to live with integrity, and make decisions and choices based on my values.

Consider the feelings below. Reflect on a time you felt each sensation and consider what it was about those circumstances that led you to feel that way.

Feeling	Time	Why?
Proud	Made a video for Mum's 60th	Took seven hours of dedicated work and she absolutely loved it
Peace	Sitting on the beach listening to the waves	Allowed myself to be in the present and appreciate nature
Joy	. . .	. . .
Appreciated	. . .	. . .
Helpful	. . .	. . .

From these occasions, think of five words or phrases that capture the themes running through the events selected to highlight some values you consider to be important.

Creativity   Caring   Wonder   . . .   . . .

BRAINTENANCE: WHO ARE YOU HELPING?

A huge factor in defining purpose is determining how your actions and goals from this mission will help others. This could be helping your family, the people you work with, your community. Or it might be helping future generations, a certain animal, plant species or the planet. Having a purpose which extends beyond yourself will give you a surface to cling to when you feel like giving up. With my PhD, whenever I had a tough day or week, I would remind myself who I was doing this for: my nan, her siblings and her mum who died with Alzheimer's disease. I was doing this for them, and for the other nans, grandads, parents and people currently living with Alzheimer's disease and other types of dementia, the hope being that in the future there are not as many individuals living with these conditions. A small hiccup or an almighty cock-up would be put into perspective when I considered that reasoning. Even if your goal feels like it is for your benefit, it will positively affect others too. Those around you will feed off your new lease of energy and be infected with your happiness. You can always view positive change from the perspective of how it benefits someone else.

. . . .

Think of yourself achieving your goal from your ideal day – who will benefit from you being in this position aside from yourself?
Goal: *Working out every day.*

Helping: *My family – keeping me healthy means more energy for when we are together, and improves my mood and well-being so I can be a good support for others.*

BRAINTENANCE: MISSION 'I'M-POSSIBLE'

With your goal, your core values and who you want to help in mind, you can craft a statement; a mission that you intend to live by. This statement should define your purpose and be a guide for how you make decisions, interact with others and take action. I like my statement to be a single sentence. And it can take time to really settle on. Think of this statement as if it were being written on a banner: short, clear, to the point. Zoom out from your goal and consider how it fits into the picture of what you want from your life. If your goal was followed by a 'because', your purpose should fit neatly to round off that sentence.

Also, don't worry too much about your mission statement being 'it'. This isn't a permanent, rest-of-life mantra, but something you can check in on, adapt and change whenever you feel the time is right. I like to reassess mine at change points in my life, like at New Year or starting a school term (even though I'm no longer in school but still, we roll). Go with what you think will bring you the most fulfilment and will positively impact others. You should think of this statement and feel like you are taking a sip on the best cuppa of your life – giving you a sense of calm, peace and joy.

Crafting your mission statement

Consider your answers to the following statements:

1. The biggest wish for your life:	3. Who you want to help:
2. Your five values:	4. The difference you want to see in the world:

Thinking about what connects these things together, play around with crafting a statement that ties together these elements.

My mission is . . .

- Say the statement out loud. How does it feel?
- Imagine telling your most trusted friend or family member your statement. Does it feel right?
- Say your goal followed by your statement. Do they align?

Once you are happy with your mission statement, you can write it out and stick it somewhere you can see it, put it in the front of your diary, in a card in your wallet, or just keep it in your head to refer to when making decisions. If you start to act in accordance with your statement, using it as a guide, you will hopefully start to feel that your actions are aligning with the person you most want to be for yourself and others.

WRAP UP

Having a clearer idea of what your purpose is, especially seeing it in relation to others, can build determination to keep going, even when you don't want to. When it comes to doing things for ourselves, we give in so easily. If you knew you had a friend waiting for you at the gym, or for you to post that video online, or for you to get out and protest, you would be much more likely to follow through. When you feel like you can't be bothered, or your thoughts are giving you every excuse to throw in the towel, say your purpose to yourself and see those thoughts hush up. Purpose doesn't mean happiness, but it does mean being able to weather periods of turmoil, to be persistent, and to have grit.

You may now look at your goal in relation to your purpose and find it is a perfect fit. Or it may need a little tweaking. Or you may have realized that your goal wasn't yours at all. After you have considered what is important to you and how you want to show up day to day, you may completely change what you currently want to be focusing on. And that is totally fine. Take a bit of time to go back to your ideal day and think about how your purpose can play out in some of those actions. Make sure your goal fits in with what you want and who you want to be so you can start to drive towards an end destination, somewhere *you* want to go.

CHAPTER 6

GET AWARE

With the end destination sorted, you next need to consider where you're starting from.

When chasing goals, we often set out on a quest of achievement without thinking about where we currently are. On these ventures, the start line matters: you can't just plug in the end point and hope you will end up where you want to be. This will likely result in you pulling over, lost and frustrated, with no better idea about how to reach your destination. Or you may turn around and end up back where you started, thinking it's better to stay where you're comfortable and familiar, even if that isn't necessarily the best environment for your well-being.

You also need to consider the state of the vehicle you are travelling in. It could have windscreen wipers that don't work properly, or one of the lights may be broken. And often, the boot is packed with unnecessary items we end up dragging along with us. Is it any surprise that, as we set off, we wonder why it feels difficult to drive?

Before we hit the road, we need to open our own hoods and do a full MOT. Being aware of the current beliefs and behaviours you are taxiing around is an essential step in separating the useful from the not-so-useful. Dropping a pin on the map to understand where you are currently at and looking inwards to recognize the strengths that will propel you forwards (alongside the less favourable, old-coffee-cup-left-in-the-door-type of ideas that may be dragging you down) can provide a more accurate reflection of how the journey might go, the challenges you might face, and what tweaks may need to be made to ensure a smoother ride.

We are a walking sack of established beliefs and behaviours, which were initially formed to help us navigate the world our brain has perceived us to be living in. Some of these may be beneficial when you are considering the goal you have set for yourself. You may be an early riser and know this provides a good chunk of time to go work out. But there may be other defaults which are holding you back. Your early mornings could currently be filled with a two-hour-long scrolling session on social media in bed, followed by a rush to get yourself together for a day of work. While the pull to the newsfeed may feel irresistible, it could be damaging our hopes of progress. Putting new goals into the context of our current lives is essential in seeing what behaviours may be doing us a disservice.

When we act, we often do so reflexively and impulsively, driven by our habitual responses, recalled memories or emotional states. In the moment, these behavioural triggers mostly drive our next steps without our full recognition. We unquestionably follow through with the action the brain offers up to us; an option which is based on the assessment of the situation we are facing through its web of established networks and programmed responses. Whether that is snapping at a friend because you are stressed, continuing to play video games until 2 a.m., or avoiding an event because of nerves.

But we don't have to accept the action our brain provides as our response to a given situation. It isn't the only option we have. If we can sit and mull it over, to question if that action is actually what we want to do, we give ourselves the ability to recognize other choices.

Slowing down and providing space to question whether the way we feel we should act is the best way to approach a situation can be achieved by becoming more self-aware. Self-awareness is a person's conscious recognition of their behaviours, feelings and traits, allowing them to identify action triggers and assess if the proposed response is going to be of use to them. This reflective period not only gives us some authority over our reactions as they arise, but can also provide an overall picture of our current behavioural patterns which are unhelpful. This insight is powerful in seeking goals as it allows us to see what we could work on in order to make our mission easier. Instead of trudging uphill dragging a weighty bag of unneeded behaviours and beliefs, self-awareness can help us to decide which items can be tossed to lighten the load during goal pursuit.

For me, becoming more aware of my own motivations and behaviours has been transformative in crafting change in my life. I have pretty strong people-pleasing tendencies, and for most of my life, I didn't see how many of my actions came from a place of wanting to be liked or seen as helpful. I would quickly surrender in conflict, never complain even if I felt things weren't okay, and agree to do things I didn't want to nor had the time for, leaving me exhausted and frustrated with myself. My default was to make others' lives easier to make sure I was liked. I am not saying I now love a fight (the opposite is still true), but when someone asks me to do something, I stop and really think 'is this something I want to do and can I fit it in' before giving an answer. The thought 'just say yes because then they'll like you' is still often the first thing to pop up in most of these interactions, but I very rarely just let that flood out anymore. Becoming aware of my need to please and interfering with my default 'yes, no problem' response has saved me a lot of time, stress and energy, set important boundaries in my personal and professional relationships which were so blatantly missing before, and allowed me to focus on working towards my goals.

SCI

Self-awareness has been associated in a variety of studies with improving aspects of people's lives. From increasing confidence to fostering better work environments, having more fulfilling relationships and improving creativity,[1] seeing ourselves in a clear way is an important step in making effective change.

The roots of self-awareness in the brain are still unknown. Self-awareness means being able to recognize the underlying push and pull experienced in certain situations using the very organ doing the pushing and pulling. The mechanisms underpinning our ability to turn inwards in this way have been assigned to certain brain regions, like the value-assigning anterior cingulate cortex and the body-aware insula, but also to more general, diffuse networks throughout the brain. An individual with brain damage to these two specific brain regions and the prefrontal cortex more generally still showed aspects of self-awareness, like recognizing themselves and thinking about thinking (metacognition),[2] hinting that our sense of self doesn't solely rely on the regions involved in solving problems and checking in on how the body feels.

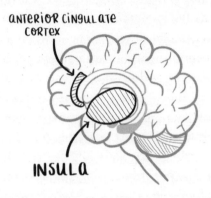

Additionally, it has been proposed that our sense of self may actually be a by-product of our evolution.[3] In social species like humans, it is important to have a grasp on what others in the group are planning and feeling in order to act cooperatively. Our brains are good at producing a 'model' for how others think based on their characteristics and circumstances, allowing us to predict how they might react in response to our actions. Our ability to model others' minds activates a network of brain regions called the default mode network, shown to be online when we are bored and daydreaming,[4] and also when we think about ourselves. Could it be that our ability to look inward and assess our own behaviours has arisen because our brains are good at modelling the minds of others? Perhaps. Even in the face of not knowing exactly how the brain generates the concept of 'self', we can still use our ability to step outside ourselves and question our actions in order to help make effective change.

Being self-aware gives us the ability to reflect and self-evaluate, which goes against the brain's desire to quickly detect what's going on and direct action. Understanding the thoughts and feelings tied to situations when you act out of alignment with your desires can help you step back and consider a different course of action. Seeing our thinking and emotional patterns in this way is a common technique used in therapy to emphasize that thoughts are not facts. Cognitive behavioural therapy, or CBT, is a method used to identify thoughts and feelings so they can be processed in a more objective way.[5] It may be that your thoughts have a tendency to jump off at the deep end in the face of a problem, going straight to the worst-case scenario. A lower essay grade than you anticipated turns into being a complete failure, a slower run becomes never being able to hit your target, a 'no' from an interview means never being able to get a job. These thoughts are not true; they have no factual evidence behind them. But when stressed, or feeling dejected, they can feel as real as gravity. The 'I'm a failure and never going to amount to anything' thoughts are all forms of catastrophizing – that is, seeing more unfavourable or undesired outcomes of an event and latching onto them as if they are a prediction. When these thoughts pop up, instead of falling into the whirlpool of 'what ifs', recognizing them and naming them as 'catastrophizing' can remove the sense of inevitability they often have. During my PhD, I went on a course at my university to help with perfectionism (another method of handling this state when working is coming up in Chapter 13) and was taught this technique to stop myself spiralling into 'my PhD is doomed' whenever an experiment went wrong (which they did *all* the time). Labelling a

negative response to an event such as 'catastrophizing', or even just as 'thought', can remove the gravitas we assign to our thinking and provide us with room to question and evaluate just how true that thinking is before taking our next step.

The voice in our head is not an encyclopaedia. It does not sprout true statements or facts. Far from it. Individuals with certain psychological conditions like schizophrenia can experience auditory hallucinations, hearing phantom voices and instructions which can be detrimental to their mental health, and some people don't hear a voice in their head at all,[6] negating the idea that our internal dialogue is giving us an accurate running commentary of the world. If you think using words, the brain displays activity in a language area of the frontal cortex. This area helps us to construct words with our mouths when speaking. Its activation during internal reflection or when sussing out a situation is believed to correspond to what some people describe as their 'inner voice', prepping us ahead of physically speaking these words out loud. And when this voice is cut off from knowing why we are doing something, it will make up any old excuse to justify the action. This has been highlighted in individuals with severe epilepsy who have undergone a rare operation to remove areas of their brain containing the epicentre of their seizure activity. One of these procedures is called a hemispherectomy, where up to one half of the brain can be removed or cut off from talking to the other side.[7] Although this is an extreme form of surgery, individuals live a relatively normal life following rehabilitation and

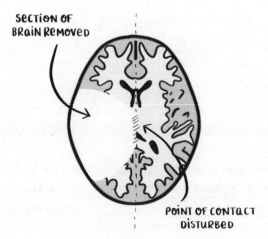

SECTION OF
BRAIN REMOVED

POINT OF CONTACT
DISTURBED

adjustment. And in a small subset of these people, the inner voice was exposed for being a complete Billy Liar.

Language centres in the brain sit on one side (in most people, the left). The two sides of our brain are always communicating with each other to create the most accurate picture of what is going on. If the sides of the brain cannot talk to each other, like in individuals after a hemispherectomy, the 'inner voice' can be in the dark about what the other side of the brain knows. The right side of our brain houses the majority of neurons controlling the left side of our body and vice versa, including the detection of vision. Our right eye sends what it sees to the left visual cortex and the left eye to the right. In individuals with severed connections between the two sides of the brain, blocking off the right eye means only the right side of their brain (via the left eye – I know, it's unnecessarily confusing. Our brains obviously just love being difficult) can perceive what is going on in the environment. And this effectively shuts off the inner voice located on the left side from this information.

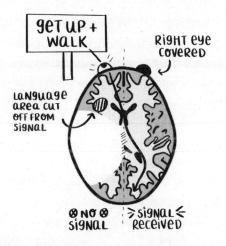

In these situations, when the half of the brain is given instructions to do something, like 'get up and walk', and the inner voice is left in the dark, it will still come up with a reason for performing that action. In one reported incident, when the researcher asked why the individual was walking, they justified their action by saying, 'I'm going to get a coke'.[8] Their inner voice came up with a reason for why they were walking, even though it was completely false. Realizing our own inner voices can pull the wool over our eyes helps us to see that whatever thoughts, justifications or assessments pop into our heads can be questioned, scrutinized or ignored, rather than taken at face value.

Knowing the influence our thoughts, feelings and circumstances have over how we act, self-awareness can help us to reframe some of these 'rock-solid' assessments. There is normally more than one way to interpret any situation. If you have a long commute to work, it can be seen as a pain in the neck, resulting in a stressful and frustrating journey, whereas others on the exact same commute see the hours outside the office as a chance to switch off, or learn something new by catching up on their favourite podcast or book. Seeing that there are options when it comes to processing a situation can influence not only how we feel about it but direct future behaviour. For example, students who were set an unpassable exam as part of an experiment were told to interpret the failure in different ways. One group was told that they were great, that the test result wasn't about their ability, whereas another group was asked to show compassion towards themselves, taking responsibility for the failure in a kind manner. After these interventions, it was found the second, self-compassionate, group spent more time studying for their next test compared to those who received the self-esteem boost,[9] highlighting how different interpretations of the same event can impact action.

This is not an 'always look on the bright side of life' or a 'think positive thoughts' mandate. Some situations are not so easy to interpret in a positive way and sugar-coating certain incidences like trauma or loss can be detrimental to mental health. But when it comes to the day-to-day resistances you come up against, like the thoughts telling you you have no time for that twenty-minute walk, or feelings we assign as negative, like being nervous to give that big presentation, these can be reassessed. Recognizing these events and thinking about if there is another way to view them may help you make effective change in your life and feel less at the mercy of your off-the-mark thoughts and emotions. Maybe that lack of time you perceive is a sign you need to break away from your current state and a walk may give you the refresh you need. Or those nerves you feel about the presentation are a sign you really care about the work you will be talking about. Reframing in your favour, or at least seeing there is another viewpoint that could be taken, may take the pressure off and allow you to get out of your head, improving your daily experiences and the experiences of others you interact with.

APPLY

Increasing your self-awareness can help identify which behaviours or beliefs are currently not doing you any favours when it comes to getting your goal.

BRAINTENANCE: I SPY

Set-ups inevitably exist in our lives which create friction when attempting to create new behaviours. With your goal in mind, have a think about what practices are acting against where you want to be. This can aid you in identifying areas to alter so you can align your common behaviours with your aims. If you are trying to spend more time working on a creative project, those four hours watching reality TV are probably something you want to cut down. Freeing up those hours in the evening to make space for a new practice can open up your mind to the benefits of altering actions.

Doing this for your beliefs is also beneficial. Our beliefs are tough to question because we think they are true. But we tend to make a lot of our life choices based on these ideals. We hold beliefs about what we should and shouldn't eat, what makes a good person, what happens to us after we leave this life. But we also hold beliefs about ourselves based on what we have experienced and been taught. Beliefs can be challenged, especially if they are doing you a disservice. If you believe you will never be successful, chances are, when things don't work out as planned, an 'I told you so' monologue starts (while anything that goes your way gets ignored). Questioning these ways of thinking can act as a first step in changing your perspective on them, making them feel less concrete. Pull all the items out of the backpack and ask yourself which ones are unnecessarily weighing you down.

Which behaviours and beliefs are currently preventing you from achieving your goals?

I am being held back by . . .
believing I will never be successful; watching an entire TV series every night until 2 a.m.

You can also try doing this one on the go. Pick a day this week and go about your normal business, but have alarms set on your phone throughout the day (between five to ten at random times). When that alarm goes off, ask yourself the question: 'Is what I am doing right now helping or hindering my mission?' I even set the alarm label as 'help or hinder' to help me identify actions or thinking patterns that are not useful to my mission.

BRAINTENANCE: IN YOUR CORNER

Self-awareness of your current state is not about knocking down every behaviour you do. It is just as much about seeing the incredible skills and practices you already have and using them to your advantage. You may know you have a knack for explaining hard concepts, or turning a dry topic into something fun and relatable, or making people feel at ease in your presence, or being a brilliant listener. You may believe you can handle adversity because of what you have been through in the past, or that you can achieve a top grade through hard work and dedication, or that you are a great friend and are there for people when they need it most. All these behaviours and beliefs, the ones you feel serve you, should be harnessed when working towards a goal. Identifying these superpowers and assigning them to the mission of getting your goal can allow you to see how many helpful tools you are already carrying around with you. Knowing you already harbour incredible skills is a powerful realization and can challenge the idea that you need to change everything about yourself in order to progress. You don't.

What are the current things you do or skills you have which will help you along the way to getting to your goal?

Look back on what you have achieved in the past, what you are proud of, what traits make you thrive. This could be the project you loved creating, the time you helped a friend feel better, or delivered a kick-ass presentation.

....

I'm a boss at . . .
Public speaking, listening, design . . .

....

This exercise can be done in your own reflection (it is a nice journal prompt) or, if you are feeling up to being showered in praise, ask those closest to you. They will have too many incredible comments about the things you do.

Once you have an idea about these assets, step back and put them in the context of your goal.

....

How can you use them to help move you along?
Incredible public speaking skills = use to present the importance of health and fitness online

BRAINTENANCE: ROOM TO REFLECT

In order to enhance self-awareness, carve out time where you can sit with minimal distractions and observe your present state of being. This can allow you to get curious about what is driving your behaviour so you can begin to create a gap before reacting. Reflective time can be made through practices like mindfulness meditation, or journaling, or taking a walk around your local park, or sitting with a cuppa listening to your favourite music. Any practice that allows you to step outside the events and drama and routines of your life and, in an objective, non-judgemental way, look at the thoughts and feelings you are currently experiencing.

Like sitting on the moon and gazing back at the Earth, these practices aim to take you out of the world you are living in to observe the comings and goings in your mind from a neutral standpoint. These practices can incorporate labelling thoughts or identifying sensations in the body that are tied to certain emotional states, dissipating their gravitas by reducing them to physical processes. While previous studies on understanding the effects of mindfulness meditation have their limitations (the practices used have varied and, most often, been trialled by small numbers of people at a single point in time), the research so far leans towards the practice being able to increase self-awareness.[10] In the rush of life, it can be difficult to identify thoughts or feelings that drive behaviour, so taking time to slow down and see your thoughts from a more objective viewpoint can be helpful in becoming aware of some of the triggers for your actions and reactions.

. . . .

Set aside a few minutes each day to have a moment of reflection.

In this time, the aim is to step off the set, to remove yourself from the action and tap into your state in this moment. During this time, you could try:

- Mindfulness meditation: you can use YouTube or an app to guide you.
- Free writing: writing a sentence, a paragraph or a page about what is currently on your mind, or use journaling prompts from the internet (there are many great questions out there to get your juices flowing).
- Take a walk: loop your block or take the dog out. Focus on what your senses are experiencing.
- Teatime: pour a cuppa and do nothing but enjoy every sip. Whack a bit of relaxing music on while you are at it and bring that spa feeling to your kitchen.
- Power shower: one of my faves. Stick on relaxing tunes and, when showering, focus on the feeling of the water as it hits your skin. I like to imagine the water washing away any emotional states or thinking spirals I have felt stuck in.

Try to schedule your reflective period for the same time every day as this will make you more likely to do it. For me, I like to do five to ten minutes of guided meditation after I have had a shower and put all the face creams on to get in a bit of mental space each day.

BRAINTENANCE: WHAT'S UP

When it comes to opening an inquiry with your thoughts and feelings, a more effective way to get an answer out of your inner interpreter is to use the word 'what' instead of 'why'. We always want to know why – we are curious and like to get to the root of a problem. And 'why' questions have their place in helping understand ourselves. But the issue with only asking 'why' questions is that there isn't a guarantee you will find an answer when it comes to gaining clarity on how certain situations make us act. And even if you think you have cracked it, the answer you've landed on could be wrong. If you want to know why you avoid doing projects until you have to rush at the last minute, you might be stumped for an answer, leaving you feeling helpless of ever changing your ways. Our brains can make things that are not real feel like they are (we have all had *those* dreams). And sometimes, instead of promoting change, finding a 'why' can give us an excuse for staying the same.

On the other hand, 'what' questions can provide feedback on the drivers of your behaviour and help derive an action plan for moving away from those which aren't serving you. 'What' questions are objective. In scientific research, most hypotheses revolve around 'what' or 'how' something happens rather than 'why', as the former narrows the search. Take as an example procrastinating on a tough project until the last minute. If you approach your behaviour with a question like 'what is it about this project that makes me not want to do it?', you can get some answers which can be actioned. This could be that you don't have the knowledge to answer the question, or that you don't enjoy the subject. These answers have solutions. If you feel you are lacking some understanding of the topic, your next step might be to spend a few days reading and making notes before you write a single word. If you're not particularly enthralled by the topic, focus on making the writing sessions more fun and manageable. Chances are, there is *something* about the work you will enjoy; it just isn't always staring you in the face.

. . . .

Look at the list of behaviours and beliefs you have thought of that are not doing you many favours in relation to your goal.

What is it about the situations that trigger these unhelpful actions? Answers could include feeling afraid of failure, not wanting to let others down, or lack of joy. This can help to find actions which can address these states (some ideas coming up in Chapter 13).

BRAINTENANCE: REFRAMING

Finally, when it comes to challenging or uncomfortable situations, seeing you have multiple options to interpret those circumstances can be useful in providing you with different ways to act. Having these options laid out, even if you don't necessarily use them, shows us our default is not the only way. Our singular interpretation isn't right or wrong; it is just one of many options. And if you are continually coming up against this situation, it might be worth trying on a different viewpoint and seeing how you feel afterwards.

....

Take a situation you currently can't stand. It could be the commute, a hard project at work, or chores around the house. Now think of five other ways that situation could be interpreted.

Task: *commute to work.* Current view: *feel like it is a waste of time.*

Time to listen to a podcast	Separation between home & work	Get my step count up	Space to try a mindfulness practice	Send emails

WRAP UP

By getting an insight into your current behaviours and identifying which ones are helpful and which are stopping you from moving forward, you can start to question what is driving these responses and find solutions to help you unpick them. Some of these changes may be easier to make than others depending on how ingrained the behaviours are in your daily life. And there is no way to be 100 per cent aware and reflective all the time. Certain impulsive reactions are guaranteed to slip through the net. But the first step is seeing these triggers. Because you can't change what you can't see.

CHAPTER 7

DIRECT YOUR FOCUS

A fundamental aspect of achieving any goal is focus. But exactly how that focus is directed is vital for both making progress and enjoying the process.

With your start and end location sorted, it's natural to want to plug in your GPS, select the first route it recommends and drive towards your target; daydreaming about how wonderful the destination will be. This outcome-focused form of travelling can make roadblocks infuriating, breakdowns frustrating and detouring disastrous.

By overly focusing on the outcomes of your goals, other opportunities can be missed which may bring you the same result faster, or end up being a better fit. It is important to have an initial vision to set your direction, but focusing on this all the time can be detrimental. Instead of your goal being a rigid, single destination, see it more like a compass; guiding you in the general direction of what you want. This can keep your mind open for opportunities that align with your desires while giving you the flexibility to adapt and reconfigure if your current path doesn't turn out as expected. Blockages can then be taken in your stride, allowing you to figure out how to handle an obstruction or pivot slightly to try a new direction.

While being hyper-focused on a singular way to achieve a very specific outcome can be inefficient, focusing on what you spend your time doing each day is instrumental in gaining momentum. Prioritization prevents you spinning twenty different plates badly. Picking one thing to be your focus and working on doing it really well is a sure-fire way to make headway towards your goal. Finding this one thing can sometimes be obvious. If you are wanting to build strength, gym sessions may be your number-one activity. On other occasions, say if you are starting a business or completing a creative project, it may take some trial and error until you find an activity that clicks. Daily practices that make it easier to work towards your goal are coming up in Section 3. But before then, it is important we find that sweet spot between too much and too little focus when it comes to making progress in your overall goal while also enjoying the ride.

WHY

All projects, no matter how small, start with a vision. We can see what needs to be changed and create an imaginary ideal of how we can make this happen. Like a sculptor standing in front of a block of marble, seeing the end product before it exists in reality is critical in bringing the statue to life. This is exactly the point of the ideal day exercise (see page 67). It helps uncover what things you currently enjoy about your day and other elements you want to change in order to create a more fulfilling experience.

If your goal is focused on starting your own sustainable fashion business, being conscious of this aim in daily life can help you to see things previously missed. That job advert that pops into your inbox for a buyer at an eco-friendly brand, the conversation you catch on the bus about opportunities to volunteer at fashion week, the friend you bump into at the park who has a contact for you to call. These random events take on new meaning in the context of your goal, allowing you to identify and explore potentially exciting opportunities.

But problems can arise when our single far-off vision becomes a daily fixation.

Having an ideal is a great place to start. But circumstances change, people change, you change, so taking new information on board and recalibrating your vision keeps your goal relevant and attainable. When a sculptor starts chipping away at the marble, their vision for the sculpture updates as they go. They may take too much off with one knock of the hammer. Instead of heaving the marble block into the bin, they think, 'How can I make this work?' That chip may make the resulting statue even better than they first imagined. But the only way for them to come to that conclusion is to keep going after their original outcome is dashed.

Another potential pitfall is that while a glamorous endpoint may act as fuel to push through a tricky task in front of you, more often than not, the big picture is too big to motivate you to do the little things. Although a dreamy vision may give some people the motivation to crack on, more likely, it will leave you stressed about the amount you need to do, anxious that you're not doing the 'right' thing, and resentful that you are still nowhere near your idealized life.

This makes for a nuanced but important line: be focused enough to have a detailed vision of where you want to be and use it as a guide, but not so fixed on that vision that it prevents you from seeing other opportunities and distracts you from doing the work required to get there. When a sculptor is working, their focus is rarely on the overall sculpture. Every so often, they take a step back to see how the piece of art is shaping up to decide what they should do next, but they then hone back in on a tiny area of detail. If after every chip they stood back, (1) it would take forever to finish, (2) they would see barely any progress and (3) they would be frustrated that the outcome they have in their mind still hasn't manifested itself into reality. Strike a fine balance between having enough focus on the big picture so you are working towards a clear vision, but not to the extent it makes the process become a chore.

SCI

Our brains are constantly bombarded with incoming information in the form of sights, sounds, scents and other sensations. Hundreds, if not thousands, of signals are ready to flood your brain to give you the lowdown of what is going on around you. But not all that information is able to get through. When you are at a bustling party, you can tune into a single conversation while suppressing the background chatter. Or if you are looking for someone in the crowd, you can pick them out among a sea of faces. The process of directing our focus is called selective attention,[1] which arises due to the restraints of our brain's processing power. If you try taking in every element of a scene simultaneously you will see your brain swing from one stimulus to the next, latching on to snippets of information at a time.

As we can only focus on limited information, our brain must decide what information should stay and what can sashay away. To do this, incoming information from the senses is filtered to allow the important stuff to get through. Sometimes, what is 'important' is an attention pull – like an incoming threat or shiny reward. Other times, our attention is directed by internal signals, like our goals. Holding a goal in mind requires working memory, that temporary storage unit created by signals in the prefrontal cortex of the brain. Whatever is being held in this storage can have sway over what we take in from our environment. If you are thinking about buying a new Mini Cooper, it suddenly seems like those cars are popping up everywhere. Unless a Mini convention has come to town, the actual frequency of those cars in your environment hasn't changed, but their importance to you has. And the more you tell yourself you are seeing those cars everywhere, the more they will seem to appear. Our brains' desire to be correct about its own predictions, known as confirmation bias, keeps that model firmly in your line of sight.

This filtering of sensory signals is thought to be mediated by a thin layer of neurons buried deep in the brain called the thalamic reticular nucleus, or TRN. Like filter paper, these brain cells are wrapped around a structure called the thalamus, a hub in the brain that receives signals from other brain areas, and the body. The job of the thalamus is to act as an operator between the brain and body, relaying important information so it can be acted on. Like a check-in attendant, the thalamus decides which incoming signals have the right ticket to ride and which are denied

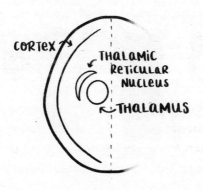

boarding. Information from our senses, like what we see, is processed through the thalamus, meaning incoming signals face this 'in-or-out' scrutiny. But it is thought the thalamic reticular nucleus influences what ends up in the thalamus check-in queue in the first place. Through work in mice, it has been shown that shutting down the TRN can heavily impede attention. And it is in the opposite way to what we might think.

Animals can be taught 'what you hear is *more important* than what you see' through training, meaning they will respond to a certain sound over a visual signal. If they are taught this but have the TRN neurons that monitor visual signals switched off, they have a tough time concentrating on what they are hearing.[2] This suggests that activation of the TRN suppresses non-important signals in order to boost the important ones. At a busy party, it isn't that the person's voice you're tuning into is necessarily amplified, but the background noise of everyone else chatting around you is dialled down, allowing you to focus on the conversation.

Our current goals influence this dampening of 'less important' information. It is thought the prefrontal cortex – where goals can be held – can tell the TRN what is currently desirable (via communicating with a set of structures buried in the brain called the basal ganglia) and this means that incoming information from our senses is potentially filtered before it even gets the chance to be processed! If our brains act in a similar way to those of mice (where most of this work has been done), shutting off the goal-holding prefrontal cortex also impacts task performance.[3] It would be like we're not taking in all the cars and then spotting the one we are keen on buying. Our thalamic reticular nucleus

is suppressing all cars *except* the one we want based on the goal in our prefrontal cortex, making it stand out from the crowd and magically appear on every street corner.

As our goals have a huge influence over the information we prioritize, this has led to the popularization of visualization, a method where you imagine yourself at some point in the future in a scenario you would like to see happen. Visualization is a powerful tool when it comes to perfecting a process, particularly highlighted in elite athletes and sports players. By mentally going through the stages of the ideal golf swing or gymnastic routine, the brain can rehearse the coordination required. If you imagine moving your arm in a swinging motion, the areas responsible for moving your arm activate despite you not physically moving a limb. This activation is below the level that triggers the arm to move, but still engages the motor pattern of the arm moving, allowing the brain cells involved to get more familiar with activating together. It's even been shown in a small study that imagining moving your little finger can improve its strength, likely down to our mental rehearsal capabilities reinforcing the pathways needed.[4] In mice, it has also been shown that they hold a mental representation of a goal location in the prefrontal cortex when navigating towards it.[5] Navigation is unsuccessful if activity in this area is disrupted, highlighting how present-moment visualization keeps them on track towards their intended destination. Our brain's ability to imagine scenarios and rehearse them in our head as if they were real gives us an advantage when in the 'real world', as we can prepare for engagement without having to use energy to practise.

Visualization has also been used to picture ideal outcomes to spur motivation and keep an end goal front and centre. Like imagining how you'll feel when you hug your teammates after winning a competition or signing the contract for your dream house. Vision boards packed with images of these ideal outcomes are used as tools to keep those big goals in mind. Imagining yourself at the 'finish line' of achieving whatever goal you have is different to the visualization used by athletes for perfecting their routines as their focus is on the process rather than the overall final outcome. And while looking towards the end result can be a good motivator for some, it may not be as effective as bringing the goals a little closer to home and focusing on how to make them happen in day-to-day life.

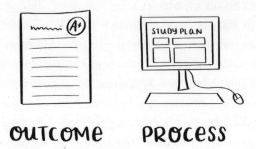

An example of this can be observed in a small 1998 study that found students who visualized themselves achieving a top grade in their final exam during the revision period did worse than students who imagined themselves studying for the test for five minutes each day.[6] The group who imagined the process of studying ended up studying more. The practice allowed them to see how to prepare for the exam and remove anxiety about studying, whereas the A-grade imagining group reported feeling less motivated to actually do the work. When your current reality differs from where you're hoping to end up, this can create a drive to close that gap, resulting in action. But too much visualization of the end result, or even telling other people about what you are planning to achieve, may mentally plug this hole and deplete your drive. This early sense of 'completeness' brings with it a sense of pride, which can make us feel good in the moment (we love to talk about our big plans for change), but then when it comes to doing the difficult work required to reach your goal, you are faced with applying effort to the harder reality.

A method used to combat fantasizing and feeling this premature completeness is called mental contrasting.[7] This technique starts with a vision – thinking about what you want to achieve normally within the next week or month – followed by a simple comparison:

What is standing in the way between where I want to be and where I am now?

If you are wanting to publish your first video online, there may be several things you need to consider before that goal can be achieved.

Maybe your schedule is packed so you need to carve out time to film, or you aren't comfortable with the editing software, so you need to block out a few hours to watch tutorials and practise. Planning to overcome the obstacles in your way should lower friction when trying to achieve a goal. However, it remains uncertain if this technique is impacted by an individual's belief in achieving their goal (as studies so far have only observed people with high expectations of success).[8] It may be important to use this form of action-setting on smaller goals that are just out of reach to make obstacles easier to identify and address. Using your dream scenario as an identifier of barriers instead of an escape could be useful in deciding what to focus on doing next.

Finally, being overly focused on a specific outcome and route towards it can put the mental blinkers on. As our attention is selective and our goals influence what we focus on, having a very restricted idea of the steps that will lead you towards a particular outcome could cause you to miss other opportunities in the environment which may be beneficial. Stepping back from your desired outcome and being more open to events going on around you will help you see different but useful paths. Nailing down your process is vital (more on this in Chapter 9), but having the ability to remove the filters from the background 'noise' every so often allows you to see opportunities in the most unlikely places.

APPLY

Try to strike the right balance between having a big goal but not being overly fixated on it. Break your main goal into smaller parts and focus on the closest target. This directs your attention into the 'goal zone' without completely overwhelming you. From your ideal day exercise, you should have the specific overall goal in mind you want to achieve. If we take a career goal as an example, this could be something specific, such as 'spend my hours from 9 a.m. to 5 p.m. in the hospital working as a reconstructive plastic surgeon', to something more vague, like 'be in a creative role where I get to be outside in nature'. First up, let's get the path down:

BRAINTENANCE: PLAN PATH

Where I am |————————————————| Where I'll be
Student at school   *Reconstructive plastic surgeon*

When it comes to the 'where I'll be', imagine what it will
be like to be in that place. How will I feel? Who else will be
there? Where will I be living? Bringing the end goal to life
in your mind can stop you feeling like it is unreachable or
unattainable. Many of our goals feel this way, like they are a
complete and utter fantasy. By getting a sense of what it will
be like at the end destination, your goal can seem more
tangible.

BRAINTENANCE: PITSTOPS

Sometimes the gap between where you are and where
you'll be is relatively small, like if you are one promotion
away from your ideal role. At other times, your goal outcome
can seem miles away. Whether the gap feels big or small, pitstops
along the way can help you reach your overall goal. Marking
these on the path can give you smaller goals to work towards
rather than always thinking about the big outcome. For me
and my career, I have known for years what I have wanted to
do but I had zero clue how to get there. By thinking of some
of the steps along the way, it became much easier to take
action.

With your 'where I'll be' specific goal, think about the
milestones, **skills** and **experience** needed to get there. Milestones
can be 'official' requirements for the goal (like degrees, or training
programmes) but can also represent significant steppingstones,
such as 'get funding from investors', 'run 10K in under 1 hour',
or 'reach 100,000 subscribers on YouTube'. Skills are the
practical methods you will need to reach these milestones (revising,
networking, animating – doing words) and experiences are ways
to build these skills (partner with friends to study biology, sign
up to mixer events, take an animation course).

Milestones	Skills	Experience
Pass school exams	Studying	Revise 30 mins per day
Get into medical school	Volunteering	Sign up to help at hospital
. . .	. . .	. . .

Go through your list and rank these skills, experiences and qualifications in the order they need to happen to achieve your goal. Start with milestones, and then add these to your plan path. For each of these milestones, you will need certain skills. Add these in before the achievement of the milestones. Finally, skills are developed from experience, so add in the experience needed to aid the improvement of the skills you are trying to build.

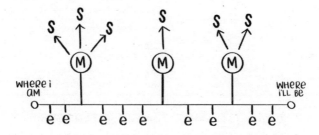

1 MiLESTONES 2 SKiLLS 3 eXPeRiENCe

Sometimes this order is obvious: if you want to be a surgeon, the first milestone you may need to hit is 'get into medical school'. This requires the skill of 'improving interpersonal patient interactions', which can be gained by the experience of 'volunteering in a hospital'. Other times it is harder to see the linear process towards a goal. In these instances, focus on the first things you need to do and add the rest in an order that feels logical for now and adapt later.

BRAINTENANCE: LIGHTS, CONTRAST, ACTION

What you have developed with these pit stops are focal points for your attention. Instead of just imagining and chasing the end goal, I want you to temporarily forget it and look to the very first milestone on your list.

That milestone should now be your main goal and the initial experience required to build the skills to get there should be where you should be directing your attention. With that experience in mind, you can devise an action plan to make it happen.

For the first experience on your list, think about what obstacles are currently standing in your way. What could be done to tackle them and get the ball rolling?

Experience: *volunteering in hospital.*

Obstacles	Strategy
Don't know how to get placement	Reach out to careers service, local hospitals and charities associated with hospitals to ask about opportunities
. . .	. . .

BRAINTENANCE: TANGIBLE TARGETS

Structuring your time using tangible targets based on your milestones can help direct focus on shorter time scales. Breaking down a milestone into action steps can enhance progress.

Check in with your current milestone at regularly spaced intervals.

I like to do this on a monthly and quarterly basis, breaking down my small goals even further to fit these time scales. I will say what I want to get out of the next three months and what three things I can work on to make that happen. For example, take writing this book. My quarterly reflection might look like this:

Milestone	Quarterly aim	Breakdown
Write book	To finish first draft	1. Draft section 2 2. Draft section 3 3. Draft section 4

I use those three small goals as **targets for each month** within that quarter. At the start of each month, I will do a short reflection to break these targets down further to get an aim for each week, and reflect on the skills and experiences I'll need to make this happen.

Monthly goal	Breakdown	How (skills/experiences)
Draft section 2	Week 1: Draft chapter 5	Writing / write each day
	Week 2: Draft chapter 6	
	Week 3: Draft chapter 7	Researching / collect relevant
	Week 4: Draft chapter 8	articles and make notes

These weekly targets give me structure and allow me to focus on the processes required to make these smaller goals happen. Weekly scheduling, covered in Chapter 11, allows me to fit these experiences into my calendar and work towards each target effectively.

Personally, I don't always hit my weekly target (probably 50:50). If I don't, I simply adjust my schedule the following week to account for the overflow. These targets aren't necessarily there to be reached within the week (although they should be small enough that they could be). They are there to give you a focal point which isn't overwhelming and enables you to see how smaller targets can be achieved through action.

As mentioned in Chapter 4, come back to the ideal day exercise quarterly, annually or at significant change points in life to check the overall goal being worked towards is still what you want.

BRAINTENANCE: ROOM FOR RANDOMNESS

Every now and again, look up. Look up from the actions which are bringing you towards your goals and see what else is happening around you. Dial up the background noise and shift your focus to other elements. Is there anything else going on that could be a fun, worthwhile experience that resonates with your mission statement and aligns with the overall direction your goal compass is pointing in? Stepping outside your routine may feel uncomfortable and out of kilter with working towards a goal, but it avoids the acquisition of tunnel vision. With the benefit of hindsight, I cannot tell you how many opportunities have come from stepping outside the routines I had set myself, like speaking to new people, asking for opportunities, attending events I'd never normally go to, or reaching out for guidance. Allowing for a bit of randomness can create the chance for more opportunities to come your way.

....

What can you do this week or month to break up your routine a bit? What event could you sign up to or is there a project that you wouldn't normally do? You never know which doors these situations could be opening.

WRAP UP

Having a clear vision for where you want to head helps you locate goal-relevant opportunities in the environment. Doing this while also focusing on the tasks directly in front of you can move you closer towards your goals. You don't have to think about the outcomes or end desires of your goals every day to make them come into your life. You have to take action and attempt to close the gap between your current state and the desired one. Allow yourself to get lost in the process and enjoy the small wins of working on a goal which is one step ahead. Direct your focus to daily doing, with the occasional look up to check you are still happy with the trajectory you're on, and you should start to see progress.

CHAPTER 8

BECOME YOUR FUTURE SELF

Be the change you want to see in the world. Or in yourself.

Your bags are packed, you know where you're going, you have your pitstops mapped out, but there is one more thing we need to consider before hitting the road to get your goal: who is going to be driving the car.

This answer may seem obvious. If the goal is yours, then who else would be driving but you? But ask yourself this: are you, as you currently are, the person who will achieve this goal? Chances are, based on the behavioural barriers we identified in Chapter 6, the you who is reading this right now has some tendencies or beliefs that may make the journey more challenging than it needs to be. Identifying some of the characteristics required to achieve your goal and taking them on board will make for a smoother ride.

You don't need to have a full transformation before you turn on the ignition. Most of the learning comes as you drive. But imagining some of the beliefs your future self might possess can help you make more aligned decisions as you go. Another way of thinking about this is to consider who you want in the passenger seat of your road trip to help navigate towards your goal. Having a role model who will make the optimal decisions on this trip, maybe because they have already completed a similar journey or have a trait you admire, will bring about your desired results. Whether this be a person you know, an idol or your future self, having a reliable reference point to internally quiz when unsure about which turn to take will enable you to pause and consider your next move from multiple perspectives.

How we define ourselves forms an integral part of understanding who we are. When faced with making a decision, a confrontation, or a celebration, we pull a response from our internal reference book of characteristics, needs, wants and past behaviours to act in a way that aligns with our sense of self. Self-identity can serve as a motivator for how you behave based on who you think you are.

Who we believe ourselves to be can come from what we've been taught, like our morals, but it also works a bit like a show and tell. If you wake up at 5 a.m. every morning by choice, chances are you are more likely to describe yourself as a morning person than someone who sleeps in until noon. If you work out every day, you'll probably see yourself as a person who cares about fitness. Depending on the action taken and the narrative you tell yourself about it, how you act can influence your identity and serve as evidence to justify who you are. This feedback loop of 'I am x $\rightleftarrows$ behaves like x' suggests that our behaviours, including habits, can help us craft identity. And if we think we are a certain type of person, we are more likely to act in a way that confirms that to ourselves.

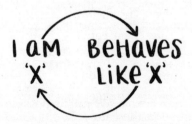

At our core, we feel we are the same person now as we were last month, last year, last decade. Self-identity projects itself as a stable construct linking past you to present you to future you. But aspects of who we are can change throughout our lives. You might look back to the 'you' of five years ago and hardly recognize that person or think the views you had a few months ago no longer ring true. The exact events and situations that prompt these fairly significant shifts may not even be obvious, but the ability of aspects of our identity to change suggests that elements of who we are can be moulded to fit the type of person we want to be. Our ability to empathize and use others' motivations as guidance can also help us decide who we need to be in order to make real change. By altering the narratives we tell ourselves about who we are and changing the language we use, we can start to walk in the shoes of our future self today and pull our goals towards us.

For me, one of the biggest shifts in my identity was around what I ate. I grew up in a Liverpool-Irish family, meaning most of our mealtimes centred around meat, potatoes and veg. From stews to roast dinners and casseroles, most of the dishes I consumed during my childhood and adolescence were packed with animal products. But when I was at university, something started to change. Others around me didn't eat what I considered 'normal' food, and although initially I didn't consciously read too much into these differences, I started to ask myself questions about what was on my plate. I continued cooking my roasts and stews but being exposed to others with different diets made me reflect on my own identity as a 'meat-eater'. I didn't even recognize this as part of my identity as it was so ingrained during my early years. But being plopped into a new environment, this characteristic was brought up to the surface. When I started dating my partner who was vegetarian, my eating habits slowly shifted. After months of us being together, I realized I never ate meat at home anymore and within just over a year, I moved from 'meat-eater' to 'plant-based'.

After this change, my family and friends from back home were shocked. 'You love meat! And how are you going to live without cheese?!' In the face of my change, they were confronted with their own identity around what they ate (more on pushback from others in Chapter 15) and were baffled that I could resist the lure of a mozzarella stick. And to be honest, it baffled me too. I was the girl who would get in from a night out and – much to my dad's horror – sink my teeth into a block of mature cheddar. I couldn't get enough dairy. But now, you could put an entire cheese board in front of me and I wouldn't even be tempted to tuck in. I had changed my internal narrative. Instead of saying 'I can't eat cheese' (implying denial, which, as we all know, hardly ever works, as not being able to have something only makes us want it more), I started saying 'I don't eat cheese'. My language had shifted along with my identity about what I did and didn't eat, and those cravings I used to have didn't bother me anymore (even after a big night out).

Now, this is not a chapter on changing eating habits or subbing beef for beans, but this particular change in my life highlighted a few things to me. Firstly, our identities are wrapped up in so many of our tiny behaviours or actions, even if we don't realize. From the time we set our alarm, to what we choose to eat, where we spend our money and how we speak to other people, little fragments of our character are spread between different actions. Certain behaviours contribute more to what makes you feel like you. Secondly, shifting a 'core belief' or a norm takes a *long* time, and it always has to feel like it was your idea. Choosing to eat more and more veggie food over many months allowed me to gradually alter this element of my life. If someone had come up to my meat-eating self and told me to go vegan, my brain would have detected this as a big threat to my current identity, leading me to feel well and truly peeved off. Thirdly, I had to show myself I could do it. I had to act 'as if' I was already veggie or vegan – purposefully picking the meat-free option on the menu when out at dinner, browsing the dairy-free section in the supermarket, and saying no to the box of milk chocolates being passed around. Each action, no matter how small, confirmed who I was, prompting me to act further in alignment with this newer identity. And finally, how I spoke to myself made a huge difference in how I acted. The words I chose to describe my choices and myself firmed up my decisions. I avoided words like 'can't', 'try' and 'might', replacing them with more firm language like 'don't', 'do' and 'will', confirming to myself that I meant business.

This example of a shift in my identity has been a great reference point for addressing who I am in relation to the goals I have. I now ask, 'Who do I need to be to make this goal happen?' Taking a goal and stripping it back to the personal characteristics that I can take on board has provided me with a solid basis for making aligned decisions and prompted behaviours that are beneficial to the end result.

The study of self-identity has been approached from many angles. Whether philosophy, sociology, psychology or neuroscience, trying to uncover our 'core' self remains a challenging feat. In the brain, it is very unlikely that our 'self' sits in one specific area due to how many functions it is intertwined with. We define ourselves based on our values, elements of our personalities, past experiences, emotional states and our analytical thinking. Therefore, our self is likely represented by several brain regions in communication with each other, when making decisions, processing events, interacting with others and making sense of emotions.

Our sense of self develops with experiences and teaching, with a big emphasis on the morals we are exposed to growing up. We are told what the 'right thing' to do is in a variety of situations based on who raised us, our culture and societal norms, and when we consistently repeat these 'right' ways of acting, they transition into habits.[1] These habits will not only sway how we act in certain situations but make these actions feel 'right', defining them as part of our character. Individually, we believe our true self is a good person, but due to the impressionable nature of the brain, the development of what we feel is moral can be false or harmful, even if there is a deep sense of these beliefs feeling right.

When looking in the brain for the components that make up our identity, we are currently still relying on models – theorized ideas which need testing to confirm if they are true or not – to try to understand the self. Identity is compromised in many neuropsychiatric conditions like schizophrenia, major depressive disorder and borderline personality disorder. By understanding how the self is represented in the brain, researchers hope this information will bring about insights into these conditions and help people grappling with a lost or altered sense of identity. One model of the 'integrated self'[2] – a term used to describe the unity between a person's projects, ambitions, emotions, desires and values – suggests this network could sit on one side of the brain due to how unified these connections seem. Like a travel network in a city which has a river in the middle; it is easier to make a quick-acting, coordinated network on one side of the water than across two using the few crossing points available.

This model suggests the self-network can address multiple lines of enquiry at once to come to a conclusion. It does this by filtering information through past memories, emotional sensations, values and goals, to make choices that are aligned. The integrated self has also been deemed responsible for allowing us to spot personally relevant information in the environment and have a deep sense of inner security and trust. This sense of self differs from what we project on the outside – named the conceptual self – which, although this is the image of ourselves that is praised by external sources, lacks the emotional and sensing insights on which the integrated self relies.

Another model of self in the brain proposes our sense of being relying on three networks.[3] The 'core self' network, associated with understanding values; the cognitive control network, reported to aid the control of social attention to external sources like thinking of

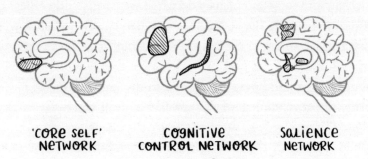

'CORE SELF'
NETWORK

COGNITIVE
CONTROL NETWORK

SALIENCE
NETWORK

others; and the salience network, thought to detect and respond to internal signals like emotions.

The involvement of these networks comes from research in psychology, neuroscience and neuroeconomics, but much more needs to be done to test if and how these networks really produce our sense of self. So far, a lot of work in understanding our true selves comes from self-reporting, which provides personal insights but is hard to accurately map onto functions. And there are still a lot of questions that need answering in terms of how our brains craft a sense of self. Like how do these proposed brain regions interact to compute this feeling of 'this is who I am'? Which exact brain cells are involved and what messengers do they use to send signals? Establishing a deeper understanding of self in the brain will allow us to better understand how we define who we are, how stable this construct is, and how elements can be adapted in conditions where the sense of self is compromised.

The notion of using identity as a tool for behavioural change is a fairly recent endeavour. A large part of understanding who we are is to look to our past behaviours and make deductions from them. We are forever using our acquired accolades and previous experiences to derive patterns which confirm who we are to ourselves. For example, I have still got the identity of being good at maths as I did the subject to a high level at school and scored fairly well on my final exams. But, if you stuck that final paper in front of me now, I would struggle. My A-level score card acts as this badge of 'I am good at maths', even if, right now, my calculating abilities are not top notch.

Looking for patterns in past behaviour to define who we are inevitably leads us to focus on a particular type of behaviour: habits. With my maths example, I know I put in the hours of work to score well in tests, so I saw my results as a consequence of my habits for doing homework and revising, rather than a one-off fluke. If I had taken a French A-level exam (I know just enough French to say hello) and got a top mark, I would not think I am good at French. I would think the test score was wrong or a complete stroke of luck as my behaviours up to that point (no studying or practice) tell me that I am not equipped to converse in *la langue de l'amour*.

When looking at how much our identity is associated with our habits, a somewhat consistent picture emerges. If a habit is tied up with your goals and values, it is more likely to form part of who you believe yourself to be. For example, in one-off studies, people who donate blood are more likely to align with the identity of being a 'blood donor'[4] and people who identified as being health conscious were more likely to eat healthier foods.[5] This has also been reported to be the case for non-beneficial behaviours, like identifying as a binge drinker and showing binge-drinking tendencies while studying at university.[6] A survey asking over 400 students to rate how automatically and frequently (aka habitually) they performed eighty different behaviours, how much each of these behaviours represented their true self, and which values they affiliated these behaviours with, found that habits were more likely to be tied to identity if they were linked to an individual's values.[7] This suggests that habits like brushing your teeth are less likely to feel like they represent you as a person, but a ritual like giving to charity would more readily be tied up in your identity. The results of this study also found that there are individual differences in how likely a person is to assign their sense of self to a habitual behaviour, meaning some people are less likely to associate who they are with what they do.

THiS iS WHO i aM...

Identity change has been used to try to help individuals move away from behaving in an unhealthy way to a more beneficial state. For example, stating you are no longer a smoker could provide the incentive to help curb the cigarette-break habit and prompt quitting. So far, there hasn't been a scientifically backed method of how to augment your identity. From the few properly conducted studies that look at using identity change to shift behaviour, the main method used has been the Social Identity Model of Identity Change.[8] This model suggests that significant life changes are better handled with social support, either from established close peers or by acquiring a new group.

Research in this area has suggested that developing connections and forming relationships is a key way to prompt identity change, helping people feel they can behave differently. Acquiring coping skills, modelling adaptive behaviours and encouraging people to act in line with their new identity led to reports of altering how these individuals saw themselves. However, almost all this work so far has relied on people's accounts of how much they feel they have changed rather than independent measurements, and there has not been enough quality research in this area yet. Better ways of defining identity, having more concrete methods of tracking identity change, and performing big studies over long periods of time to see if identity change sticks, are all needed to more firmly say if we can shift who we believe we are with intervention.

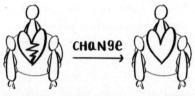

SOCiaL iDeNTiTY MODeL

While the jury is still out on the best method to shift identity to prompt behavioural change, an aspect of neuroscience which could be useful in starting to behave in a way that benefits your goals is our ability to think like other people. From ages four to six, neurotypical individuals can begin to see the world from another person's standpoint, termed 'Theory of Mind'.[9] You may have experienced this when watching a movie. You can get right inside the main character's head, feeling their emotions and sensing how they are interpreting situations. If there is a plot to kill them based on conversations between other characters in different scenes, you can hold that knowledge in your mind but still know the main character has no idea such a plan is unfolding. Our ability to model other people's minds so we can predict how they might act has been instrumental in our survival as a species. Transferring these skills to goal pursuit means you can think like somebody else when it comes to making decisions about what you should do. When we give ourselves space before reacting to a given situation, we can step into the shoes of a role model and ask what action they would take.

APPLY

Looking forward, you can begin to recognize some aspects of your identity that could shift when you achieve your goal. And you can use this mental reconstruction as a tool to question how you will act in the present.

BRAINTENANCE: WHO I AM

By envisioning the person you'll be when you have reached your current aim, you can craft some statements about that version of you and use them to help inspire action today. If you wanted to run a marathon and then did so, you will likely describe yourself as a runner. If you believe you are a runner, you should be more likely to get out and pound the pavements than if you tell yourself you are not. Internally reciting these statements when feeling resistance can help serve as a reminder of what your goal is, why you want to achieve it, and what you need to do now to get there.

· ·

Thinking about the person you will be when you have achieved your goal, complete the following statements:

I am the type of person who . . .
runs four times a week.

I never . . .
skip a run because it is raining.

I always . . .
make time for running.

I try my best to . . .
rest and recover so I can stick to my training plan.

I am a . . .
runner.

When doing this exercise, it can also be useful to consider some current elements of your identity that could be hindering your progress, like the beliefs identified in Chapter 6. For me, I didn't realize how emotionally reactive I was, especially in the face of failure, and after some reflections, I recognized a HUGE part of how I described myself was 'I am the type of person who does everything perfectly'. This aspect of how I viewed myself was a massive burden on trying anything outside my comfort zone. I took this statement and reworked it to 'I am the type of person who gives it my all', which was still in the same zone in terms of working hard, but without the unattainable outcome of perfection.

BRAINTENANCE: LIST OF WINS

The most important element of allowing yourself to believe you are who you say you are is to show yourself. Our self-perceptive abilities mean we look at what we do on a daily basis and from that make deductions about our identity. If you are trying to eat more fruit and veg but continue to avoid green things and go for crisps and chocolate, stating 'I am the kind of person who eats healthy food' isn't very convincing. By performing small actions associated with the identity you are telling yourself, you can start to take those statements on board as truths. In the book *Atomic Habits* by James Clear, he defines these actions as 'small wins' – little things which act as a 'vote' for the person you are becoming.

What would it take for you to believe the identity statement you are telling yourself? If you are wanting to eat more healthily, maybe this means having an apple as a mid-morning snack rather than a chocolate bar, or having a meal with a quarter of the plate filled with vegetables. If you are wanting to write a book, that could be sitting down for twenty minutes each morning to write. Think small with these – the tiniest actions add up to make the biggest difference (and we will talk more about getting these things to be routine in the next chapter).

What are the small wins you can do each day which will help you see yourself as your identity statement? Think of 10 things – the smaller the better!

BRAINTENANCE: BOARD OF <u>TRUSTEES</u>

Effort is initially required to make even small changes to your routine. While self-identity statements aligning with the 'future you' have the potential to give you motivation to perform these small wins, it can still feel like the statement you are telling yourself is farfetched. It is easy for your inner monologue to counter these professions with a 'yeah right, that's not true' response, preventing you from taking the action you need. In order to push through these early effort-filled stages of converting a small win into a default practice, using our ability to get inside another's head can help us choose the action we want for our future self.

Think of a person who has achieved your goal, or someone who has a quality you want to bring into your life, and then, when faced with a decision where you know what you 'should' do but temptation is pulling you towards an instantly gratifying option, imagine asking them how they'd handle the situation. Because of the Theory of Mind, we can then see our dilemma from another person's perspective and use them as a guide for how to act.

For me, this was key in building up an identity of being a person who runs. I have never been the keenest on cardio except if I am dancing in my kitchen. But I wanted to get into running and knew the way to make this part of my routine was to run consistently. It was *relatively* easy to convince myself to get outside and do a lap of the park when the weather was glorious, but when it was cold or raining, the resistance for me to jog rose extortionately. I would lose all my progress in winter, taking me back to the 'how did I ever run more than 200 metres' headspace the following spring.

The key to me making progress and being consistent was to get out come rain or shine. I set my schedule for three runs a week and would plug them into my calendar (more on this in Chapter 11) based roughly on when the weather looked like it was going to be decent. But as anyone who lives in the UK will know, we can go weeks without a 'decent' day. When it came to running on a cold or wet morning, I would say to myself, 'What would Mo Farah do?' I knew that Mo Farah, the British running legend, would not skip a run because it was raining, and putting myself in his trainers certainly helped: my running routine is pretty much locked in now. But every now and then, on a really grim day or when I am convincing myself something trivial is more important than sticking to my scheduled jog, I still ask Mo.

....

Think of someone who has achieved your goal, or a person who has a quality you think would help you to be consistent with your small wins. When faced with resistance, ask, 'What would *role model* do?' to help you decide which action to take.

BRAINTENANCE: WORD UP

A big part of identity is how we communicate who we are to ourselves and others. Language is a powerful tool. It makes people fall in love, start wars, and launch successful new businesses. Changing the words we use to describe ourselves may prompt us to act in accordance with the person we need to be to achieve our goals.

When talking about a behaviour you want to encourage, address it in a reinforcing manner. If you have started going to the gym in the morning, say 'I am the type of person who doesn't miss a gym session' or 'I am a gym goer' to yourself when you are at the gym (or to others there if that's what floats your boat) to reinforce who you are while performing the action.

When trying to prevent behaviours, be firm. If a friend is wanting you to go out on a Tuesday night and get legless, but you know drinking will hinder your gym session in the morning, say, 'I don't drink on weeknights' rather than 'I can't have a drink' to firmly take yourself out of the temptation zone. If you are struggling with motivation dips because you can't see progress yet, instead of saying, 'I can't do this anymore', say, 'I will persist'. The way you talk to yourself can change the entire mood around performing a certain task. Don't give your words the power to put up another barrier of resistance between you and your goal.

KNOW always
DON'T never
committed **DO**
must **WILL**

WRAP UP

Challenging who you believe you are now compared to when you achieve your goal can help improve decisions – both big and small – which should move you in the direction you actually desire. While it is still unclear if interventions can alter self-identity, it can be used as a tool to prompt beneficial behaviours and move away from hindering habits. Telling yourself you are the type of person who does the actions required to achieve your goals in conjunction with actually doing those actions – even in the smallest way – should firm up this belief in your mind.

Keep in mind that while playing with aspects of your identity, it is important to keep other aspects of who you are stable. If you try to do a full identity overhaul simultaneously, this will likely lead to confusion and inability to take action. Identity is an anchor, a part of us we feel is stable as we move through life, and a loss of identity is affiliated with life-altering disorders. So, pick one aspect of your life you would like to work on and try emulating the version of that behaviour you want to have, consulting your internal board of trustees and your future self to guide the decisions you make and the actions you take.

Methods

CHAPTER 9

PRIORITIZE PROCESSES

Routine is a word that can be loaded with desire or dullness. But, love them or loathe them, they rule our lives.

From waking up in the morning to putting your head down at night, our days are governed by routines. We grab a shower, take the dog for a walk, pour a big cup of coffee, go to work, eat soup for lunch, come home, crash on the couch and crawl into bed. Although routines may feel monotonous, they can be harnessed to propel you towards your goals.

If you think of your daily routines like songs on a playlist, our brains press play and listen to the entire track before moving on to the next. Some of these tunes are mildly pleasant, others are absolute belters, and a few are just downright painful. Without intervention, this personalized playlist will happily run on repeat, regardless of the music you prefer. But, with small and simple changes, the listening experience can be improved by replacing rubbish songs with better ones. When you shape your daily routine to make it uplifting, enjoyable and focused, you will move towards your goal much more easily.

When trying to incorporate new behaviours into your day, we want to make them as routine as brushing your teeth. And although the routines we perform today may feel simple, it has taken consistent reinforcement to teach the brain which actions are important. The keys to keeping consistent are simplicity, ease and enjoyment. Taking beneficial behaviours and adapting them to fit these categories can increase the likelihood that we keep performing them, improving the tunes on your day-to-day soundtrack.

Small actions add up to big results. When we are pursuing a big goal, we often fall prey to thinking that we need to make drastic changes to achieve our desired result. In actuality, it is the tiny tweaks that can have the most impact. Firstly, altering something small makes it easier to be consistent, reducing the internal pushback we experience in the face of change. Secondly, small steps encourage bigger ones. Like easing yourself into a pool of tepid water. Each bit of your body exposed to the liquid adapts and feels less cold, eventually allowing you to fully submerge. And thirdly, it is the 'insignificant' moments – where we don't really recognize the consequences of our actions – that summate towards our current state. Like the ten minutes spent scrolling on social media or taking the lift instead of the stairs. At the time, it feels like these actions have no bearing on our goals, but over days, weeks and years, these activities accumulate to a huge proportion of our time.

Although routines can appear complex, they are composed of a series of small actions smushed together, comprising different processes such as habits and behaviours. If we break our big goals down into small, simple actions, we are more likely to introduce them into our daily lives. You may boggle at someone who runs 20 kilometres every Saturday, but they likely started their fitness endeavours running for only a few minutes at a time. By stripping back our goals to the first small step, and setting that fail-safe action as a regular goal, it aids consistent practice and builds momentum, proving to yourself that you can hit milestones.

Routines can be triggered. As mentioned in Chapter 3, individual habits are often prompted by our environment in a call-and-response manner. And routines built of several steps can be the same. When we take, for example, going to the gym, this kickstart could come from an action as simple as putting your gear on – triggering the next steps of packing your bag, leaving the house and eventually working out. Alternatively, an internal cue, like feeling stressed, can trigger a whole different routine, such as reaching for the family bag of crisps and crashing in front of the television instead. Identifying these triggers, or cues, can help you see what the gateways are for certain routines and can also be used to help craft new ones. My dad always says to me that the hardest exercise when working out is leaving the house. Making these small starter actions (or stopper actions in the face of trying to prevent a behaviour) more automated is hugely beneficial, acting as a gateway for the rest of the routine.

When it comes to altering routines in my own life, the most recent change I've faced has been writing this book. I knew I had to make writing habitual. This went against my original belief that writing should be done in bursts of inspiration. And although that may be the case in an ideal world, I didn't have the time to wait for bursts. I was writing on a deadline and working full-time. If inspiration struck me at 10 a.m., it was as much use as a chocolate fireguard, because my time was committed to another cause. I had to take control of the free time I had available to me and craft a writing routine. For me, I work best in the morning and, at the time, I was using those hours to work out. I decided to shift my workout routine to later in the day and use these early hours to get some words on a page.

In order to make this new routine default, I would set up my desk the night before, with my screen open on the last page of the book I was up to and a plan for the morning already sketched out. On waking, I would do two simple things which acted as my gateway into writing: (1) make a HUGE cup of tea, and (2) stick on my writing playlist. I chose one playlist which I would listen to every time I wrote and play the same song first each morning. Over time, my brain associated this song and the rest on the list with 'writing time'. I would write at the same time every day with the small goal of writing three sentences. Some days, these sentences were all I could muster, and other days, I would go way beyond and churn out a few pages. The consistency of my 'writing routine' with a realistic, clear and achievable goal meant that I was always showing up and putting pen to paper. Sure, I would have bursts of inspiration at other times during the day, and I would capture some of my thoughts in these moments in my notebook, but I was not relying on my mood to make the work happen. I instead generated a routine that kept me coming back, with my tea and tunes acting as perfect initiators into the realm of writing, and with my small goal of writing three sentences never overwhelming me.

SCI

In Chapter 3, we met the call-and-response habit model:

HaBiT THeORY
SiTuaTioN = BeHaViOUR
[cue]   [ResPONSe]

And we discussed how changing elements of this can facilitate new behaviour in our 'go to bed = watch TV' example. If we look at these individual components in more detail, we can see how to disrupt unhelpful behaviours and instigate new ones.

Crack the cue

It has been imperative to the survival of humans that we have specific behavioural responses to internal or external cues. Say you were stung by nettles in a particular patch of woodland. Your behaviour in the same environment should be to tread slowly and carefully. Each time the patch is approached, the brain's recognition of the surrounding trees and foliage through sight, sounds of particular birds or the smell of specific leafy plants, will trigger the 'slow-and-tip-toe' motion to avoid another sting. With each repeated tip-toe experience, the connection between the environmental cues and the careful treading is strengthened. This association helps the brain to protect the body. And these connections can become so strong that if you were to walk in a completely different area of woodland but saw similar trees, or heard the same birdsong, or smelt the familiar foliage, you might find yourself automatically on your tip-toes – anticipating the appearance of nettles – because these signals have triggered their connected movements.

You may think, how does this relate to me demolishing an extra-large chocolate bar after a long day of work? Or prevent me from working on writing an article in the evening? Well, cues – whether we are aware of them or not – are constantly influencing our behaviours. There are obvious environmental signals which alter how we act – like temperature. When you feel cold, your brain will prompt you to find warmth. Just like the weather, our brains process signals to help direct what we should be doing next. These signals can be external. If you find yourself coming home from a long day at work and you stick the kettle on, you may naturally reach for that bar of chocolate. You have linked your 'end of the day tea' with 'something sweet'. Cues can also be internal. When you are extremely stressed, you may have turned to the sugary stuff in attempts to soothe your inner panic. The rewarding properties of sugar mean the brain can seek to alleviate 'feeling stressed' by 'eating chocolate', prompting a candy craving when the pressure is piling on.

Although cues and behaviours are naturally combined by our brains, when actively trying to implement new behaviours, these cues can be purposefully selected. Say you want to study in the evening. This new behaviour will currently have no 'green light' for when it should start. Picking a cue to signal 'study time' and consciously responding to this cue by sitting at your desk and opening your books can begin the linking process. Over time, the conscious effort required to sit at your desk and work can be transferred to the cue, acting as an initiator to start hitting the books.

The cues we choose can impact our likelihood of performing new actions. A study of thirty-nine young people asked to take vitamin C supplements for three weeks used a variety of cues. Some of the more successful cues were based on convenience (displaying the pills or tagging it to another routine), others were centred around previously learnt memory strategies (putting pills where you have put them in the past) and another group selected cues through trial and error (trying multiple ways to get pill-taking into routine). The least optimal cues were found to be relying on a single, inconsistent source (like taking a pill when plugging a laptop in to charge) and having non-specific cues (like leaving the pills on the table in general).[1]

Although this was a small study based on qualitative results and there were no measurements regarding whether the vitamin C-taking became habitual, the results give us some insights into the type of cues we can use to help prompt action. Low-effort cues and associating new behaviours with established events could make them easier to initiate. With more complex behaviours, like trying to get into a new study or workout routine, these will likely take longer to tag to a cue (an hour sweating vs taking one pill is a tad different on the effort scale). But having reliable, low-effort triggers should help with prompting behaviours and, over time, remove some of the conscious effort required to push us to act.

When trying to break habits we currently have, relying on cues is more difficult. Many of these habitual behaviours arise without our input, so their triggers may be very difficult or impossible to change. Like if feeling stressed is the trigger for an unwanted behaviour, it is pretty much impossible to never feel stressed again. In these instances, altering the behaviour itself is more beneficial.

Beckon the behaviour

A key way of making a behaviour routine is by repetition. Regularly repeating an action, in response to a conscious cue or not, means the brain forges strong connections between the components that form the action. If you consciously put in effort to make walking part of your daily routine, there will come a point where you no longer have to force yourself out the door.

It may sound simple, but being consistent in an inconsistent world is tough. There are periods when life happens, and new behaviours are one of the first things to fall to the wayside. So, making these behaviours as simple and as easy as possible, while still feeling like they are contributing towards your progress, is crucial for when times get hectic. There are several ways to increase the likelihood of performing a new behaviour:

Keep it small (simplicity)

When trying to change – as described in Chapter 3 – we face resistance. This can be down to the brain trying to correct for uncertainty, a pull towards familiarity, or an aversion to putting in effort. Small actions are like a backdoor, a way of tricking your brain to do something unfamiliar without slamming on the brakes. Just write two sentences; that's not so bad. Five sit-ups? That's manageable. These achievable targets make it easier to convince ourselves to act and, over time, the actions become familiar. Real-life reports of these small interventions are published in *Tiny Habits* by B. J. Fogg, demonstrating that less than five minutes of time each day dedicated to a small action can make a huge difference.

Make it the go-to (ease)

The brain has a finite amount of energy resource at any given time. We can pool our energy into executing something which is effortful, but as soon as other events crop up which are stressful or overwhelming, these can be prioritized as problems to solve. Putting your new behaviour in your way, so that it almost has to be done, can keep you performing when your resources are being rerouted. Like those alarms that can only be deactivated by solving a maths problem, making your new behaviours unavoidable solidifies them into a routine. Fill the cupboards with healthy snacks, park the car a block away from work to get those steps in, leave your computer open on the page of your essay. Making your action the obvious thing to do can help ease you into it.

Make it fun (enjoyment)

Think about an activity you absolutely love doing – why do you find it so appealing? It could be spending time with others, the opportunity to be creative and solve problems, and being able to laugh out loud.

Incorporating fun into a new behaviour can help us perform them as this signifies reward in the brain. Reward is one of the main drivers of motivation (more on this in Chapter 14) and it strongly impacts habit formation. By pairing a tricky or boring activity with something fun, we are more likely to perform the action and make it routine. This pleasure/pain pairing has been termed 'temptation bundling' by behaviour change expert Katy Milkman, and has been shown to be an effective technique for increasing behaviours like going to the gym.[2]

Consider the fringes

We look at activities as isolated events but whether we follow through with them or not can be impacted by how we are spending our time outside these windows. Other events that can influence our ability to follow through include: getting enough sleep, being fed and having down time (discussed in Chapter 16), as well as preparing in advance (planning ahead coming up in Chapter 11).

Breaking old ways

For trying to break an unhelpful habitual behaviour, you can make it difficult or near impossible to perform, and then replace the behaviour with something beneficial.

If you remove the possibility of performing the behaviour, you will notice the craving for it. Like when you really fancy a particular type of food but know you don't have it in the cupboards, all you can think about is that one dish. Non-food-related cravings are the same – whether that is watching TV or checking the news. If you delete the ability to perform that action – taking the batteries out the TV remote or removing the news app from your devices – you will feel it. That restless itching sensation. Once something is habitual, the brain cells associated with performing that action already activate in response to the cue and the body desperately tries to follow through with the orders it has been given.

To break habits, stopping the automatic repetition of performing an action is vital to weakening those connections by starving them of stimulation. So, preventing behaviours (by making them difficult or impossible) is essential. But that doesn't stop the craving. This sensation requires conscious intervention in the form of inhibition from prefrontal brain regions to suppress. Like a stream running downhill, it takes a lot of power to prevent its flow. So instead of trying to ride out a craving with no distractions, replace the behaviour with something else stimulating that fulfils the general need the unhelpful behaviour is trying to satisfy. This can prevent giving into temptation, allowing your brain the time to re-configure which connections are important.

APPLY

In order to build routines that should work in your favour when thinking about your overall goal while disrupting old habits, think small.

BRAINTENANCE: BREAK IT DOWN

Simple actions that require minimal effort are easier to fit into your day and stick to. If you are wanting a healthier diet, a simple goal might be to drink one glass of water in the morning. When selecting these actions, you want to go small, but not so small it feels insignificant. Back in Chapter 4, we touched on research that suggests challenging but achievable goals are most likely to bring about behavioural change. If your water-drinking goal was to have one sip more each day, you run the risk of this action not feeling like it is doing anything, whereas a glass is significant enough that you feel accomplished.

....

Think of your overall goal. Now scale it right back. What would be the simplest, low-effort action you could take? You could use one of your 'small wins' from Chapter 8 for this. For example:

Overall goal	Simple action
To run a marathon	Run for five minutes
To get an A in final exam	Read one page of a textbook
To start a business	Read one business article a day
To build strength	Do five reps of an exercise

BRAINTENANCE: ROUTINE FIEND

Fitting this action into your day may seem straightforward. With small actions, we often mistake their simplicity for ease when the difficulty lies in our ability to be consistent with them. Selecting a specific time or tagging this behaviour onto other things you do each day will help with this.

If you think about your day now and consider the routines you are already performing, your new behaviour can be slotted in in a few ways:

Depend: If you have a certain routine you do every day – like taking the dog for a walk – you can tag your small action to these routines. This is optimal for simple actions – like taking a supplement – as the current routine serves as a reminder to perform the action and it can easily be incorporated into that sequence without sacrifice. Just remember that if you are depending on another routine, make sure to choose something stable. If you drink a cup of tea every morning, you could do ten sit-ups as the kettle boils, but if you only inconsistently start your day with a hot drink, the crunches will likely go undone.

Deviate: This is when you take a dedicated 'routine block' that is already established in your day and use it to do your simple action. This method could be applied for small actions that are creative or physical. As mentioned before, I did this when crafting my writing routine, subbing my morning exercise block for getting words on a page. If you are trying to do something creative (like editing a minute of video footage), mentally stimulating (like reading a page of a textbook) or physically demanding (like running for five minutes), scheduling these new actions into established blocks in your day should help you fit them in.

Disrupt: This is the most extreme instance of routine change, and involves completely altering an established routine block to remove old cues and unhelpful behaviours. If your current routine block at the end of the day is to come home, sit on the couch and fall into a TV binge, but instead you want to do a few minutes of push-ups, it can be hard to resist the call of the couch. Disrupting this routine can be done in various ways: unplugging the television, hiding the remote, not entering your living room until the push-ups are done, or taking the route home that passes the gym. Disruption requires a combination of making an old routine difficult to trigger (taking batteries out of the remote) and putting the new routine in your path (dumbbells where remotes are normally kept) to break old patterns of behaviour.

Walk through your day – what are the current routine blocks that exist? Think of this as your daily playlist. What are the tracks that play and in what order?

TRACK 1	TRACK 2	TRACK 3	TRACK 4
07 00 - 07 30	07 30 - 08 00	08 00 - 08 30	08 30 - 09 00

With your small action in mind, where can this fit into your current day? Are you going to depend, deviate or disrupt a routine block? How can this be made as easy as possible?

BRAINTENANCE: CRAFT YOUR CUE

When it comes to triggering an action, you can create a cue. Try to make it visible (in your way), specific (get clear on what the cue is) and sacred (only performing that cue with this action). For example, I had a study candle on my desk when doing my PhD. I only lit this when I worked, fulfilling all three categories for making a successful cue.

With your small action in mind, think of a gateway into performing that action. How can you make it:

Visible?	Specific?	Sacred?
Trainers by front door	*Putting trainers on = run*	*Only wear these trainers for running*

BRAINTENANCE: PARTY TIME

Being consistent with your small action can also be achieved by making it fun. When something is fun, we *want* to do it. Take your small action and inject some enjoyment. If you want to drink a glass of water each day, maybe this could be done while talking with your partner. Or when you are studying, you could use drawing to bring in an element of creativity. For me, the only time I listen to two of my favourite podcasts is when I go to the gym or on a run. This form of temptation bundling has made me look forward to working out as I know I'll get my podcast fill too, and it has cemented a daily sweat as part of my routine.

If your small action was fun, what would it look like? How could you make it more appealing?

BRAINTENANCE: TIME FILLERS

No matter how consistent we become at implementing small actions, how we 'fill' the rest of our time can have a huge impact on our progress. When I had my first extended period of time working from home, my screen time shot up to six hours per day. Six hours! While I love a good scroll, spending over a day and a half per week on my phone was not how I wanted to use my time. Consciously deciding how you use your short breaks and longer periods of free time can be used to progress towards your goal and improve how you feel throughout the rest of the day. These periods should be used to get what you actually want out of them – whether that's to rest, reinvigorate, reboot or reconnect.

I had a pretty bad habit of watching TV series at night where one episode would run into the next, into the next, until it was way past the time I wanted to go to bed. Watching TV this close to bedtime not only disturbed my sleep (hello, graphic dreams) but also wrecked my ability to get on with work the next day. After one too many tired mornings, I stopped asking what I 'wanted' to do in my free evenings and instead thought about what I needed, which was to wind down, switch off and get a good night's sleep. I implemented a new rule: the only activity I could do before sleep was read. Although I technically could keep reading until 2 a.m., I find I am so knackered at night that my eyes start to close after just a few pages. This change in routine, alongside other small tweaks throughout my day, like not scrolling on my phone every time I have a ten-minute break, helped me feel rested and more on track with my goals.

When you have a break throughout your day, what do you need from that time? To rest, reinvigorate, recharge, reconnect? Are you getting it with the activity you are currently doing? What alternative activity could fulfil this need?

BRAINTENANCE: BEHIND BAD HABITS

We can flip and reverse the activities designed to implement new routines and instead use them to disrupt unhelpful behaviours (like those highlighted in Chapter 6). To prevent a behaviour, make it as hard as possible to perform, react differently to the specific and sacred cue, and make the unhelpful behaviour unappealing. Take scrolling on social media when you need to work. If you want to get a bit more space from your phone, you could leave your phone in a different room, so when the cue of 'I'm stressed, this work is too hard' pops up, your device is not in reach. Over time, the lack of device should start to break down the association of 'stressed → scrolling'.

Bad habits get a bad rep. We scold ourselves for engaging with them and talk them down. But we shouldn't be so quick to dismiss. 'Bad habits' are trying to serve a purpose, and are normally activated when we want to escape our current state, like feeling upset or bored (more in Chapter 13). If you can understand the motive behind a certain habit, you can start to find more appropriate means of fulfilling that need. For example, you might spend hours a day on your phone as a way of supplementing your desire for connection. Or you could eat unhealthily when you are bored because it stops you feeling emotions that arise in quieter moments. Recognizing these reasons means you can think of alternative ways to address them, like calling a friend for connection or picking up a book to read when you are lacking in stimulation.

....

Think of some of the habits you classify as 'bad' and uncover what need they are serving for you. What activity could replace them? How will you make this new action easy to do?

Habit	Purpose	Alternative	Ease
Watching TV for four hours at night	To disconnect from my responsibilities and switch off	Reading a book	Leave book on pillow

SIMPLE ISN'T A SUBSTITUTE

A final note: a big misconception many of us have is that because something is simple to execute it should feel easy to perform. But when pushing to improve, these tasks will still use effort. Getting yourself to the gym may become routine, but doing the reps is still hard. Making something routine doesn't magically remove the challenge from the work. Instead, it makes showing up your default behaviour. Change requires challenge, but we can augment our days to make sure we are able to face those challenges head on.

WRAP UP

We default to routines, so crafting them to encourage behaviours that will help you achieve your goals is a way to ensure you are moving in the right direction. Changing routines requires repetition. Find a specific way in, like a particular playlist or consistent routine you do every day, and set small actions as your target, like writing three lines of that book or running for five minutes, to ensure consistent commitment. The beautiful thing about small actions is they aren't restrictive. It isn't an obligation to stop at three lines or five minutes. But having a target that is pretty much fail-safe – even on busy or stressful days – makes showing up and completing the task easier. If the aim of your small action is met, you will feel that sense of accomplishment.

CHAPTER 10

REWARD EFFORT

We reserve celebration for special occasions. Whether that's a significant birthday, receiving a promotion at work, or passing our final exams. However, by only celebrating achievements, we are reinforcing the idea that the end result is all we are after when pursing goals.

Yet celebration is so much more than going to a fancy restaurant or jetting off on an exotic vacation. Celebration is a signal. The human brain uses reward as feedback. If an action or circumstance is celebrated, it is branded 'beneficial', compelling us to seek similar situations in the future. Rewarding yourself after a big win relays the message to your brain that this situation is advantageous, that being in this position is what we want. Which is fine . . . as long as you also celebrate your efforts along the way too.

The problem with achievements is they are not always reliable signifiers of hard work. Sure, if you studied loads and got a top-class mark in an exam, that result is likely a direct consequence of your efforts. But other achievements can occur through luck, chance, connections and privilege. That's not to say these achievements aren't valid – some instances of luck can require putting yourself out there – but by only celebrating the end result, the brain isn't being taught dependable methods for how to recreate that state of attainment.

On a broader note, only celebrating in the face of accomplishment is problematic. The world we live in applauds achievement: final grades determining university admission, promotions at work increasing the size of a pay packet, ripped abs on the beach getting thousands of likes online. Our culture encourages us to determine our worth based on what we achieve, making it natural for us to measure our own personal goals against these 'success' markers and feel incomplete until we hit them. The aim of goal pursuit should be to enjoy the process and celebrate the small wins along the way. Celebration is not a limited resource. And by rewarding effort, you are teaching yourself not only that it is important to keep making progress, but that you are enough as you are.

WHY

Effort has unfairly gained a negative reputation. It isn't cool to be trying too hard or pushing forward with little to 'show' for it. It isn't something we can brag about at parties or use on our CV to land a job. Effort isn't deemed sexy. We want results, and mostly without much trying. If we start a business, we want it to be a success straight away. If we start working out, we want to see the weight literally disappear during our first sweat session. If we begin dating, we want the person we like to instantly fall madly in love with us. Results give us news to share when we see our friends, content to post on our social media feeds, and a sense of accomplishment . . . for a little while.

When the highs of a win fade and the achievement is normalized, our celebration and reliance on results for validation leads us to seek the next milestone. We judge our progress on the results we are getting, but using results to track your current position is flawed in several ways:

1. *Results take time.* When starting a new venture, very little 'progress' will be seen initially. Every endeavour starts with a period of learning – a time where effort goes in to honing the craft or getting to know the ropes. If we expect instant success and then don't see it, it is much easier to justify that what we are doing isn't working and quit. Also, with new goals in particular, we have little experience of how long it takes to achieve certain results. So, setting ourselves up to hit a milestone by a specific date is hard to realistically judge.

2. *The results you see reflect your past efforts.* As it takes time for results to rear their head, any achievements you start to

see are the culmination of past efforts. An athletic reflection in the gym mirror is not because of the ten-minute run you have just finished, but the past twelve ten-minute runs you have completed over previous weeks. There is a delay between your progress and the results you see, so using them as a benchmark to track how you are getting on means your measurements will be off.

3. *You can't control results.* As the results from our efforts today sit in the future, it is very hard to have complete control over them. There are things we can do in the present to make certain results more likely to occur, but they are not something we can 100 per cent guarantee. So, waiting for a specific result to signify progress may be fruitless. It might not come, and that lack of feedback can be mistaken as things 'not working'. Showing up and putting in the effort regularly means change will happen. It just might not be exactly what you were expecting.

Instead of using results as our go-to method for tracking progress, we can shift our focus to the effort we are putting in. By ticking off the number of hours in the gym, sentences written, videos produced or time connecting, we are directing our attention to the present and to what we can control. As our results come from our past efforts, taking our eye off the prize and on to the moment allows us to put in the time and skill required to generate the results we are aiming for.

Progress doesn't happen in even steps. It's not like 'for every week of training, I am going to see x amount of gains'. Instead, progress requires a lot of effort and push initially for what seems like very little return, but with continued commitment, results will come. The capital you have invested in terms of effort pays off. And by focusing on doing the things you can control, results will begin to appear in a non-linear way. The results from your efforts begin to act as positive feedback, fuelling even more results. In this way, progress is exponential – the graph shape where initially it looks like not much is happening, but eventually, the line takes off and skyrockets.

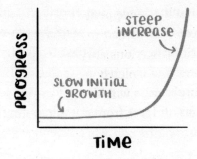

PROGRESS

STEEP INCREASE

SLOW INITIAL GROWTH

TIME

In *Atomic Habits*, James Clear describes the relationship between effort and results as 'the plateau of latent potential'. Essentially, a lot of initial effort is required to break through and see results. But once that barrier is broken, many more results should start to flood in. You can see this across many different goals. If you look at any big YouTuber account and check how their follower count has changed over time, you will see this curve repeatedly. They start off with a few subscribers, slowly acquiring a couple here and there. This phase can go on for months or years until, suddenly – BOOM. One video takes off and the count goes wild. With every video thereafter, more people watch, promoting that video, so more subscribers come. Each post acts as a positive feedback loop, with more views exposing the creator to more new people. In the present day, their high subscriber count is determined as the measure of their success. But if that metric had been used in those early days, they would have never stuck at it long enough to take off. Effort-focused measurement helps reduce the disappointment from a lack of results straight away. If we are not looking at subscriber counts, or muscle size, or completed chapters, to judge where we are at but instead make those calls based on whether we show up or not, we are almost always in control and can be consistent.

I made the switch from achievement-based to effort-based progress tracking when writing my PhD thesis. A thesis is a long slog. It requires combining results from years of experimental work and synthesizing them in the context of other work from hundreds of research papers in your field. The report starts with a summary of the current literature, which involves hours of reading complex papers, organizing them into a structure, and then discussing them in relation to your question.

Initially, I had set myself achievement-based goals to try to get myself through this chunk of work. I had milestones like 'by the end of this week, I will have written sections a, b and c'. Obviously, having never written a thesis before, I completely misjudged my milestones. Thursday would roll around and I would spend most of my writing time worried about how far off I was from completing section a, never mind b and c, rather than focusing on what I could do in that moment to move myself along.

I tried this method for a few weeks and ended up feeling frustrated and demotivated, which led to me doing less and less work. One day, I gave myself a good talking to, deciding to sack off the end-of-the-week achievement goals and instead bring my efforts to the forefront. I reasoned that if I could write for a few hours each day, the review would get done. I would start my writing sessions at 8:30 every morning and had a small goal of writing one sentence to get me started. But before I put a word on the page, I set a twenty-five-minute timer. I said to myself that I needed to complete five or six twenty-five-minute timers' worth of writing each day. That was my new target. I would open my to-do list and instead of writing 'complete section a', I would write 'section a [] [] [] [] [] []' , with each box representing one twenty-five-minute timer session. When I started a timer, I put a line in one box ([/]), and upon completion, crossed it out [x], so by the end of each morning, I'd have five or six boxes all checked off. Seeing these little crosses was like a celebration, each one patting me on the back for showing up and going for it. Some mornings, I would have to add more boxes as I was so in the flow with my work, I didn't want to stop. By switching my goal to something within my control – writing for a certain amount of time – and signifying my efforts by something as simple as putting a cross in a box, my 20,000-word literature review was completed within four weeks.

SCI

According to goal orientation theory in psychology, there are two major ways we configure the outcomes of our goals: performance or mastery.[1]

Performance goals focus on achievements – getting the top grade in an exam, winning a race, earning a high salary – and are normally driven by a desire to demonstrate personal and professional competence. On the other hand, mastery goals aim to improve a skill or increase learning, with success measured by acquiring more enhanced knowledge. Due to school systems and our normalized celebration of achievement, many of us naturally acquire performance-based goals, but flipping these to focus instead on mastery can lead to greater persistence – the key element required in the early stages of making a behaviour routine.

PERFORMANCE
Paint a
Masterpiece

Mastery
improve
painting skills

Research into goal orientation is somewhat weakened by the fact that various other factors influence success (like how hard a task is or personal circumstances of the individual trying to complete it) and these tend not to be consistently accounted for in studies. However, some studies have hinted that mastery-based goals could encourage more consistent performance.[2] One of the strongest reasons for favouring mastery over performance goals is that with performance goals, 'setbacks' and 'failures' are more readily highlighted. If you are focusing on running a fast race time and you don't hit that time in a practice race, this can be taken as a reflection of your abilities and disrupt progress. It could be harder to 'get back on the wagon' and push towards your performance goal. But with a mastery goal, for example, running three times a week to improve running skills, a 'slow' time shouldn't have the same knock-on impact on taking future action. Focusing on the learning element of a goal that you are committed to and passionate about can give the grit required to push through challenge points.

Performance-based goals have a clear element of reward tagged to them. When a milestone is reached – getting the grade, lifting the weight, pulling off the presentation – we naturally celebrate. This feed-back is how many of our habits form, even if we haven't consciously chosen them. For example, if you eat a banging piece of cake, the high sugar content is considered a reward by the brain because high sugar = high calories, which means energy. The initial value of this reward is thought to be captured by the release of a signalling molecule called dopamine.[3]

Dopamine is a chemical which opens certain gates on synapses of specific neurons and changes their chatter levels. When the brain senses reward, dopamine is released and modulates the activity, and hence connectivity, between the cells in your brain which led to you getting that reward. If you purchased the delicious cake from a new coffee shop that you pass on your daily walk, the spike of dopamine in your brain after taking a bite helps solidify in your mind what the coffee shop looks like, the smells in the air, the name of the cake – essentially, all the cues that led to this moment of delight. Next time you go out on your daily walk and wander past the coffee shop, dopamine signals in recognition of these cues, driving you to go in and buy the cake again. And over time, with repetition, the coffee/cake combo can become second nature.

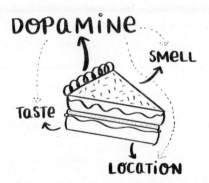

Dopamine-mediated, reward-based learning goes beyond cake. It is thought to operate when a target is hit, or a round of applause is received, or a post goes viral on social media. This signalling can act as a motivator to repeat the actions that led to our success but it also increases our desire to achieve, leading to problems with self-worth when we fall short. As reward is such a strong signal, it can be consciously used as a feedback mechanism to positively reinforce action. When performing mastery-based goals, which might not necessarily have this naturally embedded feedback, celebration can be used as a tool to lock them in. Reward-based learning has been shown to increase habit formation in rodents, like receiving a treat after performing a certain action.[4] And although this area is still under exploration in humans, a large-scale study on gym attendance found that giving participants a tiny reward for returning to the gym after a missed session was the best intervention for increasing gym visits.[5] Although the reward wasn't huge, having a positive reinforcer in the face of a potentially negative situation (missing a session) appeared to encourage behaviour.

APPLY

BRAINTENANCE: MASTERY CHEF

Research suggests that mastery goals that focus on improving knowledge and skill are more likely to encourage persistence compared to performance goals. As the start of any goal is likely to be slow on the achievement front, it might be useful to think about your big goal in a mastery-based way. If it is currently leaning more towards performance, what could a mastery alternative to this goal be?

....

What skills or knowledge do you want to improve? For help with this, you can flip back to Chapter 7 and look at your skills list.

Performance goal	Mastery goal
To complete a 10 km run in one hour	To run four times a week to improve running technique
To get 100,000 subscribers on YouTube	To boost creativity and improve editing skills by making one video each week
To achieve an A in my final exam	To study for ten hours a week to get better at maths

---

BRAINTENANCE: TRACK YOUR MILES

From Chapter 9, you came up with a small action relevant to your goal. These action-based goals are naturally focused on effort and we can use them to judge our progress rather than relying solely on the results they will bring.

Think of a unit, like time or a count, which fits best with the action you want to perform. It could be minutes put in, lines written, reps performed. Any measure that is doable and within your control. If you were trying to make videos, you might choose time spent editing, splitting it into twenty-minute chunks which you mark as tallies in your notebook during a session. Or if you are studying, for every page of the textbook you go over, you might log it with a colourful dot on your revision list. For me, my hand-drawn boxes which I cross out work a charm. I am in control of how many boxes I draw, so I am not left with that horrible 'I can't fill this out, I'm a failure' self-talk, and I use a set amount of time as my unit to represent each box (twenty-five minutes is my go-to).

. . . .

What unit can your small action be tracked in? Which of the below techniques could work for you to track your small action?

○○○○○○

| MARKiNG PROGRESS | TRACKiNG APPS | JOURNAL ENTRIES |

BRAINTENANCE: CELEBRATE GOOD TIMES (COME ON!)

Measuring effort can also serve as celebration, as it provides immediate feedback for the work we have put in. We addressed the 'green light' cue that led to small actions and how to fit them into our day in Chapter 9. But adding a celebration to an action should help solidify it into a routine. By celebrating our efforts, we are essentially teaching the brain that showing up in this way is beneficial to us.

Crossing boxes or scoring tallies works as a celebration, and I find it helps that when you make these marks, you take a couple of seconds to tell yourself 'well done' to stimulate the feeling of pride. You could make the celebration physical – like punching the air or having a little dance. You could also reward yourself with a treat. This is something that has to be done in a healthy and sustainable way (a.k.a. not a full-blown takeaway every time you complete a workout). For me, I would get myself a coffee-shop latte when I had completed a workout as a 'well done' for showing up, and ended up using the coffee as a motivator to go to the gym. Whatever the little things are that make you happy, see if you can pop them on the end of your small action as a way of celebrating what you have achieved.

Think of an activity that takes a short amount of time, anywhere from two seconds to a few minutes, but makes you really happy. A nice cup of tea, getting outside, watering plants, playing your favourite song – anything you enjoy. Tag this onto the end of your small action and internally (or externally, by all means) congratulate yourself for a job well done!

BRAINTENANCE: INCHING FORWARD

When focusing on action-based goals like going to the gym, creating content or studying for exams, we can use these activities to push ourselves towards our goals by striving for little improvements. Extra inches add up to miles over time. As they are small and in the moment, it is not overly hard to convince our brains to get on board with the activity. I did this with running – adding an extra 100 metres every time I went out when I first started, and within a few months, I was running 5 km.

Every time you engage in your activity, ask yourself 'what can I do this time to push myself a one inch further than the last session?' Start with your small action and you can finish there. But if you have the extra energy today, what will stretch you a bit?

In weight training, this technique is call progressive overload – adding a few extra kilos or reps with each session, meaning, over time, your muscles are cumulatively building up strength. Progressive overload can be applied to our goal-related activities:

Activity	One inch more . . .
Going to the gym	Add one more rep or an extra 2 kg
Studying	Read three more flashcards
Writing	Write twenty more words
Running	Run for an extra minute
Creating	Try writing one more new idea

BRAINTENANCE: MONITOR YOUR MOVEMENTS

Finally, when measuring effort, it is important you don't fall into a box-ticking hole. Monitor if this effort is actually working for you over time. Is it taking you towards your current milestone? By checking in every so often – maybe during your quarterly or monthly planning sessions from Chapter 7 – to see how you are progressing towards your goals, and analysing what is working and what isn't, you can fine-tune the effortful tasks you are performing to make them more aligned with your milestone goal.

Say you are sharing creative content online across three platforms and one is consistently bringing in more traction. At your review, you might designate more hours to that platform to grow your audience. Checking in every now and then to refine your process as you go will enable you to make the kind of change you want while still focusing on effort day to day.

Look at your unit of measure log (minutes spent, crossed boxes), your schedule (Chapter 11) and any outputs every three to six months. Are any trends emerging? Is there a particular amount of time spent on a task which brought you closer to what you want? Or doing it at a particular time of day? Or a specific type of task? From these trends, you can tweak your strategy to encompass more of what is working for you in your day-to-day endeavours.

3 MONTH REVIEW

INPUT	OUTPUT	NOTES
20 GYM SESSIONS	SQUAT 60KG	MORE ENERGY IN A.M

WRAP UP

Achievements are great, but they are not a reliable way to keep us consistent with our practices. Focusing on effort from the start gives you the power to push through when there are no results and prevents you from becoming hooked on acclaim. If we think of a unit we can define and track, this acts as an indicator to ourselves that we are doing the work and it gives us control. Ultimately, we decide if we show up and put the time in. By prioritizing effort and celebrating these actions, we are more likely to be able to build the routines required to get to our goals and beyond, and whether the results come or go, we can persevere with the actions we enjoy and know will benefit us.

A downside some might consider with effort-based goals is that not many people will see your hard work. They won't be praised in the same way as achievements because of the award-collecting culture we live in. But every time you show up and put the effort in, that is a result. And you need to celebrate yourself for coming back time and time again. When the achievements are reached or milestones hit, those around you will be ready to pat you on the back. Savour these moments. But also take those pats and pass them back to past you for all the hard work you put in to make it happen.

CHAPTER 11

MAKE DECISIONS

Think of a time you made a decision you later regretted.

I am going to almost guarantee that choice was not planned or thought through extensively in advance.

Goal pursuit can be seen as making lots of little decisions that favour your end result. Choosing to sit down to write today, saying no to that third glass of wine the night before a workout, putting the money in your savings account instead of buying another pair of jeans. The choices made in these micro-moments can stack up to favour your long-term desires, or not.

We face many decision-making crossroads every day. Sometimes making a choice is obvious (like what we should watch on TV), but on other occasions, decisions can slip under our conscious radar. We fall back on habits instead of pausing to consider what other actions we can take, or we go for a choice that gives us an instant burst of reward.

Most of the time, the brain drives you to pick the most optimal option for you right here, right now, determined by calculating a 'value' for each option it is faced with. Although we may think of ourselves as rational, logical beings, the values assigned to choices are often skewed based on how soon we will be rewarded, devaluing options where the pay-out isn't until later. This can lead to long-term beneficial choices, which take effort and hard work in the present, to fall down the ranking, while instantly gratifying options are selected instead.

Far too often, we trust ourselves to make optimal decisions regarding our future wants and needs in the present moment, without considering this flaw in the human system. There have likely been times when you had the intention to work out, but when faced with the prospect of leaving the house on a cold morning to push weights versus staying in bed to sleep for another hour, our brains will root for sleep every time. We can beat ourselves up for not following through with our intentions, but leaving decision-making to ourselves in the moment means having to repeatedly resist the lure of our warm beds.

Making decisions about your long-term goals should be done in two ways: **slowly in advance** and **quickly in the moment**. Considering your options in advance and planning out which one will be most beneficial takes the onus off present-day you – who has a skewed view of 'what is best' – at decision time. However, even with the best planning in the world, the brain can still value a more instantly gratifying option as a better choice when you have to act. In these moments, quickly deciding to go with your plan takes that tempting option off the table and allows you to follow through.

WHY

When making new routines, you must actively decide to go against your old defaults and choose to do something which is alien. Novel actions that favour your long-term goals are normally unappealing to the brain because they require effort, aren't instantly gratifying, and their selection means leaving 'better' options behind. Even with small actions, there will be times during the early days where you will face the mental pull to do something else. Whether that is lying on the couch watching TV, eating a family bag of crisps before dinner or watching Instagram reels or TikTok videos for another thirty minutes, our brains value little-effort-big-reward tasks and the defaults it already has programmed.

By planning in advance and making your small action the obvious option, you can skip the resistance of having to fight off other choices. It is natural to try to talk ourselves out of doing something new, so having answers and contingencies can help you follow through with what you know is going to be good for you. Before you arrive at a decision-making crossroads, you can work on making performing small actions as frictionless as possible. This can be done by clearly defining when you are going to do your action, having as much set up in advance as possible, and prepping how to talk back to your inner chatter. When at the crossroads, your main aim is to remove other options as quickly as possible to lessen the pull towards something more tempting.

Making decisions in advance and rapidly in the moment were vital to me establishing an early morning exercise routine. I hate going to the gym when it is really busy, and living in central London, the hours immediately preceding and following work would be absolutely heaving. I couldn't use any of the machines I wanted, there would be a queue for the showers afterwards and I couldn't get near a mirror for love nor money, so I would resort to balancing makeup on the sink of the toilets to sort my face out. I wanted to work out, but I was so frustrated with the current state of my sessions that I knew I had to change them.

I am good for nothing in the evening, so I decided to get to the gym early doors before the rush. This meant a 5 a.m. alarm to catch the train that would get me to the gym for opening. The first few attempts at this routine were a complete failure. I was staying up too late, meaning when the alarm started blaring at the crack of dawn, my inner chatter would scream, 'YOU NEED MORE SLEEP. TURN IT OFF'. So, I'd snooze until seven and end up skipping the gym entirely, feeling disappointed in myself for missing another day. I realized I couldn't rely on 5 a.m. Julia to get me to the gym, so I had to make it as easy for her as possible.

I identified that the main things keeping me from following through in the early mornings were (1) I was tired, (2) it felt like a lot of effort to get up and out the door and (3) I didn't feel like it mattered if I missed a session as I wasn't letting anyone down but me (sob). For each of these reasons, I came up with ways to offset the excuses. For commitment, I used a calendar to block out my gym time each week to confirm that what I wanted to do for myself was important and joined an online fitness regime where I had to log three to four sessions per week with a personal trainer. To get myself out the door, I packed my bag the night before, put my gym clothes on the floor next to my bed and set up a travel mug with a teabag in it ready to have on the train. For tiredness,

I went to bed before 10 p.m. and made sure my bedside lamp switch was in reaching distance so I could whack it on as soon as the alarm sounded. I also came up with an answer to my brain's 'I'm tired' talk: 'I have slept for seven hours. I am fine.' All these choices meant that when my alarm went off, I was equipped to face the excuses head on. Over time, these actions and my early gym sessions became a no-drama routine and I barely heard my inner chatter pipe up in protest anymore. By making as many decisions as possible in advance and acting quickly in the face of temptation, my morning gym visits became one of my favourite routines.

SCI

Making decisions involves a lot of brain activity, even for choices that may seem benign. Like picking what show to watch on Netflix. We may see this as a passive flick through the menu, but within the brain, a hubbub of information is being presented with each option. We are considering which show will be the most entertaining – what is the best use of the next eight hours of our lives? We also consider similar series we have previously watched and whether we enjoyed them. Our current emotional state is considered – are we in the mood to laugh or cry? From this information for each title, a value is assigned and weighted against other programmes in the list. Much of this processing happens in the prefrontal areas of the brain,[1] with three regions indicated in playing important roles:

- The **dorsolateral prefrontal cortex**,[2] important in comparing information being presented with past events to come to a conclusion on what to do next (like loving the last thriller documentary so watching another one).
- The **anterior cingulate cortex**,[3] involved in taking our emotional state into account and in detecting 'choice error' (like picking a really awful series) so we don't repeat the same bad decision in the future.

- The **orbitofrontal cortex**,[4] which weighs up the value of the reward of an action versus the effort required to perform it (watching full series vs eight hours of real life).

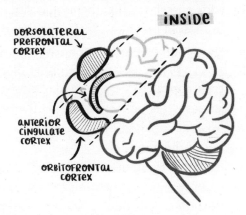

These calculations occur in many instances throughout our life: choosing what drink to have at a coffee shop, what university to go to, whether to go to the gym or not, moving jobs or staying where you are. Our choices are computed through our past experiences, emotional states, and their reward versus payoff. Chapter 10 dove into reward in the brain, and we met the chemical dopamine. Dopamine is thought to be an important signifier in making decisions, with its release in advance of a choice marking the potential reward we might get from going down that route. As the dopamine system is ancient (it was present millions of years ago in a common ancestor that humans share with other species), its definition of 'reward' is not always what we actually want. High calories, sex, safety and survival all rank pretty highly in dopamine's book, meaning we can be driven to opt for choices which serve more 'basic' human functions than logical, healthier options.

We probably make thousands of decisions every day. From what to wear, to how much milk to put into our tea, to what time we should leave the house, to whether to say hi or not to that person you went to school with who is fast approaching you down the fruit and veg aisle. As decision making is an energetically demanding process for the brain, it can be easy to default to habits or the low effort/high reward option (watching TV, having the chocolate bar) when we are stressed, tired or preoccupied by other problems.

A once-popular notion named 'decision fatigue', or 'ego depletion', suggested we have a limited amount of willpower and each decision we make eats into that until it runs out, meaning we can no longer make good choices for ourselves. This theory has since been seriously doubted, as research showed that individuals who experienced decision fatigue in a study were those who believed it was real, whereas participants who didn't believe in decision fatigue didn't display its effects.[5] Our willpower doesn't appear to be a limited, finite store. It is more likely that general fatigue, stress, distraction and other emotional states can deter decision-making capabilities due to the limited bandwidth of the prefrontal regions of the brain.

Our brains are designed to be more concerned about the here and now, meaning decision making in the moment might not be optimal for future success. In studies, we exhibit a 'present bias', meaning events going on now feel more important than those which may happen later. In fact, in research experiments, psychologists have observed that we treat our future selves not as an extended version of us, but more like a stranger. Whether that is forfeiting future money to get a smaller amount now or passing a disgusting task on to yourself in a few weeks' time, our present self can postpone responsibilities in order to get an instant reward or get-out-of-jail-free card now.

PReSeNT BiaS

ReWaRD
NOW

ReWaRD
LaTeR

Brain scan studies have also revealed that when we think about ourselves in the future, activity is not identical to when thinking about ourselves right now. Some of the brain areas recruited in envisioning 'future you' are similar to those activated when thinking of other people.[6] How much we see our future self as a stranger has been reported to depend on factors like self-esteem levels, cultural background, how close in time something is going to happen and how vivid an individual's mental imagery is.[7] Bringing our future self to life, shown in experiments using virtual reality,[8] prompts making better decisions for the person we will be, seemingly increasing our sense of connectedness with them.

APPLY

Planning ahead and making decisions in advance avoids being dependent on the state of the present brain's somewhat flawed prioritization method. By looking ahead, thinking about the friction points that may prevent you from taking the action you want, and finding ways to solve these problems now or in the moment can help you follow through in the future.

BRAINTENANCE: FRICTIONLESS

Break down your routine into a series of steps. What are the things that can be done in advance to make performing these tasks easier?

BRAINTENANCE: AIM OF THE DAY

Have one thing you want to achieve each day – whether that is something to do with your goal, a task at work or a personal endeavour – to give yourself a sense of accomplishment. Decide at the beginning of the week or the start of each day what your daily aim is and make space for it in your calendar (see page 168). I write this aim at the top of my to-do list each day with a star next to it to show it is the one thing I really want to get done.

BRAINTENANCE: PLANNING FOR FUTURE YOU

This involves three steps . . .

1. **Get organized**
   Organization may have the reputation as the destroyer of spontaneity, but it has an important role when it comes to following through with future plans: it crushes indecision. Indecision gives space for the current state of the brain and body to influence what you should do. Deciding when, where and how your actions will happen enables you to fall back on your schedule when you don't know what to do next, rather than make bad in-the-moment choices.

BRAINTENANCE: IF I COULD BLOCK OUT TIME

My favourite way to organize myself is blocking out my calendar each week to include the actions I want to do to help me towards my goals. I use an online calendar and fill out the blocks on a Sunday morning with a cup of tea, nice music and, if I am feeling fancy, a lit candle. Throughout the week, I write checklists each day from my calendar so I can physically mark off (and celebrate) following through with my plans. I started time-blocking in my PhD and it was a game changer for helping me move forward.

Mark out all your non-negotiable hours in your calendar: these are tasks like work, picking kids up, pre-arranged parties or events.

Add in your wake-up and wind-down times: thirty minutes to an hour at the bookends of your day dedicated to getting yourself up and getting ready for sleep without rushing.

Add in blocks for your small action (+ follow-through time). Block out time for your action. If very new, give yourself a thirty-minute block so you can do it and have time to chill after (or, if you feel like it, keep going with the task). If more established, you can block out the time it takes to do a 'full session', which still starts with the small action to get you into it.

Make time to move or create: if your goal is an exercise-based one, find some time each day to be creative – this could be reading a book, cooking, drawing, organizing, singing – anything that gives you a chance to check out of work mode. If your goal is more creative, add in a block for exercise. This could be a twenty-minute walk, a short run or an at-home workout. Something which you are familiar with so you can focus on establishing your new routines for your goal but still have room to give your brain space.

Add admin: got tasks that are hanging over you but keep getting pushed back? Pop sessions into your calendar to get on top of them.

Mark out downtime or free time: deciding to relax is as important as fitting in work (more on this in Chapter 16), so dedicate hours to your downtime.

Make different tasks different colours so you can see the balance of your week at a glance and you're set! The beauty about time-blocking online is you can adjust and move things around if other situations arise. But an ideal plan is in place. Keep your calendar open on your device and if you like ticking things off, write a to-do list based on your schedule so you can satisfyingly mark items as complete.

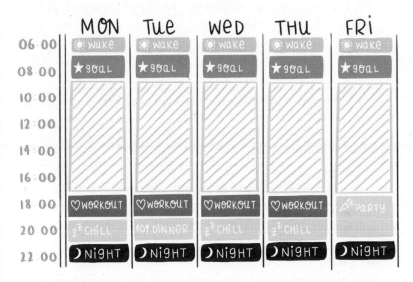

If you have a fairly regular schedule, set these generic blocks to repeat each week. Then on Sunday, you can edit the week ahead – filling out specific tasks to do in those set hours and moving things around as needed.

2. Get locked in

When you have a flight to catch or an exam coming up, your brain pushes you beyond the barrier of procrastination and into action mode (more on procrastination in Chapter 13). Now, we don't want to live in the stressed-out stage of rushing to the departure gate or working to a deadline, but if we can give our actions some sense of importance, we should be less likely to flake. Sadly, we don't really mind letting ourselves down, but if others are involved or there is a consequence for skipping, it can help keep us committed.

BRAINTENANCE: COMMITMENT PACT

There are different ways of committing yourself to follow through with your actions. Give some of the following a go:

- Meet someone: if you arrange to work out with a personal trainer or do study time with a friend, you know they are there waiting, and it makes you want to show up. It is important you do not depend on them, though – if they cancel, still follow through!

- Sign up to a plan or programme: introduce some accountability in the form of knowing you are getting checked up on every week.

- Make (somewhat flexible) deadlines: if you are trying to get something done ASAP but there isn't the pressure to get it finished, make deadlines for yourself. Like with a real deadline, the countdown can help you be consistent. But you don't want to feel guilty about not meeting these arbitrary dates. Personally, I make flexible deadlines to work towards but shift them if I need to. In my PhD I used to make Gantt charts (scheduled timelines on a spreadsheet) to give myself deadlines so I could ensure I was using my time wisely, but each week I would assess where I was up to and adapt if needed.

3. **Get vocal**
When you haven't followed through previously, what has stopped you? Identify the chatter your brain throws up when going against the grain, or the general feeling in your body making you want to resist, and craft a comeback for some of these excuses. Sometimes, skipping a planned session is the right thing to do – if you are sick, or wiped out – but most of the time, we give ourselves ways to wriggle out of doing things that are challenging or uncomfortable. Like if you got no sleep, then being tired is a real reason not to act. But if you've had eight solid hours of shuteye, tiredness can be a trump card your brain is trying to play.

BRAINTENANCE: COMEBACKS

Think of the main excuses your brain throws at you when you are trying to do something hard, and then plan what you are going to say back to help you follow through.

Excuse	Comeback
'I'm tired'	'I've slept for eight hours, I'll be fine in ten minutes'
'It's cold outside'	'I have layers and I will warm up after five minutes of jogging'
'I have more important things to do'	'My schedule is dedicated to this; I can fit in other things after'

When faced with excuses, sometimes it's easier to try to shush up the noise altogether. My favourite short-circuit exercise is to count down and then launch into action. The **'5, 4, 3, 2, 1' method**, described by motivational speaker Mel Robbins, is great for this. When the excuses or negative chatter start swirling around in your head, count back from five and then take the next step towards what you want. For me, I use this to get up on mornings when I am lying in bed worrying or when I am sprawled on the couch with dishes waiting to be cleaned. Having a countdown, or a word you use, to launch you out of 'thinking' and into 'doing' is an effective way of overriding the present brain's desire for the familiar and comfortable.

BRAINTENANCE: FUTURE FRIENDS

Our future self should not be a stranger to us. If we consider the future version of ourselves as a friend, it can help do the things that will benefit them. We so often disregard our own wants, even if this will make us feel not great. Imagining your future self as a real person you care about should help when making choices that favour you going forwards.

Who is a person you really love, care about, respect and never want to let down? Imagine your future self is this person, and that the

actions you are doing – working out, creating videos, studying, networking – is all for them. You could even think of yourself in the future and consider what they would tell you to do.

When you are battling with excuses, bring this person to mind and consider how this action will help them. When I think of my future self in these situations, I imagine them saying 'keep going'.

WRAP UP

Taking the responsibility of decision-making out of the present reduces the sway your current state has on influencing which way you go. Each choice we make is carefully valued by what is deemed important to us, what will bring us reward, how similar things have played out in the past, current emotional state and whether the effort required is worth the payout. Valuation of the exact same choice can differ depending on what the brain perceives as your needs right now, meaning leaving even small choices to the last minute can be a risky business. Being overwhelmed, stressed or tired can interfere with your plans, leaving you kicking yourself later. By being organized, committed to yourself and prepared to answer back to excuses, you can lessen the uphill battle against instantly gratifying temptations. And if an inner debate about whether you should or shouldn't follow through arises, choose fast. Count down and go, activate that cue, perform a small step immediately to take the tempting option off the table.

It is worth saying that with all the preparation and planning in the world, there will be times when your present self is victorious. The lure of the couch, or that admin task which all of a sudden seems so appealing, wins out. It is completely normal. Even when a behaviour is pretty much routine, there are occasions where you hit the alarm and turn over for more shuteye. Accept it and prep yourself so you can come back fighting tomorrow.

CHAPTER 12

BOOST BELIEF

With protocols and plans in place, we often feel ready to seize the opportunity and begin working towards a goal. But one last tool is required, which is potentially the toughest to cultivate: believing in yourself.

Every goal can be made easier to perform by breaking them down into actionable steps, planning and rewarding ourselves for carrying them out. The pixie dust of cracking-on is believing you are capable of doing these action steps and trusting that the tough work now will pay off.

It is easy enough to say, 'believe in yourself', or read quotes saying, 'you have the power', but actually fostering a deep sense of self-belief takes work. Just like other habits and behaviours, we build up an inner sense of confidence from experience. The brain takes on board feedback from a variety of tasks to give us a sense of what we are and aren't 'good' at. This can not only influence our judgements of what we are able to do, but also who we are and – via the praise, or lack thereof, we receive – what makes us worthy.

We all use external feedback to some extent to measure our self-worth and self-belief. And expectations from society, from those closest to you and from yourself, create pressure to uphold a certain standard or image, giving us little wiggle room to get it wrong. If we ever 'fail', or make a mistake, or even just think about something not going our way, we can flap – opening the floodgates to a tirade of negative self-talk.

'You're never going to make this happen.' 'You're stupid for attempting this.' 'You are a fraud and incapable of doing anything right.'

While this criticism may be designed to try to protect you and keep you away from the threat of embarrassment and social exclusion, its knock-on impact makes you stall, doubt the actions you are doing and scold yourself for even trying.

You don't have to believe you can do something miles ahead of where you currently are – that will most likely lead to calling yourself out and prevent action. But having a belief in your abilities, in your work ethic, and trust in yourself to get the job done is a fundamental aspect of working on a goal. Fostering a compassionate outlook towards yourself when things aren't going as planned can help you to move on from setbacks and push through tough periods, while giving yourself some slack by lessening the weight of expectation. Knowing how to deal with your own self-criticism and not let it get so loud that it makes you stagnate is a skill that can be utilized to keep you pursuing your passions.

WHY

When starting something new, lacking some confidence is normal. Whether that is turning up to a new gym and not knowing where anything is, starting a new job and getting to grips with new systems or reading about a new topic at school and not quite getting it. It takes time and repeated practice to build up feelings of assurance in new fields, with confidence levels increasing the more you engage with an activity. But even when unconfident in a new skill, having an underlying degree of self-belief that you can eventually do it is an important driver of sticking with it. This belief could stem from knowing that you are a hard worker, or having skills in a similar field, or bringing expertise from a different area of life. Even though you may feel a bit shaky now, you have enough belief in yourself that you can commit. This self-belief, also called self-efficacy, can drive you to build new behaviours into your routines and advance skills, increasing your confidence and promoting future action.

Even when you believe in your abilities, doubting yourself from time to time is inevitable. It is normal to question yourself, to step back slightly and assess if what you are doing is good for yourself and others. These doses of self-doubt ensure we query our own opinions or beliefs to solve problems effectively, drop practices that are not beneficial, and don't harm others. If we lived in a world where none of us questioned our actions, there would be no room for advancement and change, no space to learn and grow, with everyone more concerned about proving their competence and convincing others that their way is the correct and only way to be. Self-doubt acts as a prompt to stop, question, take on board other information and orient ourselves to act in a more efficient, helpful and beneficial way.

The ideal level of self-doubt falls into a narrow range. Like adding spice to a dish – there is a sweet spot. Too little means you can't taste it, but too much overpowers. It would be great if we could measure out our self-doubt in tablespoons, but the brain doesn't abide by the imperial or metric system. Often, the balance of self-doubt is way off, falling on the 'this-is-overpowering-and-I-can't-do-anything' side. This may manifest as your inner chatter convincing you not to do something because 'what's the point?' or telling you that you are rubbish and can't do anything right. Or you may just feel downbeat or pessimistic when trying to keep at it. And even in instances when you have truly earnt your position and have physical proof of what has led you to where you are, you can still feel that you are a fraud. Overly doubting yourself and your abilities can lead you to question yourself, feel stressed about what you are doing, prevent you from pushing forward and fail to recognize how bloody fabulous you are.

SELF-DOUBT SPOONS

Of all the chapters in the book, this was the one I needed to write the most. I could do all my planning, make my routine straightforward, incentivize myself with rewards, but if my inner chatter wasn't being my cheerleader that day, I was pretty much doomed to give in. I'd find it difficult to muster up the belief that I was capable and be plagued with self-doubt. 'Is this the right way?', 'I'm not good at this', 'No one likes what I am doing', 'If it hasn't happened now, it never will', 'What's the point? I will always be like this', 'I will never make it work'. I was so used to relying on other people's praise and feedback that when it came to me taking action without immediate external validation, I struggled.

Throughout my PhD in particular, the self-doubt was rife. Even though I worked so hard and had the results to show for it, I would find myself stunned in the face of any compliments about my work. Not just in a polite 'don't-flatter-me-but-thanks' kind of way. It was more like my brain would downright refuse to believe any of those words were true. When writing up my thesis and preparing for my final exam, everyone I spoke to about my progress would say, 'you're going to be more than fine!', reeling off a list of things I had done over the past four years, and still, I couldn't take the message on board. If anything, it made me more worried that people had such convincing expectations of me. I was so stressed that the exam would be where it all came out, that I was going to fail and break the facade of being a competent PhD candidate. As the three-hour viva exam with two world-leading experts in my field drew to a close, I remember the voice in my head saying, 'that can't be it'. Even afterwards, as we were toasting and celebrating me becoming a doctor, I said to my partner, 'I feel like they have made a mistake; there must be something I have missed.' I could not get my head around the fact that I had done it. The years of batting myself down as not being good enough and feeling like an imposter had created such a strong belief of 'this is never going to happen', that when it did, I was stunned. Even now, as I am writing this, I had the thought of 'should I put this story in, because at some point, everyone will see that I couldn't possibly have got a PhD', despite my official degree certificate hanging above my desk.

You may think because I got through my PhD that the self-doubt wasn't so much of an issue in the end. And to some extent, it did make me work harder to prove myself. But the process of consistently showing up was so much more difficult because of it. The stress before giving a talk or writing a report was so high because I never believed what I did was good enough. And with a structured course like a PhD, I felt like I sort of had to just get on with it. I had a deadline and, self-doubt or not, I wanted to complete it. But in more unstructured areas of my life like my career, my over-pouring of self-doubt has leaked over and prevented me taking action. Words like 'this isn't working, you're not good at this, others do it better' have been taken as signals to actually stop. Without external pressure or a deadline to buffer this negativity, I would just shelve things and never return. I couldn't muster up that belief that I could do it. And for me, that has been my biggest obstacle.

I recognized how much my loud self-doubt was overpowering my quiet self-belief and I wanted to try to switch the dials. I needed to have enough self-doubt to question my actions in a constructive way but allow my self-belief to give the commands. It has not been an easy 'here are five ways to increase self-belief' scenario. This element of helping myself show up is something I must actively deploy whenever self-doubt starts to raise its volume. And although responses have started to come more naturally, this mechanism of questioning my abilities is ultimately a safety mechanism, meaning I know I will face it time and time again when taking on new challenges.

SCI

As explored in Chapter 8, our sense of self dictates many of the decisions we make. Through trial, error, labels, test scores, praise, punishment, wins, losses and a whole heap of other life experiences, the brain can craft up a concept of who you believe you are, what you can do and where your limits lie. And when we try to do something new, this concept can be used as a gauge to measure whether we are up to the job.

In the pursuit of goals, you come face-to-face with yourself a lot. When striving for more, you are encountering your beliefs about yourself repeatedly, and normally must confront them in order to make change. Although our concepts about who we are grant us stability and help predict how we will fare in given situations, these ideas are malleable and, if they are not working in your favour, should be challenged. Four selfies that should be on our radar during goal pursuit are:

Self-esteem (aka self-worth)

. . . is a measure of how positively or negatively we feel about ourselves. Self-esteem is an overall deduction about how we see our 'worth' and is computed based on factors like what we are good at, what we do, how we look, our strengths and our weaknesses (assigned by ourselves or others). Individuals with lower self-esteem tend to have higher levels of negative emotions and are more likely to have symptoms associated with conditions like depression and anxiety, whereas higher self-esteem is seen in people who experience more positive states, like joy. It is thought self-esteem acts as a buffer against stress, meaning higher levels make people more resilient, and because of this, it potentially has a beneficial effect on physical health.

In the brain, experiments have associated regions involved in learning, memory and valuation with self-esteem, which makes sense as this concept requires understanding past experiences and giving them weight to generate an overall value for worth. For example, there is correlation between having a larger hippocampus – a region vital for forming new long-term memories – and higher levels of self-esteem.[1] This may be because this region contributes to making up our sense of worth, or it may be that an elevated level of self-esteem increases the size of this brain region due to the better handling of stress (which the hippocampus is particularly vulnerable to). When our self-esteem takes a hit, say in the case of social rejection, our brain registers a 'social

prediction error' and updates our measure of self-esteem, corresponding to activity in prefrontal regions.[2]

As low self-esteem is a common state in many mental health conditions, therapy often utilizes techniques to help raise the level of a person's self-worth. Challenging negative beliefs, be that through vocalizing or writing, and backing these statements up with real-life evidence like good things others say about you, is a recommended technique provided by health services.[3] Established negative thoughts are (unwantedly) repeatedly offered up as a solution by the brain when we are trying to understand challenges or why something has happened. But these thoughts, like any other, can be contested. And using real-life evidence is a good method to quieten them.

Self-efficacy (aka self-belief or self-confidence)

. . . is how confident we feel in our own abilities and skills. This is different to just general confidence. A person can feel completely fine networking at parties, or giving a speech on stage, but internally, they still do not fully believe in their own abilities. And this can be a problem when it comes to goal pursuit. In order to work towards an aim that is some distance away, you need some element of belief that you can give it a good go. So, the lower the level of self-efficacy, the less likely a person will believe they can do it, and so may stop trying altogether.

Whereas self-esteem focuses on how we feel about ourselves, self-efficacy considers whether we think we can do something. The difference is in the action. For example, a person with high self-esteem may feel like they are worthy of an opportunity because of their hard work, whereas a person with high self-efficacy might take on a role even if they don't necessarily have the skills right now, as they believe they can learn. High levels of self-efficacy can also fuel motivation and confidence, because the more you believe you can do something, the more driven you feel to want to work at it, and with this work, the more confident you become. This can turn into a positive feedback loop, with the increased motivation and confidence bringing about more results, which further proves you can do it.

MASTERY   VICARIOUS   VERBAL   EMOTIONAL
          EXPERIENCE PERSUASION & PHYSICAL STATE

In psychology, self-efficacy theory suggests that our levels of inner confidence in our abilities depends on four sources:[4] (1) mastery – challenging yourself and succeeding builds up trust; (2) vicarious experience – having role models who we can look up to and emulate; (3) verbal persuasion – hearing words of encouragement like 'you can do it'; and (4) current emotional and physical states – your overall health and well-being can impact how much you believe in your abilities. Studies have associated high self-efficacy levels with better work performance,[5] school performance and higher optimism.[6] But because self-efficacy is enhanced by all of these events, it is unclear which is stronger: self-efficacy causing success or success causing self-efficacy. So far, the underpinnings of self-efficacy in the brain are not clear, making it difficult to test beyond association.

Self-doubt

. . . is a mechanism to help protect you from making big mistakes or jumping into actions with consequences, but it often goes too far. Often self-doubt is accompanied by its friend **self-criticism**, which normally presents itself as a tirade of insults and putdowns. It is thought our inner critic is an additional way to extend control over the random events we face. If we could have just tried a bit harder and got the job, or not chatted so much and got a second date – it makes us feel like we have influence over things that don't go our way. In healthy doses, self-criticism can prevent us from hurting people and help us see our potential when we could have pushed that little bit more to get what we wanted. But there is a point at which it can become toxic. At high levels, both self-doubt and self-criticism are symptoms of debilitating conditions such as depression and anxiety, fuelling an inwardly directed negative disposition.

A manifestation of heightened self-doubt is the imposter phenomenon. This is when, despite having the evidence to back up exactly why you are where you are, you feel like a fraud. Many people with an array of accolades under their belts, including Academy Award and Nobel Prize winners, experience this inner conflict. Feeling like you just 'got lucky', or someone was easy on you, or, at any moment, someone will expose you as a con, are common reports. Not much neuroscience research has explored this psychological state, but it has been theorized that imposter feelings may arise as a form of anticipatory anxiety – enabling us to plan for a 'worst-case scenario' if our current structure were to crumble.[7] In the brain, imbalances in the reward system have also been proposed to contribute to imposter-like thoughts, preventing the true scale of an achievement to be registered internally and, hence, not being able to accept it externally.[8] While the imposter phenomenon and other forms of self-doubt and self-criticism can act as a driver to work hard and to prove that you are worthy of your position, high self-criticism was a predictor for less positive events in a large sample of teens.[9] Plus, in the state of heightened anxiety and stress that accompanies imposter syndrome, people are more prone to failure and reduced productivity.[10]

Self-compassion

. . . is the antidote to self-criticism and self-doubt. Being self-compassionate is essentially treating yourself as you would a friend. You don't need to have high self-esteem or self-efficacy to be self-compassionate. It is not about only being unrealistically positive, but instead approaching internal conversations in a similar tone to the chats you would have with the people you care about. Say you didn't make it to the gym today because you were run off your feet at work. Instead of calling yourself lazy and a quitter, consider what you would say to your best mate in the same position (more like 'you've had a really busy day; don't be hard on yourself'). This can help cultivate a healthier internal narrative.

Neuroscience research into self-compassion and the tone of our inner monologue is starting to pick up. In a brain-scanning study of forty healthy people reading self-critical and self-reassuring statements such as 'I fail to keep up with my commitments in life', vs 'I keep up with my commitments in life', engagement with the reassuring statements led to decreased activity in areas associated with threat detection like the amygdala and anterior cingulate cortex.[11] Although not a perfect measure for self-compassion, this study indicates that altering the way we speak to ourselves could help us move beyond negative self-talk to a more productive, healthy headspace. This technique is also going to be tested for people with high levels of self-criticism, such as individuals with anxiety and depression, to see if it could provide long-term benefits.

Addressing bumps in the roads and setbacks with statements like 'we all make mistakes' does more than blunt the sting of self-criticism; it can also help us follow through with plans and move us towards our goals. Having higher levels of self-compassion is associated with looking after your health and well-being better,[12] being more pro-active, having more resilience in the face of failure, and showing more willingness to correct mistakes.[13] If you had a teacher at school who always told you how rubbish you were, calling you a useless failure, how motivated do you think you'd be to keep working at that subject? On the other hand, if you had a teacher who was patient, reassuring, encouraging and realistic, telling you it is just one test, pointing out the things that went well and where you can improve, it is much more likely you will keep trying. Being that teacher for yourself when addressing challenges can help you to keep going in the face of adversity.

APPLY

Boosting belief is a case of show and tell. You have to show yourself that you are able to take on challenges and follow through with commitments while telling yourself how things are in a compassionate way. Ultimately, you need to build up trust in yourself and your abilities so that, when in the midst of a crisis, where everything seems to be going wrong, you can fall back on the belief that you can handle it and make it through.

BRAINTENANCE: LITTLE PROMISES

In any relationship, a way to build up trust and belief in the other person is if they stick to their word. And we can apply the same method to start trusting in ourselves more. Making and keeping little promises to yourself builds up a belief that you are capable of following through with plans, respecting your own commands as much as you respect others, and can act as physical evidence when having to believe in yourself. Examples of little promises are:

WAKING ON ALARM **MEET ON TIME** **COOK DINNER**

CLEAN WHEN PLANNED **WATCH 1 EPISODE** **LEAVE PHONE WHEN WORKING**

What little promises could you make and keep for yourself?

BRAINTENANCE: BACK IT UP

When we are experiencing self-doubt or low self-esteem, looking back on past accomplishments can help show what we're capable of. Take a negative thought like 'I am so uncreative' and follow it up with a 'well, actually . . .' and add a statement that contradicts the thought. You could imagine these examples, or write them down, or find the physical evidence in the form of records like photos, videos, certificates and past projects to show yourself you can do it. When I'm making a video, if I feel like I am completely rubbish at it, I sometimes watch one I have created previously to remind myself I am capable.

What evidence would you use to respond to:

'I don't deserve to be in this position.'
Well, actually . . .

'I never succeed at anything.'
Well, actually . . . .

'I can't do this, it is too hard.'
Well, actually . . . .

BRAINTENANCE: IF–THEN–AND

When we are confronted with self-doubt and self-criticism, we can end up in a 'what-if' spiral. *What if this doesn't work? What if I can't finish it? What if I am not good enough?* Although we ask ourselves many questions in these internal battles, we very rarely respond to them with concrete answers, fuelling anxiousness and worry. Giving yourself a potential answer to these enquiries, even if it is a 'worst-case scenario', can help shift you out of the spiral and into action mode. With some of the scarier answers, saying 'and I'll handle it' afterwards could help calm inner panic.

When you find yourself facing criticism, try the following:
IF [criticism] THEN [what will happen/what I'll do] AND I'LL HANDLE IT

For example . . .

IF I fail this exam THEN I will take it again AND I'LL HANDLE IT.

The worst-case scenario is very unlikely to happen, but if it ever did, a plan is now in place, meaning you can more readily quieten those 'what if?' thoughts and instead focus on the work you need to do.

BRAINTENANCE: MASTER–MODEL–MOTIVATE

According to self-efficacy theory, the ways to build up self-belief are to master challenges, have a role model to look up to, and be encouraged along the way. While these methods have been tried in schools and workplaces, we can also turn them in on ourselves in a few simple ways.

- **Mastery**: Set yourself easy wins – little challenges that you can take on and accomplish to show yourself you can succeed (your small action from Chapter 9, or small wins from Chapter 7, or little promises from this chapter are perfect for this).
- **Model**: Like with our role models back in Chapter 8, think of a person who has already achieved your goal, or has qualities you admire, and consider how they would handle the challenges you are facing.
- **Motivate**: Be your own cheerleader. Say 'good job', 'well done for getting through that' and 'I am improving' as you work towards your goal to create your own internal support system. As in Chapter 10, it is all about celebrating your efforts.

BRAINTENANCE: QUESTION THE CRITIC

We can often take the words or deductions about feelings that our brain makes as truth (which, as we know from Chapter 4, is not wise). But these interpretations, whether they feel like it or not, can often come from a place of trying to protect yourself. By questioning the motivation of the internal criticism coming your way, you can start to see that its motive is to prevent you from doing something for – what it thinks is – your own good. Like a villain in a film, when you learn their back story, you can see how they have come to their warped interpretation of the world. Understanding where this criticism is coming from and what it is trying to do will help us to take it less seriously and deploy compassion.

Inner chatter	Reason
'I am rubbish at this'	I don't want to embarrass myself and have people laugh at me
'I am a terrible human being'	I don't like how I have acted before and feel it defines me
'I should just give up now'	I don't want to try and not succeed

BRAINTENANCE: NEXT SMALL STEP

A problem I often find when trying to work towards a goal is that I try to make myself believe I can do the very end stage right now and when I go to take action, I realize how far away from that 'end ideal' I am. It helps to scale back the expectation and muster the belief that you can achieve the next small step in front of you. For example, if you want to be a champion body builder, the next step to believe in might be 'I can lift an extra 5 kg'. When the goal posts are shifted so close you can't miss, you are more likely to believe you can do it. This should increase self-efficacy (via mastery) and enable you to craft a belief that you can always go one step further.

Using your 'one inch more' criteria from Chapter 11, can you believe you can do that next step? This should encourage you to take action and start a snowball effect of boosting self-belief through getting results.

BRAINTENANCE: COMPASSIONATE CHATTER

We would never talk to others the way we talk to ourselves, so call yourself out on it. When self-criticism or self-doubt come up with explanations for why things haven't quite worked out or why carrying on with our action plan is fruitless, address these concerns as if you were talking to someone you care about. Think of this person now – it could be a friend, teacher, partner or parent – and imagine how you would react to them being in the following situations.

- **Made a mistake?** That's part of being human, no one is perfect, and everyone makes mistakes.
- **Missed out on a job?** There could have been someone internal who got it, the team may not have been a good fit or there may be a few skills you can work on. But it means in the future you will be free for the right opportunity, and you can work towards that.
- **Forgotten to pack your socks for the gym?** We all forget things, especially when we are busy. Let's pop to the shops, grab you some new ones and next time, we'll pack our bag the night before, so we don't have to rush.

Many of us aren't used to giving ourselves a break. But pausing to recognize when you are beating yourself up, and intervening with a kind, compassionate statement, can help disrupt negative self-talk.

BRAINTENANCE: WHY NOT ME?

When pursuing a big goal, it is easy to sit there and think 'why me?' We question what makes us so special to think we could possibly do this, and our brains will automatically rattle off a list of reasons why we can't. In these situations, I like to flip the question from 'why me?' to 'why not me?' Instead of filling your head with self-critical negatives, this question changes the tone to one of hope. Chances are that your goal has been achieved by someone before. It can be done. So why can't it be you who does it as well? Look at those who have come before you and achieved, learn how they did it and then put your own spin on it. 'Why not me' helps you see the power you hold and believe that if they can do it, so can you.

WHY NOT ME? I am . . . *determined, passionate, hardworking . . .*

WRAP UP

Believing in your abilities, whether that be particular skills, how you take on challenges or solve problems, or your ability to work and get a job done, is often underestimated when trying to change elements of your life. This isn't something that can be easily built into a schedule or measured, and is unique to every person, making it difficult to generate blanket methods to foster a sense of self-efficacy. But recognize that your thoughts about yourself and your capabilities can be challenged. You can prove your abilities to yourself through small wins and in challenging situations basing your behaviour on role models. By talking to yourself with compassion, you can quickly quieten the doubt that arises in your mind. Treat yourself the way you treat others – with kindness and understanding – by being gentle with yourself when going through difficulties. This can provide the encouragement so many of us need. *You* can give yourself permission to try, *you* can cheer yourself on when you are working at it, and *you* can celebrate your successes while consoling your defeats. Believe that you can take the next step forward and watch your progress snowball.

Maintenance

CHAPTER 13

BEAT PROCRASTINATION

We often know what we need to do to reach a goal. It should just be a straightforward case of following through with your plans and, hey presto, you're in the running to reach it. But instead, we often find ourselves procrastinating on the things we want to do, despite knowing the disappointment this will bring in the long run.

On the surface, procrastination doesn't really make sense. It isn't advantageous to unnecessarily or irrationally postpone tasks we want or need to do. Yet, procrastination is something most of us face. We scroll on social media, refresh our emails, watch more episodes, spend hours gaming, clean our rooms – all in the name of avoiding doing the task we need to do, and often end up blaming our laziness or poor organizational skills for not being able to push through.

Research in psychology and neuroscience suggests that we procrastinate – and sabotage ourselves in the process – due to a failure in the systems directing our self-control. Overriding the control we need to stay focused on a task and blocking out distractions means we are more susceptible to giving in to emotional demands. Our attempts to solve the discomfort generated when trying to perform a task that requires effort is to seek out a more pleasant state, which normally comes in the form of immediately rewarding activities. In this regard, procrastination appears to be a regulatory mechanism to help us deal with and move away from uncomfortable states. And even when we know these feelings are a normal part of trying to pursue something hard or new, the urge to procrastinate still pops up as a defence against stepping outside our comfort zone.

By recognizing the reasons that might lead us to procrastinate and using a few simple tools, we can avoid losing the precious hours we have dedicated to showing up and doing the work. Instead, we can trust that when procrastination comes knocking – which it will – we are able to close the door and follow through with the tasks we have set.

WHY

Procrastination is sneaky. It steals our time by making us feel like our current intention isn't that significant, but in the long run, it can add up to hours' worth of lost time. Like having a jar of coins. If you take out a small amount each day, the odd 50p or £1, it doesn't really feel like it will make a dent in the total, until the day arrives when the jar is empty, and you have no idea what you spent all your money on.

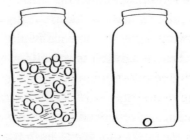

Procrastination leads to us making similar miscalculations, fostering a sense that the present moment isn't adding up to a grand total. By taking odd hours here and there, procrastination quietly robs us of making progress, while postponing stress and frustration to our future selves. Unfortunately for long-term goals, procrastination normally arises when we are doing something difficult and deemed not necessary for survival. It is very easy to convince ourselves that postponing now is not the end of the world – because technically, it isn't. Unless a deadline is looming or you have a lot at stake, skipping on today's intentions won't obviously hinder progress. If you are consistent the rest of the time, missing a day here and there is completely fine. But as procrastination often takes each moment as a stand-alone entity, the consequence of sacrificing today's plans on tomorrow's results is easily excused. The more we put something off, the more anxious we tend to get about doing the work, making it even more difficult to get going.

Like any action which is repeated, procrastination can become more than just an innocent quick fix to a negative emotional state – it can become habitual. If a certain task – like going for a run – is put off day after day, and instead we watch TV, the brain will likely start to associate these two activities. So, our intention of running instead triggers the urge to procrastinate. This can occur in many contexts, whether it is an often-avoided task, or an emotional state, like fear of failure. The brain can link avoidance to these states. And the procrastinating task of choice isn't always 'bad' – it could be cleaning your room or redoing your schedule. But doing anything that takes you away from the task you want to do is procrastination. So situations where we have procrastinated before will make us crave procrastination again, meaning we face an uphill battle to actually do the work we know will be good for us.

Consistently delaying tasks we know we should do is not only costly for progress, it is also thought to block momentum. Momentum is built from uninterrupted effort, allowing development on a project to gather pace with the more time spent on it. Procrastination slows this drive, making you switch gears out of work mode. Even the smallest of procrastination activities, like a quick check of the emails, can potentially compromise your work efficacy, as your brain has to reorient itself back to the task at hand. Procrastination has also been associated with unpleasant states like experiencing more stress, low self-esteem and health problems. So, breaking a procrastination habit could have more benefits outside your goal-seeking pursuits.

My biggest vice for procrastinating is my phone. I have been hooked on my phone since I was about sixteen years old when I got an unlimited text messages contract. I would be on it day and night, in class, in bed, constantly checking for messages. Unbeknown to me, I was forming a dependency on my device. To my brain, my phone meant messages, which meant connection or school gossip or invites to parties, which made me feel good. As phones became more advanced, I had no hope. With social media apps, shopping online and constantly updated news feeds, my phone became my crutch. Whenever I felt any sort of negative emotion, I would scroll. The scrolling didn't feel particularly good; it was more that my brain had associated 'feel bad = pick up phone' as a habit, triggering this response whenever I was facing a challenge.

As I was in education for a long time, I was repeatedly coming up against challenges, having to sit exams or prepare for assessments, with my phone at my side in the library or on my desk for a comfort-click. During my PhD, there was the added stress of having to collect data and present it to my department every three months. When things weren't going right in the lab, I would find myself at my desk scrolling away. I started to realize that once I was on my phone, I found it hard to not keep checking it. So, as a trial, I started putting my phone in a locked drawer in my desk until lunch to give myself time away from my screen. When my stress levels would rise or I was trying to solve a complex problem, I would find my hand deep inside my bag searching for my phone before I was even aware I was doing it. As my phone wasn't in grabbing reach, I would 'wake up' from my automatic search and begin to recognize the feelings and situations that were driving my procrastination. This was often when I found work too difficult, bringing up a fear of 'I'm never going to get this right, I am going to fail'. Looking back on my schooling, I could see this thought pattern triggering procrastination over and over again: leaving assignments until the last minute, revising with a week to go before my exams, or pulling an all-nighter to finish my third-year dissertation. While I convinced myself I worked well under pressure, it was more like I needed pressure to push myself to do *any* work, and that work was definitely not my best.

We know procrastination is detrimental to us, yet when we do it, it gives us an excuse for our work being sub-par. 'I left it to the last minute' was the most common phrase spoken on my university campus. Last-minute-itus meant that if things didn't go well, you had an excuse, but if things did go well, you could feel super-assured in yourself that even with limited time, you had pulled it off. I wanted to cure my own last-minute-itus. I didn't want the stress and worry of not meeting a deadline to be the thing that got me to work. Like with my PhD thesis or this book. If I had waited until 'deadline fear' hit me to write, I would not have been able to finish. Or I would have not been able to sleep for a week. I wanted to enjoy the process, to show up every day and work on making my projects the best they could be. I took on my procrastination urge with tactics (and my phone continues to stay as far away from me as possible when I am working).

SCI

When we focus on a task, we are exerting control. This enables us to hone in on what we are doing but also to block out distractions. Getting into the zone is a case of keeping our emotional and mind-wandering states at bay so we can be present and fully immersed in what is in front of us.

Procrastination is thought to occur due to imbalances in the relationship between our ability to exert control on where we are putting our efforts and attention, and how we feel about the situation at hand. In other words, procrastination is a type of decision. We can decide whether to do this hard, difficult task now, which isn't critical or urgent, or we can instead do something that requires less effort and will make us feel good. When put like that, it literally is a no-brainer what choice we would prefer. Our present-biased brains will value the second option as higher and ignite a craving to follow through. This relationship is described in the emotional regulation theory of procrastination.[1] There is also the temporal motivation theory behind why we procrastinate, where our motivation to perform a task is influenced by how far away the deadline is.[2] If far in the future, this time period will discount our desire to act, but when fast approaching, we can motivate ourselves to get in gear. A newer theory, called the temporal decision model, incorporates the influence of how useful and how aversive the task is

WHY WE PROCRASTINATE...

LACK OF
REWARD

FAR AWAY
DEADLINE

NEGATIVE
EMOTIONS

when deciding to act.[3] These factors affect the values our brains assign to choices, often making procrastination feel like the better option.

The brains of procrastinators at rest have given us some insights into this battle between doing what is good for us versus putting it off until later. Brain activity of people who were self-described procrastinators versus people who didn't tend to put things off differed in two networks: the cognitive control system, which helps drive goal-directed behaviour, and the affective processing system, which reacts to emotional and self-important information.[4] Collectively, these networks underpin our self-control. With high activity in the cognitive control system and low activity in the affective processing system, we are able to focus on our goals and not let other incoming information, especially emotionally charged signals, distract us.

cognitive
control

vs

affective
processing

In this study of 132 students, it was found that the procrastinators tended to have decreased resting activity in the front section of the prefrontal cortex, known to be important in the control of social emotions. They also had increased activity in areas involved in making decisions based on value (ventromedial prefrontal cortex) and areas thought to trigger prospection – or future thinking (parahippocampal cortex).[5] Prospection can have a negative tinge – for example, you could be faced with doing a difficult task and picture yourself failing. These results suggest that procrastinators may experience increased negative thinking about future events which influences the value-encoding decision-making areas to push towards doing something immediately satisfying.

Studies have also looked at procrastinators in action to observe brain activity when people are given a task to do. In a situation where individuals could win or lose money based on pressing a button in response to specific signals, high procrastinators – selected based on survey data about procrastination activity – were found to be more impulsive in the task and more sensitive to punishment (losing money). Using brain scanners, the group of high procrastinators showed, on average, impaired ability at processing errors and a decreased ability to up their self-control in more intense situations.[6] This could suggest that in a 'to-procrastinate-or-to-not-procrastinate' dilemma, they may be less able to resist temptation. Similar results were found in a different cohort when measuring brain signals using electrodes rather than a brain scanner, noting that procrastinators especially struggled in situations that require more effort to act.[7] From these small studies, plus the brain activity from procrastinators at rest, it looks like a tendency to procrastinate in high-effort situations may come from selecting less beneficial behaviours due to reduced cognitive control, as well as emotions having a heightened influence over action.

Research so far has relied on grouping people as procrastination-prone or not. How these procrastination tendencies arise is still being unpicked. Some research has suggested people could be genetically predisposed to procrastinate, with one study finding women with higher procrastination tendencies were more likely to have a certain mutation in a gene that influences dopamine levels.[8] As dopamine is involved in promoting motivation, the conclusions of this study suggested higher levels of dopamine could enhance 'cognitive flexibility', which is the ability to switch from one task to the next. Although this is a useful skill, increased cognitive flexibility can also enhance distractibility, i.e. looking out for the next thing to work on. This genetic relationship was not seen in men in the study, and a problem with trying to link our genetics to behaviours is this work is mostly based on associations: self-reported questionnaires versus changes to DNA. We don't know if these women have higher levels of dopamine as the researchers weren't looking in their brains, meaning these findings remain inconclusive.

Association studies have also found procrastination tendencies to be associated with low conscientiousness, low self-efficacy and high neuroticism.[9] Procrastination has also been explained in the context of perfectionism – setting unrealistic standards on which self-worth is measured – inducing a fear of failure. As procrastination is likely to be influenced by how people manage emotion, this could be innate due to genetics or can be shaped based on experience and action. How much individuals use the frontal areas of their brains to exert control over their attention and direct it towards the task at hand also plays a part.

As procrastination impacts productivity, work has been conducted to see if there are mechanisms to reduce it. One study found procrastination levels were reduced in completing five written tasks when the task was 'gamified'.[10] The written tasks – which, upon completion, would earn the participants $20 – where either given to people on a plain 'to-do' list, as a list with each task given the same value in terms of 'points', or on lists where more difficult tasks earnt participants more points, representing a larger proportion of the $20 reward. Those with the ranked-reward lists were more likely to complete the task, especially those which were more challenging, and wrote more words, showing how rewards – even ones that make no difference to the final outcome – can spur action.

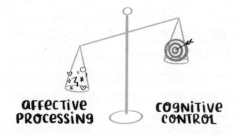

Some research has hinted mindfulness may be a good way at addressing procrastination.[11] Mindfulness can help identify the feelings driving procrastination, and visualizing yourself a few months in the future twice a week has been shown in one study to help prevent avoidance. Other methods suggested for tackling procrastination are removing distractions to physically prevent procrastinating, and having a gateway to get going, like just doing five minutes of work. Many of us feel overwhelmed in the face of a challenging task and stall, so easing in with a short period (like your small action) can help break the stalemate of getting started.

APPLY

No matter how much self-control we think we have, we will likely face a procrastination paradox at some point in our lives, especially when working towards goals. At these decision points, certain methods can be deployed to follow through with our plans.

BRAINTENANCE: REMOVE AND PLAN DISTRACTIONS

You might have a go-to distractor when you procrastinate. This could be your phone, the internet, planning and scheduling – anything that takes you away from the task at hand. When you work, try to make this thing and other fall-back distractors as hard to access as possible. For objects, put in a drawer or leave in a different room. For devices, switch off or block certain apps. And then schedule in when you will do these distractions. Instead of abstaining completely, have a five-minute phone check in your calendar or a ten-minute cleaning session to rationalize not using them in the moments you want to procrastinate.

What distracts you when you are trying to get on with a task? How can you make this thing less easy to engage with?

BRAINTENANCE: TIMER TIME

Starting a challenging task can be tricky. We can end up procrastinating because we expect a task to be hard before even giving it a go. By using a timer, you can get over the overwhelming urge to delay.

Depending on how resistant you feel, pick a length of time (the more resistance, the lower the number) to work for, and after this time is up, you can stop.

Once you start working, you can keep going beyond the timer. I use an app called 'Focus To-do' and go with a twenty-five-minute timer followed by a five-minute break. This way of working – the 'pomodoro' method – means you work for a good chunk of time but with the knowledge a break is pending. The more familiar you are with a task, the more time you can work for. As well as helping you get started, this method also gets your brain used to working distraction-free for extended periods. With consistent practice, it will be easier to work, and you won't feel the constant need to reach out for your phone for a scroll as much.

BRAINTENANCE: SYSTEM-OUT STRESS

When faced with a big task, we can feel overwhelmed by its seeming complexity. But tasks like these can be broken down into raw components and followed like a recipe to make them more digestible. For me, I like to take a task – such as writing a chapter of this book, as described in Chapter 9 – and write it as a step-by-step protocol. I always try to make a system when I start something new and refine it with each practice to generate the steps I need to follow, preventing it feeling like one huge daunting task.

WRITE BOOK CHAPTER

INGREDIENTS

LAPTOP   PEN‡PAPER   TEA   PLAYLIST   RESEARCH   SCHEDULE   TIMER

INSTRUCTIONS

① MAKE TEA
② OPEN DOCUMENT
③ CHECK SCHEDULE
④ START PLAYLIST
⑤ SET TIMER

⑥ WRITE 3 SENTENCES
⑦ WORK UNTIL TIMER
⑧ 5 MIN BREAK [OPTIONAL]
⑨ REPEAT 7-8 [UP TO 5 TIMES]
⑩ SWITCH OFF MUSIC, CLOSE COMP

If you were to write a recipe or guide to follow for your task, how would it go?

BRAINTENANCE: POP-UP LIST

Preventing procrastination is not just about keeping focused on a task; it is also about preventing distractions from disturbing your efforts to work. You may notice that when you are trying to work, you get the urge to check the weather for your run later or ring the dentist to book in your hygienist appointment. These urges are like pop-ups. Some are useful, but most are just attempts to distract you and take you off course.

Instead of acting on these impulses, which can slow momentum, you can capture them.

Put a blank piece of paper and a pen next to you as you work and record all the pop-ups.

This could literally be anything from 'what time is it in New York right now' to 'call up friend and tell them I'm free this weekend'. Once you reach a designated break time or, even better, after you have completed your task, go through this list and action any of the important pop-ups. Chances are 90 per cent of them will be things you no longer want to know or really care about, illustrating just how many times distractions crop up when you are working.

BRAINTENANCE: GAMIFY

Making things fun is a great way of getting new behaviours and activities into your routine. In Chapter 9, we discussed temptation bundling – bringing elements of what you find enjoyable into tasks so you look forward to doing them and feel more compelled to act. Turning these tasks into a game can also help tackle procrastination. Like a kid with a sticker chart, seeing the accumulation of badges or points can act as a motivating force in the face of a challenge.

Think about the task you keep putting off. Is there a way to make it into a game?

I have noticed this gamification on my running app. When I go on a run, I get rewarded medals for certain distances or times, and there are challenges you can take on – like 24 km in twenty-four days – with a bar on the top of my home page marking the progress I have made.

Find an app for your task that gives you this gaming element, or make your own chart to fill out, and by giving yourself a record to beat or a target to hit each day, you can incentivize taking action.

BRAINTENANCE: UNDERSTAND WHY

When we procrastinate, we often brand ourselves as 'lazy', accompanied by a showering of insults and put-downs. But normally, when we are avoiding doing a task, there is an understandable reason behind our aversion.

. . . .

When you find yourself on the verge of procrastinating, stop for a moment and ask yourself: 'What is it about this task that is making it hard for me to follow through?'

Your answer could be that the task requires effort, which you are struggling to muster, or it feels really difficult or you want it to be perfect and are scared it is not going to be. Getting to the root of why you are procrastinating can help with tackling it in the future.

. . . .

Struggling to put in effort? Ask yourself: when was the last time I ate? Have I been skipping on sleep? Is this task unfamiliar?

If you are scared about not being perfect, you can rationalize this fear by thinking about how doing some work now – even a small amount – is going to make it better than not doing anything at all. Or you can purposely set out to do the task 'badly' (a 'for-my-eyes-only', or imperfect, draft) to get cracking. Be compassionate and view your desire to procrastinate as a mechanism to help you avoid negative states, which can help you tackle the underlying cause and prevent future procrastination episodes.

BRAINTENANCE: VIABLE ALTERNATIVE?

Sometimes when we go to procrastinate, our brain concocts a story about needing to do something 'more important' than what we had planned. Like those pop-ups, more often than not these alternatives are not something we should prioritize.

....

If wanting to procrastinate, ask yourself: 'If I don't do *this task*, what will I do instead?'

This can help highlight how what you think you need in the moment can be a cover-up for procrastination. This happens to me when I am going out for a run. My brain tries to convince me it will be better to 'rest'. But when I actually ask myself what I will do instead of that thirty-minute jog, the normal answer is to faff on my phone – which is not particularly restful or a great use of my time. Defining the alternative, unhelpful action can help you follow through with your intended plan.

BRAINTENANCE: CONSEQUENCES

Our brains prioritize the present. We seek what feels good now and avoid what brings us immediate discomfort. By thinking about the long-term pain procrastination brings, we can help contextualize how a small price to pay now can lead to avoiding larger disappointment.

....

Think about the project you are struggling to work on, or the task you keep putting off. What would happen if you skipped this activity:

Ten times?

Fifty times?

A hundred times?

Forever?

It is important to remember that the more you procrastinate on something, the more likely procrastination will become habitual. Skipping on the gym ten times may not change your life that much, but those ten missed sessions will more likely turn into fifty or one hundred unless you start to tackle procrastination. Write down or think about the answers to these questions to remind yourself of the pain that will come from procrastinating in the long run when you are considering giving an activity a miss.

WRAP UP

Procrastination is the preferred option for our brains when faced with a challenging situation. We deem it more beneficial to avoid engaging in tasks that may be difficult or require effort, even though logically we know that putting them off is to our own detriment. The interplay between the brain's ability to exert self-control and manage emotional signals is a battle where control loses out in procrastinating, increasing the value of less optimal behaviours to provide us with a 'quick fix'. Understanding what it is about the task in front of us that is making it less appealing to engage with and tackling that root issue rather than giving in to the short-term pleasurable option the brain offers up should help us with managing procrastination more generally. Removing and scheduling distractions, breaking down a task to make it systematic, easing yourself over the start line with a timer, aiming for imperfection and gamifying your work can all be deployed to tackle procrastination. And this will mean that over time, avoidance behaviours are disrupted and less automatic when trying to manage emotions. Expect those procrastination urges to win out from time to time, but know you have an arsenal of tools to break out against them when they next rear their head.

CHAPTER 14

FORGET MOTIVATION

The magic ingredient we all search our mental shelves for when working on goals is motivation. A sprinkling of the big M is what we think we need to act. On some occasions we are met with heaps of the stuff, making us eager to get going, whereas at other times, not a scrap can be found. As we often take motivation as a sign to get going, its absence makes it easy to think we can't follow through, or that we are no longer interested in our long-term pursuits.

The key to making lasting change is to forget about motivation and show up anyway.

Motivation is a fleeting state. Its purpose, from humans to worms, is to drive organisms towards favourable situations and away from threatening encounters, maximizing chances of survival. Our brains are built to follow motivational signals towards sources of potential gain, seeking out rewards and logging their feel-good sensations to refer to in the future. Be it foraging food, having sex or finding shelter, motivation is a core element of advancing any species.

In modern-day life, motivation has gained a whole new identity. Instead of an innate drive towards pleasure and away from pain, motivation's 'glow up' has branded it as the essential component of success. Whether it is working more on a project, revising for a test, cooking a healthy dinner, or getting out to exercise, motivation is the antidote to inaction. We find ourselves wishing we could be more motivated. And when it doesn't show up, we wait. Maybe until next week, or next month, or next year. We reason that when our motivation gets a boost, we will finally be able to get going.

There is nothing wrong with using significant time points to incite change. These landmarks may provide the push you need to take the leap. But constantly deferring your plans to a distant place in the future because of low motivation in the present is going to prevent you from making progress. Motivation does not come from thin air. As the actions required to achieve long-term goals are often challenging, the urge to initially 'seek' them is pretty low. Instead, motivation can be created by taking action. When you start before you feel ready, or push yourself to follow through when contemplating swerving, your actions provide the 'this is good for me' feedback that the brain is looking for. Showing up when your motivation stays home helps repeat behaviours, enabling their integration into your routine and, over time, motivation will barely be a consideration when deciding to act.

WHY

Taking the onus off motivation to get the job done is hard. It feels good to feel good about wanting to get up and go. When we set out on a new venture, motivation is high. We can imagine how these new interventions will change our lives and we use these visions to commit to the early starts, the difficult workouts and the challenging sessions. This way of working may be sustained for a few days or a few weeks, but eventually the gleam of future change fades and, with it, motivation wanes. Like with a new year's goal, the first few weeks of January can see motivation carry us through but when the work continues to be hard and the 'results' remain few and far between, motivation dips. The sessions we were so excited to start become activities we dread. Visions of how these tasks will eventually make a difference to our lives are no longer enough to muster up the desire to keep going. And even the things we think will give us a motivation boost – a new plan, workout clothes, diary or devices – only temporarily push back the incoming resistance to act.

No matter how much warning we give ourselves that we aren't always going to feel motivated with every workout, writing or study session, we still often fall into the trap of using motivation as a signal of our desires. If we aren't motivated, is this really what we want to do right now? The answer comes up as a firm 'obviously not'. Instead, we feel we want, or need, to chill out and skip our plans. This is the natural order of how hard tasks transition: from life-changing actions to time-sapping, energy-robbing chores. Only consulting our motivation when deciding how to act is destined for doom. Until a task becomes routine, or we start to see progress or results, motivation's opinion can further confirm that we shouldn't take action.

See motivation as a bonus, a nice to have, rather than a necessity. Focusing instead on being dedicated and determined will help with consistency. If you are determined, a lack of motivation is seen as something to tackle, rather than a red light. Sadly, it is too often the case that motivation only kicks in once a person is at rock bottom. When the pain of our present is too much to bear, we finally get the impetus to try to alter our behaviour. This is exemplified in addiction disorders, where the seeking of pleasurable substances in the present leads to the formation of habitual behaviours which can destroy relationships, damage health and ruin lives. Unfortunately, it takes hitting a real low – whether that be in terms of health issues, losing loved ones or hating your current situation – to muster the will and try to change.

We don't have to go to rock bottom to be able to transform an aspect of our lives. We don't need to go through hard times to gather enough motivation to make a change. We can choose to change right now. We need to accept that it won't all be sunshine and rainbows and we won't be enthusiastically bounding out of bed every day raring to go. We have methods to fall back on to keep us going when we don't feel motivated, and we can hopefully keep consistent enough in our behaviours so that they start to become more routine and rely less on our willpower. Knowing what drives motivation and realizing that there will inevitably be occasions when you will have to start work without it is imperative to pressing on.

Personally, I have previously read way too much into motivation. When I felt motivated, I could take on the world. Revising for a hard exam topic? No problem. Getting up at the crack of dawn to work out? Sure thing. Putting a new creative project plan into action? Bring it on. Motivation was a signal that I was ready and on the correct path, making it frictionless to follow through.

This overly weighted positive assignment of motivation's role in my life meant that when it didn't appear, the opposite felt true. Revising for a hard exam topic? Absolutely horrendous – can't face that right now. Getting up at the crack of dawn to work out? Nope, not happening – back to bed I go. Putting a new creative project plan into action? Urgh, this feels hard – maybe it isn't right for me and I should go back to the drawing board. A lack of motivation was interpreted as 'I obviously can't/shouldn't/don't want to do this right now' and I would put the task off to not waste my time.

But the more time spent postponing hard tasks, the less motivated I felt to crack on. This continued until I reached that 'pain point' – the fear of missing a deadline, or letting someone down, or compromising my own health and well-being – and motivation would kick in. It is why we procrastinate until the last minute, as discussed in Chapter 13. Waiting for motivation to give me the green light got me nowhere. All the build-up and excitement of planning a project, driven by motivation to make a real change in my life, would come crashing down when the reality of hard work was faced.

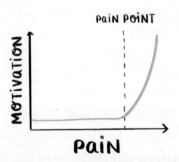

I realized I had to seriously reconfigure my relationship with motivation to disrupt its influence over my outlook and actions. I had to stop translating my lack of motivation in the moment as an indicator of what I shouldn't do, and also stop acting only when motivation was around. All this was doing was teaching my brain that I only work when I feel this seeking, pleasurable sensation. I had to show up consistently whether motivation was there or not to demonstrate to myself that motivation isn't the determining factor of whether I follow through with my intentions. If I was motivated, that was cool, but not the reason I was acting. It was like a cherry on top of a cake. By reconfiguring my interpretation of motivation, I have stopped using it as a gauge of my interest or competence for tasks I face. This has led me to act long before I felt 'ready', resulting not only in fun opportunities and adventure, but also increasing my motivation for engaging in these activities. Acting when lacking motivation has been the ultimate boost for my will to work. And by refocusing my attention onto the task at hand and understanding how it fits into the bigger picture, motivation often shows up for the ride.

SCI

Motivation has been essential for human survival. It allows us to seek out states which will keep us safe, advance our species and fend off threats. Motivation can arise due to external accolades, like earning a reward or praise, or it can be internally driven. This intrinsic reward is when people seem to act in the face of no obvious acclaim for completing an action.[1]

A key moderator of both types of motivation is dopamine. There are pockets of dopamine-producing neurons in different areas buried deep in the brain, including in brain circuits involved in reward and movement. Dopamine's function is determined based on (1) where it is released, (2) how much is released over a certain time period and (3) the brain cells it interacts with.[2] All of these factors lead to different changes in brain cell activity and can alter how an organism acts. A big

DOPAMINE PATHWAYS

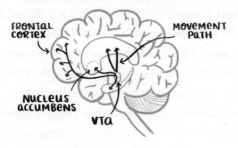

release of dopamine from an area called the ventral tegmental area, or VTA, before performing an action is thought to signal the high estimated value that activity could bring upon completion.

Addiction disorders are an extreme example of dopamine's role in extrinsic motivation.[3] Addiction to a substance or activity usually starts off as a pleasurable pursuit. The target – say drugs, alcohol, food or gambling – triggers the release of dopamine, prompting the brain to take a mental snapshot of the cues and associations that led to the reward. Following an initial experience, dopamine is subsequently released pre-emptively, igniting a craving. This craving drives an individual to seek the substance again. Over time, seeking can turn into a compulsion, taking advantage of the brain's ability to transform repeated actions into habitual behaviours, even as the 'pleasure' from the addictive substance wanes. Tolerance can build, meaning more extreme interactions are needed to get the same hit of pleasure, and a reduction in the level of dopamine receptors in the brain has been noted in several addiction disorders.[4] This can disrupt a subject's ability to be interested in, or motivated by, other things. Addiction disorders essentially hijack the motivation system in the brain to create inflexible and often damaging behaviours.

In intrinsic motivation, dopamine systems are also implicated in the drive to pursue actions. Chasing actions without definitive rewards – like painting, or writing, or volunteering for fun – aren't obviously advantageous to survival. They use energy and resources without getting a tangible 'payback'. Yet, as a collective, we spend a lot of time engaging with these endeavours. Intrinsic motivation has been proposed to persist in humans due to our tendency to move towards growth. The criteria for facilitating such growth is outlined in the self-determination theory,[5] which states competence (having skill for doing an activity and experiencing mastery), autonomy (using free will to engage in a task) and relatedness (a sense of being connected to or helping others) drive action. An ultimate form of feeling intrinsically motivated is flow. This is when you are so absorbed in a task that time seems to zip by, making progress with a project based on the love of doing the activity.

SELF-DETERMINATION THEORY

COMPETENCE　　　　**AUTONOMY**　　　　**RELATEDNESS**

In the study of intrinsic motivation, dopamine systems have been found to play a key role. Results from research have highlighted a potential increase in dopamine receptors in reward areas for people who experience more flow. Some people have a genetic mutation that increases the availability of certain dopamine receptors, and they were found to be more likely to experience flow states.[6] It's been proposed that intrinsic motivation leads to a steady release of elevated dopamine, keeping people driven to engage in the task at hand.[7] In brain-imaging studies, brain areas rich with dopamine-producing neurons and areas associated with value are active in intrinsically motivated tasks.[8]

Across several studies, it's also been shown that intrinsic motivation coincides with decreased activity in the large brain network associated with thinking about ourselves and daydreaming (default mode network), and increased activity in networks associated with performing demanding tasks (executive control network) and directing attention (salience network)[9], generating an all-encompassing focus on a task. The salience network is thought to consider the significance of signals to decide where an organism should focus its efforts. One brain area in this network, called the anterior insula, has been found to house specific brain cells which increase mice's motivation on tasks without prompting addiction-like behaviours,[10] suggesting their role in driving general motivation in these animals. In intrinsic motivation, a reduced focus on 'the self' and an increased shift in attention to the external task

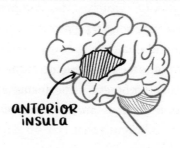

ANTERIOR INSULA

through changes in brain network activity could be how we are driven to perform without reward.

Motivation is not constant. Some days we can be raring to go and on others we will be completely disinterested. Motivation can be impacted by conditions like depression, schizophrenia and Parkinson's disease. It is also subject to degradation when fatigued. One study found that even in the face of reward, people are less likely to be motivated to perform when tired. And although short rests can help boost motivation initially, the more prolonged the task and the fatigue, the less likely immediate rest is to recover motivation levels.[11] In the brain, these fluctuations in motivation were mirrored with changes in brain activity in frontal regions (valuing 'is this worth our efforts?') and in the dopamine-housing VTA. Making effective change has also been associated with when people have 'fresh starts'[12] – New Years, moving house, a birthday – so jumping on the motivational wave and riding it could help with instigating new behaviours.

As a component of motivation requires directing attention and is impacted by energy levels, there can also be different times of the day where a person can feel more motivated to act. The human body runs on a near 24-hour clock, with cycles for sleeping and wakefulness, as well as timely fluctuations of different hormones, body temperature and blood pressure. Included in these peaks and troughs are our levels of alertness,[13] making how easy it feels to be productive change throughout the day. For most people, it's thought alertness peaks a few hours after waking, dips slightly in the afternoon and picks back up again in the early evening (yes, the afternoon slump does indeed seem to be real). Scheduling your day so your toughest activities align with your more motivated hours may help with following through.

APPLY

Not relying on motivation for following through with plans is no easy feat. When we get to the moment of performing a task, we naturally turn to our motivation level as an indicator of whether we should act or not. So having techniques that rely on defaults instead of your motivation can help us to stick to our plans when motivation decides to bail.

BRAINTENANCE: SAME TIME, SAME PLACE

In Chapter 11, we covered scheduling your day to know exactly what time you would be performing certain activities, to remove indecision from your day. Now think about when you feel most alert and most productive: **schedule your new behaviour to as close to these hours as possible and repeat this block every day.**

For me, I have an exercise block in my calendar from 6 a.m. until 7 a.m. every weekday, and from 10 a.m. until 11 a.m. on weekends. I feel the least resistance to act in the morning, so it is much easier for me to get myself moving at the times scheduled than waiting until the evening after work. Also, as it repeats every day, I don't have an excuse to skip. Some days I go to the gym in this slot, other days I go for a run or pop out for a quick walk. Showing up every day and exercising at these times – no matter how intense or chilled that movement is – reinforces 'this is when I exercise', removing dependency on motivation.

- -

What block could you add to your calendar at the same time each day? It could be an exercise block, a creative block, a writing block, a study block, or a downtime block. Think of two or three alternative activities with varying degrees of effort you can do in that time so you can show up consistently.

BRAINTENANCE: DO IT NOW

Sometimes we look for motivation to do the smallest tasks: washing the dishes, making the bed, writing one more sentence. Considering their completion time can help you to act. A productivity method coined by author David Allen called the two-minute rule states that if a task takes two minutes, it should be done when you are considering whether to act or not. For example, if you have finished cooking and have a few pans to wash, it is easy for them to sit in the sink for hours. But if, when you have finished, you execute the two-minute rule, the pans will be clean and drying on the rack before you have a chance to build up resistance to washing them. I say to myself, 'If it takes two minutes, do it now' when faced with putting my clothes away at the end of a long day to prevent a growing floordrobe taking over my room.

The two-minute rule can be applied to execute your small action, or cue the lead-up to your small action.

. . . .

When deciding whether to act or not, what is something that takes two minutes or less to do?

This could be doing those five push-ups, or writing one sentence, or making your study cup of tea, or getting dressed for that workout. Knowing that within two minutes that small task will be complete can help spring you into action without the helping hand of motivation. As two minutes is a relatively short period of time, it makes the perceived effort required for completion seem low, reducing the barrier to entry and altering the brain's valuation of whether the task ahead of you is worth the reward you'll get.

BRAINTENANCE: AUTOMATIC REPLY

Like having an automatic reply on your emails if you are out of office, having an automatic reply to a lack of motivation can help you to take action regardless. This reply could be a statement ('motivation is fleeting'), an action (jumping up quickly), or a countdown (like the '5, 4, 3, 2, 1' from Chapter 11). For me, when I don't feel motivated, I repeat to myself, 'I don't need motivation to do this' as I ease into my small action or when executing my cue. This helps move me away from using motivation as a sign I should or shouldn't act.

. . . .

When lacking motivation, what will you say to yourself? Or what will you do straight away to take the significance away from motivation?

BRAINTENANCE: FRESH STARTS

We want to reduce the weight motivation has on us performing a task, but **we can also take advantage of 'fresh starts', when motivation is more likely to be elevated, to implement new behaviours**. Use times like New Years, or moving house, or starting a new job to try switching up your routine slightly, as you will already be in a headspace that is more open to change.

This is not to say wait until next January to start working on your goals. It is more about using these peaks in motivation to supercharge your actions. Like surfing waves, there are times where you have to push against the currents and other times when the waves carry you. Using these waves of motivation can help solidify or implement routines, getting the wheels in motion before motivation decides to exit stage right.

Fresh starts can be obvious, like the change in date, or you can make them yourself, like calling the Monday you want to start 'change day'. Either way, when you feel motivation naturally rise due to external circumstances, don't see it as the only time you can act, but do use it as a bonus to turbocharge your change.

BRAINTENANCE: SHOW & TELL

Dopamine signals in the brain are stimulated when we experience rewards from doing something, which then leads to dopamine being released in the future to motivate us to perform a similar sequence of actions again. To replicate that initial reward, we must act.

We often expect to be motivated before we start. But, like those initial dopamine signals, we often need to take action to get rewarded. Action increases motivation. As described in Chapter 12, when we do a task, we are showing ourselves that we are capable, meaning next time we go to act, we already have some confidence in our ability to do so. This creates a positive feedback loop: the more action we take, the higher our motivation to act. It is the opposite of what we expect.

....

What action do you feel like you have been putting off because you are waiting to feel motivated or don't feel 100 per cent ready?

Add this action to your schedule as a short time block (fifteen to thirty minutes) for the next two weeks and follow through to ramp up motivation. You won't be perfect, it will probably be messy, but every new venture is. But by simply showing up for yourself, you should begin to build momentum.

BRAINTENANCE: BIGGER PICTURE

When we look for motivation to act in the moment, we are considering the one action at hand. 'Do I feel like I want to do this now?' Chances are, not really. There will often be a more appealing option. Instead of thinking about individual actions, consider the bigger picture. Like a massive jigsaw puzzle that depicts your goal, this small action is fitting a piece in place.

Contextualizing your action into the bigger picture can help bring a sprinkling of motivation dust. **Thinking about how it is adding to your overall goal, its small but significant contribution, can provide impetus to act.** Small actions offer incremental improvements – a 1 per cent boost to your skills here and there – so focus on how inching forward today will add up to miles in the future.

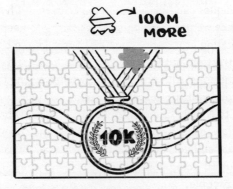

BRAINTENANCE: INTRINSIC IMPETUS

Whether we openly recognize it or not, many of our goals have an element of external reward. These rewards can be used as motivation – the picture glued on the fridge, the phone background of the beautiful apartment, the dreams of lifting the trophy. As discussed in Chapter 7, although these scenarios can be useful in providing the push we need, they can make it difficult to do the more challenging, less rewarding daily actions that will eventually lead to their fruition.

Instead of looking to external accolades to motivate us, we can instead try to foster a sense of intrinsic motivation – engaging in a task for the joy of doing it rather than what it will bring to us. To this end, we can use the self-determine theory's three criteria to foster a sense of growth with the activities we are trying to pursue:

Categories	Meaning	Apply to task
Competence	Improving skill & increasing mastery	Improve form when deadlifting
Autonomy	Choosing to engage	Wanting to go to gym as improves mood
Relatedness	Connecting to others	Join group strength challenge

BRAINTENANCE: FINDING FLOW

Starting an activity can be hard when lacking motivation, and the previous techniques can be used to help get over this hurdle. But sometimes, once we get started, it can be tricky to keep on task. The tips for beating procrastination in Chapter 13 can be deployed to destroy distraction, but we can also try to find a state of flow – getting into 'the zone' with an activity – when working to keep motivated throughout the season.

According to Mihaly Csikszentmihalyi, in his 1990 book of the same name, 'flow' occurs when one's skill level and the challenge of the task are matched. If a task is too hard, you are likely to feel worried and put off doing it, but if it is too easy, you will end up bored and distractible.

Think about the activity you are trying to get into the zone with in terms of your skill in that area and the challenge the task presents. Raise or lower the challenge level to fit your current skill and see if you can find flow.

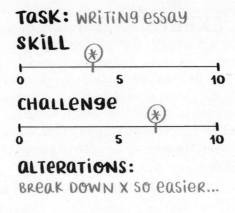

TaSK: WRITiNG essay

SKiLL

0　　　　5　　　　10

CHaLLeNGe

0　　　　5　　　　10

ALTeRaTiONS:

BReak DOWN X so easier...

WRAP UP

Relying on motivation to carry you to your goals is a losing battle. Motivation's transient nature, its desire for immediate reward and sensitivity to fatigue means it is not a reliable coach to consult on whether to show up. If you are trying to engage in a new task beyond your comfort zone, you are very rarely going to feel ready. But most people who have been successful start anyway and figure it out as they go. The action taken builds the confidence and motivation we lack initially, and with consistency, these new tasks will start to feel like part of the furniture.

Our motivation is fickle. If we don't see instant results, it can fade. If we are tired, it can exit. If another event comes up that feels like a priority, it can be redirected. Instead of looking towards the initial motivation level as an indicator to act, use techniques to help get you started and stay on task. Considering how each small action is contributing to the bigger picture can help you take the action you planned and build momentum with your work, allowing you to make progress whether motivation is present or not.

CHAPTER 15

EXPECT PUSHBACK

When we are working on new ventures and putting plans in place to make change in our lives, it is an exciting time. We see how these changes will benefit our lives, but also the lives of those we love. So, when those closest to us don't necessarily share the same level of enthusiasm for our ideas, it can be extremely frustrating.

While we expect internal resistance from our own brains in the pursuit of goals, we rarely anticipate the resistance we can experience from our environment – be that the place you work, where you live, the people you casually interact with or those closest to you. When we are trying to change, these places and people can push us back into old routines.

As we have learnt with habits, our brains make associations between aspects of our environment and how to act. These signals may be obvious, like the smell of smoke igniting a craving for a cigarette, or more subtle, like staying in your childhood room and acting like a teenager again. And, as discussed back in Chapter 6, our brains make models of other people so we can harmoniously interact with them. Just as we model others, they model us. Individuals across many different areas of your life have a certain idea of what to expect from you. So, if you start to make big changes, you can experience some people trying to force you back into the version of you that feels familiar.

Our interactions with others can be extremely influential in trying to make change. While some may be initially (or perpetually) hesitant when you step outside your comfort zone, other people can be absolute rocks of support when you are aiming for something new. Having a community or specific individuals who cheer you on throughout your endeavours can give you the power to push on with your efforts when in a face-off with your own internal resistance. Recognizing how powerful who and what we surround ourselves with is when working towards a goal and understanding why certain places and people can unintentionally act as barriers can help us be compassionate and move beyond these pushbacks.

WHY

Our goals are often considered a solo pursuit. We focus on what we can do to change ourselves to make them happen. But we exist in a dynamic world of interactions with others and our environment. We often look to the weather to decide whether we should go on that bike ride, or find ourselves being convinced by our friends to stay for one more drink, or cannot concentrate when trying to work from home. We are constantly interacting with entities outside ourselves, and these impact our actions, with or without us realizing.

It is therefore false to think that going after a goal is all about controlling ourselves. Our environment pulls us. Past experiences and familiar associations with a space both tailor your options for how to act, and you may find yourself pushing against resistance which seemingly comes from nowhere. It may be that the living room where you are trying to start your new home workout regime is where you normally relax, so you feel an urge to sit on the couch instead of crunching. Whenever I go back to my childhood home, I find it so much harder to get up early and exercise because I associate my teenage bedroom with sleeping in until noon. Other people are also rarely thought about as impacting our progress unless directly involved in making goals happen. We carefully select the perfect coach, trainer, business partner or study buddy, but when it comes to those closest to us, we don't bat an eye, despite their opinions heavily influencing our personal endeavours. While we may get some nods of approval when divulging our plans, we can also face questions about our motives and how we will feel if it doesn't work out, which can make us reconsider our decisions.

This resistance is a natural reaction to change. Your parents, your partner, your friends, your family all have an expectation of who you are, so the idea of you altering a significant element of your life can make them panic. If the shoe was on the other foot, and your best friend who you love partying with discloses their grand plans for a health kick, meaning no more 'big nights out', you can't help but consider how their new actions will impact your life. Your thoughts might spin about how your relationship will change because of this altered dynamic. We like predictability and familiarity in our relationships as well as in our own actions, so proposed shifts in behaviours from those around you can result in guards being put up.

I have been on both sides of the table with pushback. Deciding to jump out of academia and into a creative career was definitely one of these moments. I was really excited to have found something I wanted to do and was eager to share my plans, but was met with many expressions of concern. While congratulations were given, I also faced a tirade of questions: 'Is this a stable career? How will you get a mortgage? What is plan B if it doesn't work out?' Although I knew these questions were coming from a good place of caring about my well-being, it still made me think that my loved ones were doubting my abilities. And if those closest to me didn't believe I could do it, then who was I to kid myself? I took the pushback as a sign that maybe this career choice wasn't the best idea.

On the other hand, I have also been the person pushing back. When my partner decided to go vegan (in the middle of a supermarket on a random Tuesday night), I lost it. 'What will we eat now? We can't have that dish anymore. How will you get your nutrients? I don't know if this is wise while studying for your exams . . .' My mind saw change and I fought it like a dog in the dairy produce aisle. Even though I could see his intentions were valid, I couldn't help but dwell on how this change would impact our lives and relationship. My internal expectation of who he was clashed with this new information, and my outburst was an attempt to cling to the familiar.

Because of our innate urge to resist change – especially change that is outside our control – finding others who are pursuing similar aims in their lives and who have normalized your aspirations can be super helpful. This is not saying exclude your family and friends from your ambitions, but avoid using them as a sounding board to decide if your ideas are valid, as you could be met with doubting questions and queries from a place of protection. Personally, I have found friends online who are pursuing similar careers to me, and it is great to chat to them about roadblocks. With some of my family and friends, I talk about active projects I am working on and events that I have completed so they are in the loop and celebrating with me, but I don't openly chat as much about what my big future plans are. This helps me stay focused and not overly question whether I am doing the 'right' thing before giving it a go.

SCI

It would be great to live in a bubble where only our decisions influence how we behave in pursuit of our goals. But the human brain contextualizes us as part of the world we live in – tying up places, people, systems, societies, events and emotions into bundles which can be recalled when needed, so who and what surrounds us impacts our actions.

This makes places we visit so much more than houses, restaurants, parks, beaches, towns and cities. They are triggers for thoughts, feelings, actions and memories. Like a giant game of 'Guess Who', when you walk into a particular space, like your favourite restaurant, most of the options on the board are flipped down to leave a pattern of memories, emotions and thoughts associated with your current location.

When we go about trying to incorporate new behaviours into our routines that align with our goals, we rarely consider the combination of cards flipped up in our brain based on where we are or who we are with. Many of these associations can be outside our awareness – their context lost to the passage of time. But they can influence how we act. If you are trying to instil a new behaviour which goes against these associations – like working where you relax – you are going to be fighting with established behaviours. Like trying to flip up a card in the 'wears glasses' category when that option has already been wiped off the board.

With our goals in mind, we can prime our environment to make it more likely we will act in the way we want, from removing all junk foods from the cupboard, to setting up a designated workspace, or joining a gym five minutes' walk away from home. One framework that attempts to measure how changing environments alters behaviours is called TIPPME (an acronym for the very catchy 'typology of interventions in proximal physical micro-environments').[1] The TIPPME model involves six interventions which could potentially be deployed within an environment to impact behaviour: position, availability, functionality, presentation, size and information.

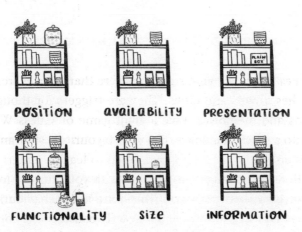

POSITION   AVAILABILITY   PRESENTATION

FUNCTIONALITY   SIZE   INFORMATION

Take, for example, using the interventions of TIPPME to alter eating habits. If a person is trying to reduce their biscuit intake, they could move the biscuits to a high shelf (position) or take them out of the house altogether (availability). If the products remain in the kitchen, they could be stored away from the tea to alter their association (functionality), or put in an unappealing jar (presentation). A smaller packet could be bought (size) or calorie labels added to the biscuit tin (information). So far, research using aspects of TIPPME has mostly focused on changing eating behaviours, and it is still early days with regards to having strong evidence to back up how effective the model is. However, in this work, altering the availability and size of objects have been the main interventions used to change behaviour. For example, regarding availability, increased numbers of vegetarian options in several university cafeterias led to increased selection of plant-based food, boosting sales from 41 per cent to 79 per cent.[2] When it comes to size, giving people larger portions of food leads to them eating more.[3] As this research field grows, we may see if combining these interventions – like reducing portion size alongside a campaign about the damage of eating too much junk food – has even more impact, and if it could be a useful tool for altering behaviour en masse.

Modifying other aspects of the environment has also been shown to facilitate different behaviours. One study showed that working in a clean and tidy room increased an individual's ability to 'do the right thing' (give more to charity and eat fruit after the task), whereas a messier space increased a person's creativity.[4] A further study found that the impacts of an orderly and disorderly environment on self-control and creativity were altered by an individual's baseline self-control. Those with low levels had self-control increased in orderly spaces, whereas those with high levels had creativity increased by being in disorderly rooms.[5] Studies have also hinted that light exposure (altering blue light levels by wearing specific glasses[6]) and music[7] could impact work performance. Therefore, by tailoring the environment, task performance may be altered.

When it comes to other people in your environment, your ideas for change can cause them upheaval. This is especially true for those closest to you. They have a more detailed internal model of 'who you are' from witnessing and absorbing a fuller range of your behaviours over long periods of time.

HOW REACT IN SCENARIO:

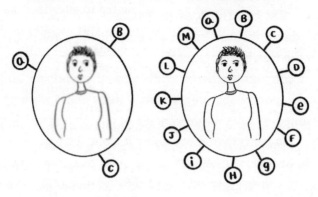

When we decide to make changes in our lives, presenting our ideas to others can cause a conflict with their already established model of you. Their perceived ability of being able to interact with you and make predictions about your behaviour is put under threat. Your change means a change in their associations of you. How you fit into their world could be compromised. And different people can display different levels of resistance. A study found that in romantic relationships (majority heterosexual) where each partner had to consider a time where their other half had changed, individuals with low self-concept clarity were the most resistant to these occasions.[8] Low self-concept clarity represents a person's lack of coherence about who they are due to having inconsistent or contradicting beliefs about themselves. These individuals – identified through questionnaires – struggled more with their partner's changing as they felt they would have to change too, leading to them offering less support. This work suggests that pushback from others in the face of change is likely down to their own resistance to change rather than lacking belief in the change itself.

While it is important not to take the pushback from close friends, family and colleagues as gospel, support and feedback is still incredibly useful in the pursuit of goals. Feedback provides awareness of how things are going and what choices should be made next. In a study where partners provided each other with feedback that supported their growth, long-term relationships were strengthened.[9] In an exam setting, positive feedback from examiners enhanced self-belief, whereas negative feedback improved self-assessment.[10] And in an experimental setting, the most effective form of feedback was framed in terms of losses and didn't include information about how other people performed on the task being tested.[11]

Having a community that provides objective feedback and support can aid goal pursuit. Regarding fitness, a study found working out with friends resulted in a higher percentage of completing an exercise programme (95 per cent) than those doing it alone (76 per cent).[12] Talking about goals to others in similar groups can make goal pursuit more intense,[13] and telling a person who is further along the path than you about your goal may make a goal more likely to be reached.[14] Thinking about the reasons why individuals are giving you help and support (that they care about you and want to see you succeed), rather than just focusing on the supportive actions they are doing, has also been found to increase work towards goals.[15] Having supportive individuals around you is not about competing with others on similar pursuits (this was found to reduce progress in one study, as the focus shifted to 'beating' others[16]), but instead about having understanding people who can see your struggles and cheer you on. As a social species who have relied on others for survival since the evolution of our prehistoric ancestors, having a support system of people to help get you through times of crisis can boost well-being, which should help you to keep going.

APPLY

Expecting pushback from your environment and others is useful knowledge in helping to set yourself up for success. Understanding these signals are coming from a place of established patterns and avoiding unfamiliarity allows you not to take them as signs to stop.

BRAINTENANCE: READ THE ROOM

When you are trying to incorporate a new behaviour or action into your routine, think about what came before in the space you are in. You may be trying to start a new fitness regime in a gym which you have bailed on twenty times in the past, or trying to start a creative project in your kitchen, which you associate with together time. **What is your space associated with?**

These revelations are not to make you completely switch environments – in some cases that may not be possible (hello writing a PhD thesis in my bedroom during a global pandemic). It is more to make you aware of some of the reasons you may be experiencing friction when attempting to start a new activity in that space. If you want a completely fresh start and it is an option, you can change the environment. For example, you could move to a new gym where you don't have the association of giving up in the past or set up your desk in a different room designated for working only. But if you are staying where you are, you can still tweak or moderate your environment to make it more appealing for your new activity.

BRAINTENANCE: PREPPIN'

With associations in mind, altering your environment to promote doing your new activity can help reduce barriers to act. The interventions in the TIPPME framework – although they are still theoretical – could be trialled to see if you can edit your environment to make it easier to perform your action.

Let's take me writing my thesis in my bedroom, a place I associate with relaxing and chilling out. Six interventions I could try to make my writing easier are:

Intervention	Intervention in action
Availability	Having my computer open on my thesis the night before a work session
Position	Only writing my thesis when sat at my desk
Functionality	Ensuring all notes are organized so can be easily accessed for writing
Presentation	Lighting a candle to signify writing time and having a tidy desk

Size	Using a timer to break down writing time
Information	Having my schedule on display with detailed instructions for each day

It is unlikely all of these interventions will be useful, but some environmental changes will make it easier to act. Trial different options and see which you find best for getting on with the task at hand.

BRAINTENANCE: EASE IN

The pushback we experience from those closest to us when we talk about our grand plans can be a case of too much too soon. If your goal is somewhat distant from your current self, telling this to our loved ones can startle their model of you, creating resistance in anticipation of this potential change. Like with anything unfamiliar – new foods, new music, new places – easing people in with little snippets of information or familiar elements can help acclimatize those around you to new ventures.

If you start to act slightly differently around those closest to you and show little pieces of your new lifestyle, their model of who you are and how you act will be subconsciously updating, reducing resistance to your new behaviours.

Say, for example, you have a goal to move to a plant-based diet, but all your family eat meat. There are a few steps you can do in their presence to warm them up to the idea of your new way of eating:

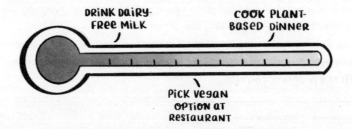

Using the temperature gauge, think about the small, incremental actions you can do to acclimatize your loved ones to your long-term goals.

These may align with the experiences and skills you established back in Chapter 7, or may be a conscious action which is a few steps behind where you actually are – talking about a recent milestone you completed, or mini goal you hit – to warm them up to this new element of you.

BRAINTENANCE: REFRAME RESISTANCE

When faced with resistance from others, recognizing that it is often coming from a place of them not wanting to change or wanting to protect you from disappointment can be useful in dealing with pushback. While some concern from others is valid (like if this new venture is going to be damaging or hurtful), if you have really thought through your goals, this hopefully shouldn't be the case. If friends or family show their concern about your plans, you can try telling yourself:

- Their response is a reflection of their fear of change.
- Their concerns are because they are worried about the impact on them.
- These questions are because they don't want me to be disappointed.

You can also try talking about your goals to others from your 'why' standpoint in Chapter 5. Emphasizing why you are wanting to make a change, and how it will make a positive impact on your life, can help make those conversations easier.

All of this is caveated with: if someone is really unsupportive and trying to keep you where you are, don't tell them your plans. No one else's opinion of what you should do with your life should impact what you want. Put your plans into action and prove those people wrong with the progress you make.

BRAINTENANCE: FIND YOUR CIRCLE

Finding people who are pursuing similar goals to you or interested in the same field can be great for getting advice, support, making friends and helping others. Some ideas for finding these people could be:

LOCAL CLUB   **ONLINE COMMUNITY**   **GROUP CLASS**

Also, having a supportive circle who are a bit removed from the detail to share your big plans with and who you can lean on when you are feeling doubtful and frustrated can be great. I have friends who have more faith in me than I do when it comes to my career, and they are incredible listeners when I am talking through challenges. Sometimes it is not about getting advice or guidance, but to talk aloud to people who can listen and remind you of your capabilities.

WRAP UP

When working on our goals, we put so much of the onus on ourselves. We set our schedules, put our plans in motion, show up time and time again, and push ourselves when we face resistance. But if we look outside our own efforts, we can see how aspects of our environment and the people around us can also put up invisible barriers between us and our intentions. And this is without even considering the systemic walls many establishments and societies have when it comes to pursuing ambition, especially for underrepresented groups, where control over success is dramatically reduced due to established, flawed protocols.

If we consider associations we personally have with certain environments and tweak or change them, friction can be reduced. And if discussions about your goals are met with pushback, reframe this as a rejection of change from the other person to remove its importance. Easing people into your plans with small actions or keeping your goal sacred might be options for getting people familiar with the new aspects of your life. And finding a community that understands your aims, and who will support you through your endeavours, can provide you with a cheer squad to keep you moving forward when you feel like giving up.

CHAPTER 16

RECHARGE WITH REST

Goal pursuit has gained a reputation of being all go. We prioritize maxing out our working hours and think about how we can use our spare time to edge forward, feeling a pressure to constantly 'grind' and get things done. And when we take a break or rest, we can be left feeling guilty. But recovery is essential for making progress.

Time 'offline' – away from tasks – is crucial for the human brain to run. From sleep, to play, to downtime, rest alters brain cell activity, provides a boost to energy levels, increases productivity, enhances creativity and improves memory. Treating rest with as much respect as action in goal pursuit is imperative for sustained effort, allowing physical and mental energy supplies to be replenished to facilitate long-term progress.

There are two big problems when it comes to resting. We either sideline it and don't get enough, or we rest inefficiently. With a world of entertainment in our pockets, much of our downtime can be absorbed with screen hours: scrolling, checking, streaming or watching. While devices can be used in restful ways and entertainment like watching videos or films help us switch off, we can unintentionally lose hours of our evenings by mindlessly stimulating ourselves. It is not uncommon for someone to be sitting on the couch with the TV blaring, phone in hand, eating snacks which will keep them wired, and call it 'relaxation'. While it may feel good in the moment, this combination of activities can often lead to elevated stress, poor sleep and increased lethargy.

We need to reset our relationship with rest. By carving out time to do activities which will give you the real recharge you need, you'll not only feel better, but you'll be able to give more focus, attention and energy towards your goals. Rest doesn't mean lying in a spa listening to whale music. Moving your body, getting out in nature, catching up with friends and solving problems can all be deployed as activities to recharge your batteries. Resting with intention to give your brain the space it needs can be one of the most important things you do for yourself, for those around you, and for actualizing your aims.

WHY

Hustle culture has branded rest as weak. The 'sleep when you're dead' mentality has permeated through many industries, and with the improved ability to work from home, it's easy to be 'always on'. In this state, sixteen waking hours means 960 minutes of continuous output, pumping out work at a constant rate. Taking a break is seen as slacking off and any attempt at rest comes with a side order of lingering guilt. No matter how tired you are, there is always a way to push through and keep grinding.

A problem with the 'always on' mentality is it does not match up with our biology. We have not evolved to be always on. We have actually developed allotted periods of being definitively off. Every day, we can take anywhere between five and eleven hours to be pretty much unconscious. Sleep is thought to be a near-universal process across species, a dedicated period of purposeful rest despite it leaving us vulnerable to the elements. Exactly why we sleep is still being unravelled by science, but it is known that catching Zs is essential for health and effective functioning. Skipping even one night's shuteye can lead to dramatic reductions in reaction time, fluctuations in mood and increased anxiety. And, over time, consistent poor sleep is linked to increased risk of diabetes, heart disease and dementia. We are designed to switch into an unconscious mode within each 24-hour period.

Sleep is not the only rest we are built to have in a day. Our attention levels can experience peaks and troughs within waking hours, which also potentially indicate times when we would have naturally taken a break. We now largely ignore these internal 'chill' signals as our commitments and schedules are outside our control. Whether that is being at school or university with dedicated class times, working on shifts or in a nine-to-five job, our hours are dedicated to other causes; keeping us 'online' when, internally, we're being told to slow down. Our current work schedules are an artefact of the industrial revolution, where technically, hours on the line equalled products produced. Transferring this linear relationship of 'hours = output' to more creative and cognitively demanding tasks is not as neat a fit as our schedules would have us believe.

Sadly, a lot of us cannot change our timetables around our ideal break times. But when it comes to thinking about our goals, we can strive to strike a balance between when we work and when we rest. Whether this is a quick break to recharge or a prolonged period offline, taking time away from the goal-related activities should improve our abilities when showing up to complete tasks and avoid burning out. Burnout is caused by prolonged periods of stress and can lead to complete exhaustion, preventing you from doing anything at all for days or even weeks. And while there are periods in life with deadlines and other duties where you may have to push yourself a bit beyond your barriers, ensuring rest is solidified into your routine will mean you are more productive in the long run.

Burnout is sadly a friend of mine. I am very guilty of taking way too much on. I love working on projects and being in the thick of creativity, which means when I am not at work-work, I like to spend time doing other creative endeavours. It is fine when balanced, but I often go too far and find myself working around the clock. I am fortunate in that I physically cannot avoid sleep – when it gets to around 9 p.m., it becomes painful to keep my eyes open (I tried one all-nighter at university, and it was honestly the worst I have physically and mentally felt in my life). My body forces me to get a good seven to eight hours of sleep a day. But when I am awake, I can use my time unwisely. Of the sixteen hours I am up, there have been times I find myself working for about thirteen of them. And when I wasn't working, I was thinking about work, or feeling guilty for not doing work. I tended to spend my spare time doing instantly gratifying things, like watching absorbing TV or playing on my phone, to take my mind off my responsibilities. During these periods, I would find myself less and less enthused about doing my creative work, which normally resulted in taking more 'breaks' (on my phone or binge-watching a series), which led to me doing less work and feeling more guilt. It wasn't until I physically marked out periods of rest in my calendar that I took time out as seriously as my work. During these periods, I tried a lot of different activities to see which would leave me feeling the most refreshed. I found taking a walk, folding laundry, working out and cooking were some of the best things I could do to unwind. By treating rest as I treated work – non-negotiable and important for me – my progress with my projects accelerated, I enjoyed work more and found a greater sense of balance in my life.

SCI

Our brain activity is different when we are awake and when we are asleep. If we think of our brain like a football stadium packed with fans, our waking hours are when the crowd members chat among themselves – pockets of individual conversations which as a collective generate a noisy racket. When we are awake, neurons across many areas of the brain are receiving and sending signals to help us deal with incoming information to navigate and interpret the world.

When we are asleep, there is a huge shift in brain activity. Instead of the noisy pockets of different signals, the brain is dominated by synchronous activity for a large proportion of slumber. Like when a match is in play and football fans cry out as one. Or, more accurately, like if the fans did a standing wave which rippled around the stadium: synchronous activity starts in one area of the brain and moves through the others in a wave-like pattern. Although there are portions of noisy chatter throughout our sleep which increase as we approach waking (believed to be when many of our dreams happen), these unified waves of brain-cell activity are what really distinguish the sleeping brain.

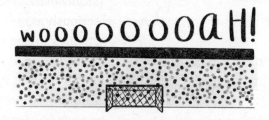

The synchronized waves experienced during sleep can vary in speed, going from quicker 'alpha' waves to huge, slow 'delta' waves. The exact function of these waves is hard to measure in humans as they occur when we are offline, but the slow waves which arise during sleep are thought to be important for consolidating and reorganizing memories.[1] This type of brain activity has been found to increase in areas used to learn in a pre-sleep task,[2] and when boosted using electrical stimulation in a research study, memory retention was enhanced in humans.[3] When slow-wave sleep is purposefully disrupted, again in experimental settings, people experienced reduced performance in motor and perception tasks.[4]

Periods of slow-wave sleep appear to decrease with age and are found to be particularly disrupted in Alzheimer's disease,[5] a progressive condition which causes dementia. People with Alzheimer's disease experience accumulations of 'junk' proteins in the brain. Disruption to slow-wave sleep in mice with some features of Alzheimer's disease experienced increased 'junk' build-ups, hinting slow-wave sleep is important for clearing unneeded proteins and acts as a prompt for optimal functioning.[6] This more specific work on the importance of slow-wave brain activity complements the more general observations that lack of sleep decreases brain activity when awake, impairs cognitive functioning, decreases productivity and can increase 'behavioural microsleeps'[7] – periods of unresponsiveness during a task due to fatigue. The consensus is optimal sleep optimizes waking performance.

Outside of sleep, the human brain also has altered activity when resting during the day. When we are 'doing nothing', the human brain

LaCK OF SLeeP

iNeFFiCieNT WaSTe CLeaRaNCe

DeCReaSeD PRODUCTiViTY

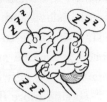

iNCReaSeD MiCROSLeePS

is still pretty active. The default mode network has been found to be switched on when we are resting or bored. Disruptions to this resting state activity have been associated with cognitive decline, ageing and disease.[8] Additionally, how quickly an individual can engage their default mode network has been correlated with making quick, automated decisions in predictable environments,[9] and is thought to be involved in coming up with creative ideas.[10] Activity in this network was originally linked to self-reflection and future planning, but more recently, the role of the default mode network has also been considered as vital for making sense of events as they unfold;[11] applying context from current knowledge and past experience to novel situations. As rest appears to be when this network is primarily activated, ensuring we have periods of downtime is important for the healthy functioning of the brain.

When it comes to breaks, taking time throughout the day to have brief respites from tasks has been shown to increase productivity[12] and reduce stress.[13] From having a quick chat, to exercising, to even taking a short nap, these rest periods can provide some replenishment of energy and enable better working. One tech company self-reported that their most productive employees worked for an average of fifty-two minutes before taking a seventeen-minute break, where they completely disconnected from the task at hand.[14] To properly break away from a task, standing up or walking were proposed as ways of making the most of this lull (although this data was not peer-reviewed, so how effective these numbers and interventions are outside this one set-up is unknown). Many big companies have recognized the importance of breaks, adding game rooms or nap pods to the office, or letting employees work in more flexible ways to enable them to work in the hours which suit them best. Studies have suggested that self-described 'night owls' (sleep and rise late) can have compromised performance in the standard nine-to-five working day versus 'early birds' (sleep and rise early), with one small study highlighting lower connectivity in the default mode network of owls versus early birds during working hours.[15] Having more flexible working hours, which consider people's lifestyle and sleep preferences, may enable individuals to perform more optimally at work and improve well-being (but how this would universally apply across all jobs is another story).

Outside of work, it is important to make the most of the downtime you have to boost relaxation. Activities like walking, being outside, or even just looking at nature are associated with positive effects by relaxing the body. Exercise also brings brain benefits, boosting brain blood flow and reducing levels of distress.[16] Mindfulness meditation – focusing on being present – has been implicated in improving emotional regulation and alleviating stress.[17] Other mindful activities (although not fully explored using research) are also turned to for relaxation, such as cleaning, cooking and gardening. Engaging in a mindful activity, where you are fully focused on the task at hand, is thought to avoid too much default mode network activity. Although we want periods of offline downtime, excessive mind-wandering can promote negative states like rumination. Mindful techniques where you absorb yourself in the task at hand is called behaviour activation, and this is currently being tested as a form of therapy for people with major depressive disorder.

Different activities mean different things to different people and thinking of personal associations with tasks can help pinpoint ways to relax and unwind. It could be that reading a book, listening to music or seeing friends are activities that have been personally associated with time off. Or watching TV or going online. If using devices, consider the type of content being engaged with and for how long. With television shows, it has been shown that while watching high-stress programmes like the news can take our mind off the present, they can leave certain people feeling more anxious.[18] With phone use, extreme cases of scrolling on devices for too long can lead to cybersickness[19] – reported nausea and dizziness from too much time online. Thinking about our personal connections to activities and how we feel during and after them can aid in selecting downtime tasks which leave us feeling genuinely rested.

APPLY

Rest is as important as time on task when pursuing goals. Looking after yourself and enabling proper time to unwind will make pursuits sustainable and enjoyable. Taking our rest as seriously as our work can help cement it into daily routines and make us less likely to skip out on time for us.

BRAINTENANCE: WIND DOWN (& UP)

The list of reasons why sleep is important for our health and productivity is endless, so perfecting our sleep preparation can make travelling to the land of nod as smooth as can be. Setting a wind-down routine which is relaxing and performed every night can settle you before sleep and, with repetition, also act as a cue for bedtime.

How I set my own wind-down routine was to think about what I find relaxing and enjoyable, and to do these things from 9 p.m. every night. I set three evening alarms each morning: half an hour and fifteen minutes before I want to wind down so I know sleep is coming, and then the final one rings at the time to get ready for bed. My routine currently is to switch on the little lamps in my room, make a peppermint tea and stick on a chilled, conversational podcast. I normally fold my clothes and put them away, tidy up anything I have got out that day, prep for the next day, put on all my face creams and brush my teeth. I then switch off the podcast and settle into bed with a book. Within about three pages, my eyes start to close, and I fall asleep. Before implementing this routine, I would be scrolling on my phone for hours, fighting sleep for one more info burst. I now try my best to avoid social media or the news before bedtime to enable me to follow my body's natural urge for slumber (although I definitely don't always succeed).

What is your current prep for bed? What could be changed up to make it more relaxing?

I also have a wind-up routine (not a routine to get me stressed out, don't worry) to ease myself into the morning following sleep. I used to start my day with a scroll session in bed, but I now use a podcast alarm to wake me up. This plays any podcast of my choice at a set time. I normally pick short ten-minute episodes, which means I can slowly wake up to something interesting, rather than being startled by an alarm and then scrolling through the news to keep my eyes open. I also use a meditation app which has a five-minute morning video, so I tend to watch that while getting myself up; heading straight to the kettle to get my cuppa brewing.

Think about how you currently wake up. Is it startling or soothing? How would you like to wake up?

BRAINTENANCE: DEDICATED DOWNTIME

In Chapter 14, we discussed how we have different times of day where we may feel more productive and, if possible, using those hours to do goal-oriented activities. Now if we think of the reverse – times we feel least alert – and use these for rest, we can make sure we are consistently getting downtime.

Some of our low-alert hours unfortunately fall in the working day, making it harder to properly disengage. But if you have some flexibility over your calendar, you could try doing some admin or collaborative tasks in these hours to get space from more intense jobs. You could also try moving your lunch break. I often take my lunch around 2 p.m. and use this hour to exercise or do something creative when I find it more difficult to concentrate.

If you have flexibility with your schedule, how can you place your breaks in your working day to help you recharge?

If flexibility at work isn't an option, ensuring you are resting properly outside these hours is even more important. For me, outside of work I treat my downtime like my goal-related activities:

I schedule it into my calendar for the same time each day. What I do in that time changes (ideas for activities coming up), but knowing I have a block which is dedicated for me to chill on a daily basis not only helps me handle procrastination in the day, as I know downtime is coming, but also helps me switch off and feel refreshed for work the following day. Consistently showing up at this time and doing something for your own benefit should start to make rest routine.

BRAINTENANCE: MICROBREAKS

When we are working on a task, we can sometimes feel like we need to be all go. But taking short breaks to refresh can be beneficial. You can schedule these breaks at regular intervals (five minutes 'off' after fifty-five minutes 'on') or take them as you feel your attention levels dip to help keep on task throughout the day and get done what you need to get done.

Microbreaks – which I define as anywhere from a few seconds to several minutes – should be used to fully disconnect from work. Not to send that email or ring that person, but to step away and press refresh. What you can do on these breaks depends on where you are (home, office, different facilities), but some disconnecting short activities you could try are:

GO FOR WALK

SUN ON FACE

MAKE A TEA

CHAT TO FRIEND

PLAN FOR WEEKEND

FOLD LAUNDRY

PREP FOR DINNER

LOOK OUT WINDOW

BRAINTENANCE: EMBRACE BOREDOM

We often avoid boredom at all costs. It is a state we itch to get out of. But having some blocks of time where you can just sit and let your mind wander can enable ideas to flow. As boredom or rest without stimulation is thought to prompt default mode network activity, this may lead to some breakthroughs as we mull things over. These moments could just be sitting still for five minutes, having a shower without listening to anything, or walking with no music or a companion. Any activity where there isn't really an aim to give your thoughts freedom to roam.

Try pencilling in a few boredom breaks per day to allow your mind to wander.

BRAINTENANCE: INTENTIONAL SCROLLING

Many of us feel joy when using our devices, whether that is connecting with friends, getting fashion inspiration, creating content or being entertained. A problem with our phones is they are designed to keep us scrolling. With never-ending feeds, variable rewards and the sense that, at any moment, something really interesting might happen, we are left staring at our screens for much longer than we anticipate, which can eat into our downtime hours without providing that true sense of relaxation.

Being intentional with what you are using your device for before picking it up can be a good way of not falling down a scroll hole.

Selecting how long you think this task will take and setting a timer can serve as a reminder to stop when you are feeling the pull to keep absorbing content. The same attitude can be applied to watching TV – what is it you want to watch, why and for how long? Setting your intentions before interacting with technology can allow you to enjoy your devices without falling into the trap of losing hours to apps which are built to hook you in.

Having dedicated time to chilling is one thing, but what to fill that time with is another. Relaxing is not just about sitting in a quiet space and deep breathing (although this is definitely an option). There are other activities which can help reduce stress and can be performed when you have chill time. Examples of these include:

BATH OR SHOWER   CLEANING   COOKING

MEAL WITH FRIENDS   READING BOOK   EXERCISE

GOING TO MOVIES   MEDITATE   PUZZLE

For me, I find taking a bath to be a great recharger, as I physically cannot go on my phone and so I am less likely to think about work. I also enjoy prepping a nice dinner, spending time with my friends, cleaning or getting lost in a book. The variety of activities you can do to relax means chill time never gets dull.

WRAP UP

In order to sustain ourselves and pursue goals in a healthy way, we need to consistently take time to switch off. Creating routines that enable us to get proper sleep, so we can better consolidate what we have learnt and function more efficiently, taking breaks throughout the day to re-energize us, resting so we can have those creative breakthroughs, and scheduling downtime so it is harder to compromise should help strike a balance between work and rest. It is not selfish to have time for yourself. It is a necessity for living a healthy, balanced life. And taking it as seriously as goal-related actions should enable you to be re-energized and fresh when you come to act.

CONCLUSION

One grey Saturday afternoon, sat overlooking the gardens of suburban Liverpool, surrounded by the baby pink walls of my sister's childhood room, I was in the midst of writing a chapter of this book, struggling to get words on the page. My partner was sitting on the floor next to me, revising for his upcoming exams, and so, naturally, I turned to him to express my frustration. I lamented my discouragement with the current chapter, leading to a full 'I don't want to fail' monologue. He listened to my catastrophizing, and eventually responded with, 'The way we look at failure is so wrong. We should be actively encouraged to fail over and over again, because failing is the way we actually get anywhere.'

As soon as those words came out of his mouth, I knew I had to end this book talking about failure, which, I'll admit, may seem contradictory for a book on goal pursuit. We purposefully seek to avoid failure. We never want to be seen as giving something our all only to miss, or to let our ideas out into the world to see them flop. Instead, we store up our dreams and wait until the perfect moment, when everything is ready and 'failure-proof', to take action. But those perfect moments very rarely manifest. We sit, and wait, and wait some more, keeping our goals cocooned from the harsh reality of actualizing them.

As well as experiencing heightened fear and decreased motivation, the more time we don't act on what we want, the more something else grows: potential.

It is a compliment to be told you have potential. Whether that is looking at current skills and predicting a future outcome, or recognizing that you have talent that you aren't using, having potential makes us feel good. It can be soothing to know we have it in us to succeed and can help us push on when times are tough. But as potential builds, so does our need to protect it. If we try going for the thing we have been branded 'gifted' in and it doesn't work out, that ability to dream can be tarnished. The 'what if' imaginary scenarios are ripped away. You often hear people say, 'If I wanted to, I could've been the best *insert profession here*'. These individuals still have that escapism of what could've been available to them because they protected their potential. Whether intentionally or through circumstances beyond their control, something got in the way of them truly pursuing that goal. And maybe it does feel nicer to live in a space where you are sat on bags of untapped talent, knowing you had it in you to be the best of the best and still being able to slip into that alternative scenario whenever you fancy. But personally, I believe this makes potential one of the biggest barriers to getting to where you want to be.

In order to take a really good shot at your goal, forget potential and promote failure. Give yourself the permission to give it a good go and if it 'doesn't work', tweak. Reorientate. Alter the strategy and go again. Take learnings away from what happened last time and apply them to the next. Every person who you look up to and who you admire has got to where they are because they have accepted failing as part of the process. Failure is a sign you are putting yourself out there, and so when trying a new endeavour, expect it. Face it. Relish it. The more opportunities you put yourself out there for, the more it becomes a case of **when**, not if, you will make it to where you want to be. Yes, the heightened number of opportunities means you'll likely taste the experience of not getting the outcome you wanted. But you are also drastically increasing your odds of success.

Potential can be bruised by failure. It's easy to interpret these events as signs we maybe aren't as 'good' or 'gifted' as we have been led to believe. That's why it can help to pop potential into a bag and leave it at home. We can peek in the bag from time to time and use our beliefs in our abilities as fuel to push forward. But day to day, forget it. Better to focus on putting one foot in front of the other, taking the next right step, and measuring yourself up against your efforts rather than the ideals our minds craft.

Failure also builds resilience. If you avoid failure, when it eventually hits you, it weighs you down like a ton of bricks. It takes time to recover, to come back from, to try again. And you may find it hard to fully shake the fear it has left behind. But if failure is taken as something to be expected and seen as a sign you are pushing yourself outside your comfort zone, then it won't knock you with as much force. You will be able to adapt and bounce back quicker, making you less afraid to try again. Setbacks no longer set you back, but instead give you drive to move on to the next endeavour. Build up your failure tolerance, push yourself beyond the bounds of what you expect from yourself to learn from what works and what doesn't, and you will find yourself moving through 'failings' with a much lighter step.

It is also imperative that throughout your journey of moving towards a goal, you are seeking joy. That is not to say you should love every moment – on the contrary, there will be many moments that feel tough and are hard – but overall, you should feel good about what you are working towards. And if your overarching aim is aligned with a purpose you truly believe in or know will make a beneficial difference, this should be the case. Acting with integrity and listening to how certain actions make you feel should help keep you moving in a direction you are content with. Find the fun in the effort you are putting in. Enjoy the process of creating and doing. Seek pleasure in the moments of hard work. Because although it will feel good when you achieve a goal, it will fade. It will become normal, even with our best efforts, and we will be looking towards what we can strive for next. If we can find some element of joy or fun in the doing, the process of working towards an aim becomes what we look forward to. And if we shift to improving and learning instead of achieving, results seem to materialize by themselves.

As mentioned in the introduction, this book is not about sitting back and wishing results into existence. It is about putting the power of change into your own hands and working on the small things you can control to move you in the direction of your desires. Hopefully, if you have reached this page, you now have an idea of what you want and why it is you want it, and you can see some of the obstacles standing in your way. And you have a plan in place that brings your focus closer to the moment, action steps for how to build the behaviours that should help you move towards where you want to be, and more belief in yourself and the mechanisms for keeping you on track. By peeking into the human brain and becoming familiar with how it works, you should now see why change feels difficult, but that it is possible. The science explored here only scratches the surface of this incredible organ, so keep reading, watching and listening for new advancements with curiosity and an open mind to go deeper in getting to know your brain. You can revisit this book and its exercises time and time again, whenever you want to set a new plan in motion. With small actions and consistency, you can make big changes. And through the tools in these pages, I hope it is slightly easier to take those first steps.

Be kind to yourself when moving towards a goal. Have self-compassion and show yourself the understanding you so easily afford to others. The onus isn't all on you. We exist in a society of unequal systems that can make it more challenging for some individuals to get to certain milestones. You may be fighting against stereotypes or 'norms' by trying to do something different, meaning pushback will be rife. Access to certain rooms, spaces and resources might be more difficult to attain. Focus on the things you can control, master them, and let your brilliant work speak for itself. When working on these goals, there are going to be times when you don't follow through, or life gets too busy or other priorities take precedence. And that is completely fine. In the final stages of writing this book alongside having an intense full-time job, it was very difficult for me to keep up elements of my routine, like exercising and having proper downtime. There were moments when that nagging voice would rear its head and berate me for not being able to 'do it all'. But instead of sinking into that hole of self-deprecation, I made a plan. I knew this crunch time was temporary and within a few weeks, I would be back in my routine. And that plan acted as a rebuttal to my inner voice. There will be times in life when it is more difficult to keep up with routines. By explaining to yourself why that is and having a plan in place ready to execute once this period is over can help remove the sting of feeling like you aren't doing 'enough'.

A final note: you are enough. As you are right now. You are enough, and you are deserving of happiness, joy and love as you are. Chasing the goal or trying to improve certain elements of life can be all-encompassing, and it is easy to fall into the trap of feeling not good enough until that milestone is reached. But who you are at this moment is worthy of celebration. So celebrate yourself every day, for what you have been through, for showing up, for being kind to others, for persevering, for being kind to yourself, for seeking joy, for just being you. No accolade or achievement can match your inner greatness. And you are carrying that with you wherever you go. Celebrate the you of today and, achievements aside, know that you are worthy.

ACKNOWLEDGEMENTS

Bringing this book into existence was made possible by so many people and I could not have got to this stage without all their help, guidance, advice and assistance.

Braintenance first came to life in December 2020, when Sara Cameron asked me, 'If you could read any book now, what would it be?' I described a book about how to set and stick to goals because I was feeling a bit lost in life at the time, and those ideas were embraced with so much enthusiasm. Thank you for encouraging me to put a proposal together to write the book I needed so much myself, sending it out to publishers, and for being a huge support throughout the writing process. And thanks to both Sara and her husband, Humphrey, for invaluable feedback on those initial thoughts about what *Braintenance* could be.

A massive thanks goes out to the Pan Macmillan team, especially my editor Matt Cole. You saw potential in those early plans and have been there every step of the writing process to guide me through putting together my first book. Thank you for always reminding me who I was writing *Braintenance* for and for helping me transition from academic writing to telling stories for those who will read the book. Your edits massively elevated *Braintenance* and I am so grateful you shared the same vision for what this book could be. A huge thank you also goes to the editors and proofreaders who helped to give this book flow, including Victoria Denne, Lesley Malkin and Samantha Fletcher, and to the publicity and marketing teams, including Josie Turner and Jamie Forrest, for your time put into spreading the word about my book. To Pan

Macmillan as a whole, I am so grateful you took me on as a new author and trusted in my ideas enough to have them printed.

I wrote this book alongside editing my PhD thesis and working full time. I have such thanks for my PhD lab in the Prion Unit at UCL, who always championed me doing creative projects outside of the lab, and the research communications team at Alzheimer's Society, who created such a supportive environment for my first job and always checked in on how the book was going. I am also so grateful to my colleagues at the BBC and the BBC Radio Cambridgeshire team, who have encouraged my work and provided another great support network over the past year while I moved house and job during the writing and editing process.

I have written this book all over the place, from my childhood home in Liverpool, to my partner's student house in Oxford, to my sister's house in London, to my partner's family home in Bermuda, to an empty flat with just a desk and a chair in Cambridge. All of these spaces will now always hold a bit of *Braintenance* and I am very thankful for the people who welcomed me and my crack-of-dawn cups of tea into their spaces.

My family and friends are the pillars in my life and, no matter how busy I am, I always have their support.

To the school girls, the dancing girls and my Gee, thank you for listening to my problems and being constant cheerleaders in all my endeavours. Our times together – whether wild, weird or chilled – make me forget my work and remind me that I am loved for who I am, not what I do.

My partner's family – Barb, Len, Brian, Gene and Sylvia – you have given me breathing space year on year by letting me stay in your home and switch off for a few weeks at a time. I really appreciate you asking about the book and letting me talk through any sticking points over a glass of rosé at the kitchen counter.

My extended family – my incredible aunties, uncles, cousins, my brother-in-law Jez, and, of course, Grandad Tony. At every family gathering, you always show such interest in the work I am doing, and I value that you listened to my plans for this book before a single idea was down on paper. Aunty Lisa, your constant support and love is so appreciated. Uncle Gary, your cheeky spirit lives on in our memories.

Braintenance is dedicated to three members of my family who are sadly no longer with us, but without whom this book would not exist.

Aunty Moira – the first Dr Ravey, who fought against stereotypes to be one of a handful of women who qualified as a medical doctor in the 1960s. Your career in psychiatry is what made me fascinated with the brain and behaviour, and your kind-hearted nature and unwavering support of me throughout my life meant I had the confidence to also be a woman in science. Thank you for being my role model.

Uncle Mike – the funniest, most creative man I have ever met – whose doodles and artwork in every birthday and Christmas card I would copy until I could draw in exactly the same style. The illustrations in this book are all down to you. Thank you for showing me how fun art can be and how warm it can make others feel.

Nanny Celia – a strong, loving woman who took no nonsense and whose sass levels I could never match. My desire to study neuroscience came down in part to try to help you, your siblings and your mum with Alzheimer's disease. Without doing my PhD, this book would not have been written. I will always keep fighting for a world without Alzheimer's disease, in your name.

To my mum, dad and sister Rosanna, the Ravey Family Unit. The facetimes, tea sessions and long conversations are what have given me clarity, focus and determination to keep going and believe in myself throughout this project. Whenever I need advice, you are all there 100 per cent, and whether celebrating or going through hard times, we always pull together and have each other. Thank you for your support in all I do.

And finally, the biggest thanks to Matt, my best friend and partner. You never fail to make me feel like I have got it – whatever the problem is – and have me smiling every day. Thank you for always listening, being patient and at my side throughout this project and all the others. I am so grateful to have you in my life.

SOURCES

As well as the example studies mentioned in each chapter, I have also added a list of other readings used to help me write *Braintenance*, including a mixture of sources, articles and other books. Enjoy!

CHAPTER 1

1 Tseng, J., & Poppenk, J., 'Brain meta-state transitions demarcate thoughts across task contexts exposing the mental noise of trait neuroticism', *Nature Communications*, *11*(1), 3480 (2020)

2 Ponce de León, M. S., Bienvenu, T., Marom, A., Engel, S., Tafforeau, P., Alatorre Warren, J. L., Lordkipanidze, D., Kurniawan, I., Murti, D. B., Suriyanto, R. A., Koesbardiati, T., & Zollikofer, C. P. E., 'The primitive brain of early Homo', *Science*, *372*(6538), 165–171 (2021)

3 Neubauer, S., Hublin, J.-J., & Gunz, P., 'The evolution of modern human brain shape', *Science Advances*, *4*(1) (2018)

4 de Zeeuw, C. I., Lisberger, S. G., & Raymond, J. L., 'Diversity and dynamism in the cerebellum', *Nature Neuroscience*, *24*(2), 160–167 (2021)

5 Constandi, M., 'Phineas Gage and the effect of an iron bar through the head on personality', *The Guardian* (2010)

6 Annese, J., Schenker-Ahmed, N. M., Bartsch, H., Maechler, P., Sheh, C., Thomas, N., Kayano, J., Ghatan, A., Bresler, N., Frosch, M. P., Klaming, R., & Corkin, S., 'Postmortem examination of patient H.M.'s brain based on histological sectioning and digital 3D reconstruction', *Nature Communications*, *5*(1), 3122 (2014)

7 Adolphs, R., 'The Biology of Fear', *Current Biology*, *23*(2), R79–R93 (2013)

8 Nummenmaa, L., Glerean, E., Hari, R., & Hietanen, J. K., 'Bodily maps of emotions', *Proceedings of the National Academy of Sciences*, *111*(2), 646–651 (2014)

9 Willyard, C., 'How gut microbes could drive brain disorders', *Nature*, *590*(7844), 22–25 (2021)

Further reading and sources

Gawdat, Mo, *Solve for Happy* (Bluebird, 2017)

Thiagarajan, Tara, 'Deconstructing a Thought', sapienlabs.org (2017)

Society for Neuroscience, '3D Brain', brainfacts.org (2017)

Alzheimer's Society, 'Frontotemporal Dementia', alzheimers.org.uk

Lago-Baldaia, I., Fernandes, V. M., & Ackerman, S. D., 'More Than Mortar: Glia as Architects of Nervous System Development and Disease', *Frontiers in Cell and Developmental Biology*, *8* (2020)

Kahneman, Daniel, *Thinking, Fast and Slow* (Penguin, 2011)

Südhof, T. C., 'Towards an Understanding of Synapse Formation', *Neuron*, *100*(2), 276–293 (2018)

CHAPTER 2

1 Reser, D., Simmons, M., Johns, E., Ghaly, A., Quayle, M., Dordevic, A. L., Tare, M., McArdle, A., Willems, J., & Yunkaporta, T., 'Australian Aboriginal techniques for memorization: Translation into a medical and allied health education setting', *PLOS ONE*, *16*(5), e0251710 (2021)

2 von Bartheld, C. S., Bahney, J., & Herculano-Houzel, S., 'The search for true numbers of neurons and glial cells in the human brain: A review of 150 years of cell counting', *Journal of Comparative Neurology*, *524*(18), 3865–3895 (2016)

3 Cellier, D., Riddle, J., Petersen, I., & Hwang, K., 'The development of theta and alpha neural oscillations from ages 3 to 24 years', *Developmental Cognitive Neuroscience*, *50*, 100969 (2021)

4 Stein, R., & Swan A., 'Personality Tests with Deep-Sounding Questions Provide Shallow Answers about the "True" You', *The Conversation US* (2018)

5   Polderman, T. J. C., Benyamin, B., de Leeuw, C. A., Sullivan, P. F., van
    Bochoven, A., Visscher, P. M., & Posthuma, D., 'Meta-analysis of the
    heritability of human traits based on fifty years of twin studies', *Nature
    Genetics, 47*(7), 702–709 (2015)

6   Zwir, I., Arnedo, J., Del-Val, C., Pulkki-Råback, L., Konte, B., Yang, S. S.,
    Romero-Zaliz, R., Hintsanen, M., Cloninger, K. M., Garcia, D., Svrakic,
    D. M., Rozsa, S., Martinez, M., Lyytikäinen, L.-P., Giegling, I., Kähönen,
    M., Hernandez-Cuervo, H., Seppälä, I., Raitoharju, E., Cloninger, C. R.
    et al., 'Uncovering the complex genetics of human character', *Molecular
    Psychiatry, 25*(10), 2295–2312 (2020)

7   Bleidorn, W., Hill, P. L., Back, M. D., Denissen, J. J. A., Hennecke, M.,
    Hopwood, C. J., Jokela, M., Kandler, C., Lucas, R. E., Luhmann, M.,
    Orth, U., Wagner, J., Wrzus, C., Zimmermann, J., & Roberts, B., 'The
    policy relevance of personality traits', *American Psychologist, 74*(9),
    1056–1067 (2019)

8   Dias, B. G., & Ressler, K. J., 'Parental olfactory experience influences
    behavior and neural structure in subsequent generations', *Nature
    Neuroscience, 17*(1), 89–96 (2014)

Further reading and sources

Mora-Bermúdez, F., Badsha, F., Kanton, S., Camp, J. G., Vernot, B.,
    Köhler, K., Voigt, B., Okita, K., Maricic, T., He, Z., Lachmann, R.,
    Pääbo, S., Treutlein, B., & Huttner, W. B., 'Differences and similarities
    between human and chimpanzee neural progenitors during cerebral
    cortex development', *ELife, 5* (2016)

Shultz, D, 'Humans can outlearn chimps thanks to more flexible brain
    genetics', science.org (2015)

Basic Biology, 'Introduction to genetics', basicbiology.net (2020)

Tottenham, N., 'The Brain's Emotional Development', *Cerebrum: The
    Dana Forum on Brain Science* (2017)

Wessel, L., 'Early Experience Shapes the Brain for Life', brainfacts.org
    (2019)

Mattson, M. P., 'Superior pattern processing is the essence of the
    evolved human brain', *Frontiers in Neuroscience, 8* (2014)

Hedman, A. M., van Haren, N. E. M., Schnack, H. G., Kahn, R. S.,
    & Hulshoff Pol, H. E., 'Human brain changes across the life span:

A review of 56 longitudinal magnetic resonance imaging studies', *Human Brain Mapping, 33*(8), 1987–2002 (2012)

Begus, K., & Bonawitz, E., 'The rhythm of learning: Theta oscillations as an index of active learning in infancy', *Developmental Cognitive Neuroscience, 45*, 100810 (2020)

Packard, P. A., Steiger, T. K., Fuentemilla, L., & Bunzeck, N., 'Neural oscillations and event-related potentials reveal how semantic congruence drives long-term memory in both young and older humans', *Scientific Reports, 10*(1), 9116 (2020)

Williamson, J. M., & Lyons, D. A., 'Myelin Dynamics Throughout Life: An Ever-Changing Landscape?', *Frontiers in Cellular Neuroscience, 12* (2018)

Thomason, M. E., & Marusak, H. A., 'Toward understanding the impact of trauma on the early developing human brain', *Neuroscience, 342*, 55–67 (2017)

Dubois, J., Eberhardt, F., Paul, L. K., & Adolphs, R., 'Personality beyond taxonomy', *Nature Human Behaviour, 4*(11), 1110–1117 (2020)

Lacal, I., & Ventura, R., 'Epigenetic Inheritance: Concepts, Mechanisms and Perspectives', *Frontiers in Molecular Neuroscience, 11* (2018)

CHAPTER 3

1 Crego, A. C. G., Štoček, F., Marchuk, A. G., Carmichael, J. E., van der Meer, M. A. A., & Smith, K. S., 'Complementary Control over Habits and Behavioral Vigor by Phasic Activity in the Dorsolateral Striatum', *The Journal of Neuroscience, 40*(10), 2139–2153 (2020)

2 Lally, P., van Jaarsveld, C. H. M., Potts, H. W. W., & Wardle, J., 'How are habits formed: Modelling habit formation in the real world', *European Journal of Social Psychology, 40*(6), 998–1009 (2010)

3 Korteling, J. E., Brouwer, A.-M., & Toet, A., 'A Neural Network Framework for Cognitive Bias', *Frontiers in Psychology, 9* (2018)

4 Grupe, D. W., & Nitschke, J. B., 'Uncertainty and anticipation in anxiety: an integrated neurobiological and psychological perspective', *Nature Reviews Neuroscience, 14*(7), 488–501 (2013)

5 Magistretti, P. J., & Allaman, I., 'A Cellular Perspective on Brain Energy Metabolism and Functional Imaging', *Neuron, 86*(4), 883–901 (2015)

6   Petruo, V. A., Mückschel, M., & Beste, C., 'On the role of the prefrontal cortex in fatigue effects on cognitive flexibility – a system neurophysiological approach', *Scientific Reports*, 8(1), 6395 (2018)

Further reading and sources

Amaya, K. A., & Smith, K. S., 'Neurobiology of habit formation', *Current Opinion in Behavioral Sciences*, 20, 145–152 (2018)

Humeau, Y., & Choquet, D., 'The next generation of approaches to investigate the link between synaptic plasticity and learning', *Nature Neuroscience*, 22(10), 1536–1543 (2019)

Averbeck, B. B., & Costa, V. D., 'Motivational neural circuits underlying reinforcement learning', *Nature Neuroscience*, 20(4), 505–512 (2017)

Malvaez, M., & Wassum, K. M., 'Regulation of habit formation in the dorsal striatum', *Current Opinion in Behavioral Sciences*, 20, 67–74 (2018)

Davis, M., Walker, D. L., Miles, L., & Grillon, C., 'Phasic vs Sustained Fear in Rats and Humans: Role of the Extended Amygdala in Fear vs Anxiety', *Neuropsychopharmacology*, 35(1), 105–135 (2010)

Social Change, 'An introduction to habit theory', social-change.co.uk (2020)

Mendelsohn, A. I., 'Creatures of Habit: The Neuroscience of Habit and Purposeful Behavior', *Biological Psychiatry*, 85(11), e49–e51 (2019)

Mateos-Aparicio, P., & Rodríguez-Moreno, A., 'The Impact of Studying Brain Plasticity', *Frontiers in Cellular Neuroscience*, 13 (2019)

Luetz, J. M., Margus, R., & Prickett, B., 'Human Behavior Change for Sustainable Development:', *Perspectives Informed by Psychology and Neuroscience*, 419–434 (2020)

Lewis, M., 'Why we're hardwired to hate uncertainty', theguardian.com (2016)

Peters, A., McEwen, B. S., & Friston, K., 'Uncertainty and stress: Why it causes diseases and how it is mastered by the brain', *Progress in Neurobiology*, 156, 164–188 (2017)

Grupe, D. W., & Nitschke, J. B., 'Uncertainty and anticipation in anxiety: an integrated neurobiological and psychological perspective', *Nature Reviews Neuroscience*, 14(7), 488–501 (2013)

Schölvinck, M. L., Howarth, C., & Attwell, D., 'The cortical energy needed for conscious perception', *NeuroImage*, 40(4), 1460–1468 (2008)

Bruckmaier, M., Tachtsidis, I., Phan, P., & Lavie, N., 'Attention and Capacity Limits in Perception: A Cellular Metabolism Account', *The Journal of Neuroscience, 40*(35), 6801–6811 (2020)

CHAPTER 4

1   Epton, T., Currie, S., & Armitage, C. J., 'Unique effects of setting goals on behavior change: Systematic review and meta-analysis', *Journal of Consulting and Clinical Psychology, 85*(12), 1182–1198 (2017)

2   Ludwiczak, A., Osman, M., & Jahanshahi, M., 'Redefining the relationship between effort and reward: Choice-execution model of effort-based decisions', *Behavioural Brain Research, 383*, 112474 (2020)

Further reading and sources

Satpute, A., Ochsner, K. N., & Badre, D., 'The Neuroscience of Goal-Directed Behavior', Goal-Oriented Behavior, Chapter 2: 49–85 (2012)

Duan, L. Y., Horst, N. K., Cranmore, S. A. W., Horiguchi, N., Cardinal, R. N., Roberts, A. C., & Robbins, T. W., 'Controlling one's world: Identification of sub-regions of primate PFC underlying goal-directed behavior', *Neuron, 109*(15), 2485–2498.e5 (2021)

Yoshida, K., Drew, M. R., Mimura, M., & Tanaka, K. F., 'Serotonin-mediated inhibition of ventral hippocampus is required for sustained goal-directed behavior', *Nature Neuroscience, 22*(5), 770–777 (2019)

Uddin, L. Q., 'Cognitive and behavioural flexibility: neural mechanisms and clinical considerations', *Nature Reviews Neuroscience, 22*(3), 167–179 (2021)

Shilton, A. C., 'You Accomplished Something Great. So Now What?', nytimes.com (2019)

Fontane Pennock, S., 'The Hedonic Treadmill – Are We Forever Chasing Rainbows?', positivepsychology.com (2016)

Armenta, C., Bao, K. J., Lyubomirsky, S., & Sheldon, K. M., 'Is Lasting Change Possible? Lessons from the Hedonic Adaptation Prevention Model', *In Stability of Happiness* (Elsevier, 2014), pp 57–74

Schippers, M. C., Morisano, D., Locke, E. A., Scheepers, A. W. A., Latham, G. P., & de Jong, E. M., 'Writing about personal goals and plans regardless of goal type boosts academic performance', *Contemporary Educational Psychology, 60*, 101823 (2020)

CHAPTER 5

1   Brosch, T., & Sander, D., 'Neurocognitive mechanisms underlying value-based decision-making: from core values to economic value', *Frontiers in Human Neuroscience*, 7 (2013)

2   Brosch, T., Coppin, G., Scherer, K. R., Schwartz, S., & Sander, D., 'Generating value(s): Psychological value hierarchies reflect context-dependent sensitivity of the reward system', *Social Neuroscience*, 6(2), 198–208 (2011)

3   Georgellis, Y., Tsitsianis, N., & Yin, Y. P., 'Personal Values as Mitigating Factors in the Link Between Income and Life Satisfaction: Evidence from the European Social Survey', *Social Indicators Research*, 91(3), 329–344 (2009)

4   Hill, P. L., Sin, N. L., Turiano, N. A., Burrow, A. L., & Almeida, D. M., 'Sense of Purpose Moderates the Associations Between Daily Stressors and Daily Well-being', *Annals of Behavioral Medicine*, 52(8), 724–729 (2018)

5   Park, C. L., Knott, C. L., Williams, R. M., Clark, E. M., Williams, B. R., & Schulz, E., 'Meaning in Life Predicts Decreased Depressive Symptoms and Increased Positive Affect over Time but Does not Buffer Stress Effects in a National Sample of African-Americans', *Journal of Happiness Studies*, 21(8), 3037–3049 (2020)

6   Sutin, A. R., Luchetti, M., Aschwanden, D., Stephan, Y., & Terracciano, A., 'Sense of purpose in life, cognitive function, and the phenomenology of autobiographical memory', *Memory*, 29(9), 1126–1135 (2021)

7   Buchman, A. S., 'Effect of Purpose in Life on the Relation Between Alzheimer Disease Pathologic Changes on Cognitive Function in Advanced Age', *Archives of General Psychiatry*, 69(5), 499 (2012)

8   Lee, M.-A., & Kawachi, I., 'The keys to happiness: Associations between personal values regarding core life domains and happiness in South Korea', *PLOS ONE*, 14(1), e0209821 (2019)

Further reading and sources

Thierry, G., 'Life's purpose rests in our mind's spectacular drive to extract meaning from the world', theconversation.com (2018)

Brooks, A. C., 'The Meaning of Life Is Surprisingly Simple', theatlantic.com (2021)

Martela, F., & Steger, M. F., 'The three meanings of meaning in life: Distinguishing coherence, purpose, and significance', *The Journal of Positive Psychology*, *11*(5), 531–545 (2016)

Taylor, S., 'The meaning of life – a psychologist's view', theconversation.com (2020)

CHAPTER 6

1 Ackerman, C., 'What Is Self-Awareness and Why Is It Important? [+5 Ways to Increase It]', positivepsychology.com (2020)

2 Philippi, C. L., Feinstein, J. S., Khalsa, S. S., Damasio, A., Tranel, D., Landini, G., Williford, K., & Rudrauf, D., 'Preserved Self-Awareness following Extensive Bilateral Brain Damage to the Insula, Anterior Cingulate, and Medial Prefrontal Cortices', *PLOS ONE*, *7*(8), e38413 (2012)

3 Deleniv, S., 'The "me" illusion: How your brain conjures up your sense of self', *New Scientist* (2018)

4 Danckert, J., & Merrifield, C., 'Boredom, sustained attention and the default mode network', *Experimental Brain Research*, *236*(9), 2507–2518 (2018)

5 NHS, 'Overview – Cognitive behavioural therapy (CBT)', nhs.uk (2019)

6 Hinwar, R. P., & Lambert, A. J., 'Anauralia: The Silent Mind and Its Association With Aphantasia', *Frontiers in Psychology*, *12* (2021)

7 Wolman, D., 'The split brain: A tale of two halves', *Nature*, *483*(7389), 260–263 (2012)

8 Gazzaniga, M., *The Ethical Brain* (Dana Press, 2005)

9 Breines, J. G., & Chen, S., 'Self-Compassion Increases Self-Improvement Motivation', *Personality and Social Psychology Bulletin*, *38*(9), 1133–1143 (2012)

10 Tang, Y.-Y., Hölzel, B. K., & Posner, M. I., 'The neuroscience of mindfulness meditation', *Nature Reviews Neuroscience*, *16*(4), 213–225 (2015)

Further reading and sources

Sahakian, B. J., Langley, C., Stamatakis, E. A., & Spindler, L., 'Consciousness: how the brain chemical "dopamine" plays a key role – new research', theconversation.com (2021)

Riehl, J., 'The Roots of Human Self-Awareness', neurosciencenews.com (2012)

Jabr, F., 'Does Self-Awareness Require a Complex Brain?', scientificamerican.com (2012)

Vago, D. R., & Silbersweig, D. A., 'Self-awareness, self-regulation, and self-transcendence (S-ART): a framework for understanding the neurobiological mechanisms of mindfulness', *Frontiers in Human Neuroscience*, 6 (2012)

CHAPTER 7

1   Lindsay, G. W., 'Attention in Psychology, Neuroscience, and Machine Learning', *Frontiers in Computational Neuroscience*, 14 (2020)

2   Wimmer, R. D., Schmitt, L. I., Davidson, T. J., Nakajima, M., Deisseroth, K., & Halassa, M. M., 'Thalamic control of sensory selection in divided attention', *Nature*, 526(7575), 705–709 (2015)

3   Ibid.

4   Ranganathan, V. K., Siemionow, V., Liu, J. Z., Sahgal, V., & Yue, G. H., 'From mental power to muscle power – gaining strength by using the mind', *Neuropsychologia*, 42(7), 944–956 (2004)

5   Basu, R., Gebauer, R., Herfurth, T., Kolb, S., Golipour, Z., Tchumatchenko, T., & Ito, H. T., 'The orbitofrontal cortex maps future navigational goals', *Nature*, 599(7885), 449–452 (2021)

6   Taylor, S. E., Pham, L. B., Rivkin, I. D., & Armor, D. A., 'Harnessing the imagination: Mental simulation, self-regulation, and coping', *American Psychologist*, 53(4), 429–439 (1998)

7   Wang, G., Wang, Y., & Gai, X., 'A Meta-Analysis of the Effects of Mental Contrasting With Implementation Intentions on Goal Attainment', *Frontiers in Psychology*, 12 (2021)

8   Ibid.

Further reading and sources

The Picower Institute, 'Scientists identify specific brain region and circuits controlling attention', neurosciencenews.com (2020)

Cepelewicz, J., 'To Pay Attention, the Brain Uses Filters, Not a Spotlight', quantamagazine.org (2019) van Ede, F., & Nobre, A. C., 'Toward a neurobiology of internal selective attention', *Trends in Neurosciences*, 44(7), 513–515 (2021)

Nandy, A., Nassi, J. J., Jadi, M. P., & Reynolds, J., 'Optogenetically induced low-frequency correlations impair perception', *ELife*, 8 (2019)

Rosen, J., 'Bat Brain Behavior Offers Insights Into How Humans Focus Attention', hub.jhu.edu (2016)

Pillay, S., 'Can Visualizing Your Body Doing Something Help You Learn to Do It Better?', scientificamerican.com (2015)

Chu, M., 'Research Reveals That Publicly Announcing Your Goals Makes You Less Likely to Achieve Them', inc.com (2017)

Tang, M. F., Ford, L., Arabzadeh, E., Enns, J. T., Visser, T. A. W., & Mattingley, J. B., 'Neural dynamics of the attentional blink revealed by encoding orientation selectivity during rapid visual presentation', *Nature Communications*, 11(1), 434 (2020)

CHAPTER 8

1   Hulsey, T. L., & Hampson, P. J., 'Moral expertise', *New Ideas in Psychology*, 34, 1–11 (2014)

2   Kuhl, J., Quirin, M., & Koole, S. L., 'Being Someone: The Integrated Self as a Neuropsychological System', *Social and Personality Psychology Compass*, 9(3), 115–132 (2015)

3   Sui, J., & Gu, X., 'Self as Object: Emerging Trends in Self Research', *Trends in Neurosciences*, 40(11), 643–653 (2017)

4   Charng, H.-W., Piliavin, J. A., & Callero, P. L., 'Role Identity and Reasoned Action in the Prediction of Repeated Behavior', *Social Psychology Quarterly*, 51(4), 303 (1988)

5   McCarthy, M. B., Collins, A. M., Flaherty, S. J., & McCarthy, S. N., 'Healthy eating habit: A role for goals, identity, and self-control?', *Psychology & Marketing*, 34(8), 772–785 (2017)

6   Gardner, B., de Bruijn, G.-J., & Lally, P., 'Habit, identity, and repetitive action: A prospective study of binge-drinking in UK students', *British Journal of Health Psychology*, 17(3), 565–581 (2012)

7   Verplanken, B., & Sui, J., 'Habit and Identity: Behavioral, Cognitive, Affective, and Motivational Facets of an Integrated Self', *Frontiers in Psychology*, 10 (2019)

8 Barnett, G., Boduszek, D., & Willmott, D., 'What works to change identity? A rapid evidence assessment of interventions', *Journal of Applied Social Psychology*, *51*(7), 698–719 (2021)

9 Grosse Wiesmann, C., Friederici, A. D., Singer, T., & Steinbeis, N., 'Two systems for thinking about others' thoughts in the developing brain', *Proceedings of the National Academy of Sciences*, *117*(12), 6928–6935 (2020)

Further reading and sources

Snippe, M. H. M., Peters, G.-J. Y., & Kok, G., 'The operationalization of self-identity in reasoned action models: a systematic review of self-identity operationalizations in three decades of research', *Health Psychology and Behavioral Medicine*, *9*(1), 48–69 (2021)

Emamzadeh, A., 'How Identity Change Happens', psychologytoday.com (2021)

Ruhl, C., 'Theory of Mind', simplypsychology.org (2020)

Ereria, S., 'How the brain builds a sense of self from the people around us – new research', theconversation.com (2020)

Clear, J., *Atomic Habits: Tiny Changes, Remarkable Results* (Cornerstone Digital, 2018)

CHAPTER 9

1 Stawarz, K., Gardner, B., Cox, A., & Blandford, A., 'What influences the selection of contextual cues when starting a new routine behaviour? An exploratory study', *BMC Psychology*, *8*(1), 29 (2020)

2 Kirgios, E. L., Mandel, G. H., Park, Y., Milkman, K. L., Gromet, D. M., Kay, J. S., & Duckworth, A. L., 'Teaching temptation bundling to boost exercise: A field experiment', *Organizational Behavior and Human Decision Processes*, *161*, 20–35 (2020)

Further reading and sources

Fogg, B. J., *Tiny Habits: The Small Changes that Change Everything* (Virgin Digital, 2019)

Milkman, K., *How to Change: The Science of Getting from Where You Are to Where You Want to Be* (Ebury Digital, 2021)

Society for Personality and Social Psychology, 'How we form habits,
change existing ones', ScienceDaily (2014)

van der Weiden, A., Benjamins, J., Gillebaart, M., Ybema, J. F., & de Ridder,
D., 'How to Form Good Habits? A Longitudinal Field Study on the Role
of Self-Control in Habit Formation', *Frontiers in Psychology*, *11* (2020)

CHAPTER 10

1   Vandewalle, D., Nerstad, C. G. L., & Dysvik, A., 'Goal Orientation: A
    Review of the Miles Traveled and the Miles to Go', *Annual Review of
    Organizational Psychology and Organizational Behavior*, *6*(1), 115–144
    (2019)

2   Ibid.

3   Walton, M. E., & Bouret, S., 'What Is the Relationship between
    Dopamine and Effort?', *Trends in Neurosciences*, *42*(2), 79–91 (2019)

4   Nicola, S. M., 'The Flexible Approach Hypothesis: Unification of Effort
    and Cue-Responding Hypotheses for the Role of Nucleus Accumbens
    Dopamine in the Activation of Reward-Seeking Behavior', *Journal of
    Neuroscience*, *30*(49), 16585–16600 (2010)

5   Milkman, K. L., Gromet, D., Ho, H., Kay, J. S., Lee, T. W., Pandiloski,
    P., Park, Y., Rai, A., Bazerman, M., Beshears, J., Bonacorsi, L., Camerer,
    C., Chang, E., Chapman, G., Cialdini, R., Dai, H., Eskreis-Winkler, L.,
    Fishbach, A., Gross, J. J., Duckworth, A. L. et al., 'Megastudies improve
    the impact of applied behavioural science', *Nature*, *600*(7889), 478–483
    (2021)

Further reading and sources

Clear, J., *Atomic Habits: Tiny Changes, Remarkable Results*
    (Cornerstone Digital, 2018)

Grogan, J. P., Sandhu, T. R., Hu, M. T., & Manohar, S. G., 'Dopamine
    promotes instrumental motivation, but reduces reward-related
    vigour', *ELife*, *9* (2020)

CHAPTER 11

1   Broche-Pérez, Y., Herrera Jiménez, L. F., & Omar-Martínez, E., 'Neural
    substrates of decision-making', *Neurología (English Edition)*, *31*(5),
    319–325 (2016)

2   Coutlee, C. G., & Huettel, S. A., 'The functional neuroanatomy of decision making: Prefrontal control of thought and action', *Brain Research*, *1428*, 3–12 (2012)

3   Lavin, C., Melis, C., Mikulan, E., Gelormini, C., Huepe, D., & Ibañez, A., 'The anterior cingulate cortex: an integrative hub for human socially driven interactions', *Frontiers in Neuroscience*, *7* (2013)

4   Torregrossa, M. M., Quinn, J. J., & Taylor, J. R., 'Impulsivity, Compulsivity, and Habit: The Role of Orbitofrontal Cortex Revisited', *Biological Psychiatry*, *63*(3), 253–255 (2008)

5   Job, V., Dweck, C. S., & Walton, G. M., 'Ego Depletion: Is It All in Your Head?', *Psychological Science*, *21*(11), 1686–1693 (2010)

6   Ersner-Hershfield, H., Wimmer, G. E., & Knutson, B., 'Saving for the future self: Neural measures of future self-continuity predict temporal discounting', *Social Cognitive and Affective Neuroscience*, *4*(1), 85–92 (2009)

7   Kapogli, E., & Quoidbach, J., 'Stranger or a clone? Future self-connectedness depends on who you ask, when you ask, and what dimension you focus on', *Current Opinion in Psychology*, *43*, 266–270 (2022)

8   Ganschow, B., Cornet, L., Zebel, S., & van Gelder, J.-L., 'Looking Back From the Future: Perspective Taking in Virtual Reality Increases Future Self-Continuity', *Frontiers in Psychology*, *12* (2021)

Further reading and sources

Robbins, M., *The 5 Second Rule: Transform your Life, Work, and Confidence with Everyday Courage* (Mel Robbins Production Inc, 2017)

Beaton, C., 'Humans are bad at predicting futures that don't benefit them', theatlantic.com (2017)

Eyal, N., 'Have We Been Thinking About Willpower the Wrong Way for 30 Years?', hbr.org (2016)

Jones, D., 'Your true self: The future is a foreign person', *New Scientist* (2017)

Hershfield, H. E., Goldstein, D. G., Sharpe, W. F., Fox, J., Yeykelis, L., Carstensen, L. L., & Bailenson, J. N., 'Increasing Saving Behavior Through Age-Progressed Renderings of the Future Self', *Journal of Marketing Research*, *48*(SPL), S23–S37 (2011)

Pataranutaporn, P., Danry, V., Leong, J., Punpongsanon, P., Novy, D., Maes, P., & Sra, M., 'AI-generated characters for supporting personalized learning and well-being', *Nature Machine Intelligence*, *3*(12), 1013–1022 (2021)

CHAPTER 12

1 Lu, H., Li, X., Wang, Y., Song, Y., & Liu, J., 'The hippocampus underlies the association between self-esteem and physical health', *Scientific Reports*, *8*(1), 17141 (2018)

2 Will, G.-J., Rutledge, R. B., Moutoussis, M., & Dolan, R. J., 'Neural and computational processes underlying dynamic changes in self-esteem', *ELife*, *6* (2017)

3 NHS, 'Raising low self-esteem', nhs.uk (2020)

4 Bandura, A., *Self-efficacy: the exercise of control* (New York: W.H. Freeman and Company, 1997)

5 Stajkovic, A. D., & Luthans, F., 'Self-efficacy and work-related performance: A meta-analysis', *Psychological Bulletin*, *124*(2), 240–261 (1998)

6 Chemers, M. M., Hu, L., & Garcia, B. F., 'Academic self-efficacy and first year college student performance and adjustment', *Journal of Educational Psychology*, *93*(1), 55–64 (2001)

7 Chrousos, G. P., Mentis, A.-F. A., & Dardiotis, E., 'Focusing on the Neuro-Psycho-Biological and Evolutionary Underpinnings of the Imposter Syndrome', *Frontiers in Psychology*, *11* (2020)

8 Ibid.

9 Shahar, G., Henrich, C. C., Blatt, S. J., Ryan, R., & Little, T. D., 'Interpersonal relatedness, self-definition, and their motivational orientation during adolescence: A theorical and empirical integration', *Developmental Psychology*, *39*(3), 470–483 (2003)

10 Neureiter, M., & Traut-Mattausch, E., 'An Inner Barrier to Career Development: Preconditions of the Impostor Phenomenon and Consequences for Career Development', *Frontiers in Psychology*, *7* (2016)

11 Kim, J. J., Parker, S. L., Doty, J. R., Cunnington, R., Gilbert, P., & Kirby, J. N., 'Neurophysiological and behavioural markers of compassion', *Scientific Reports*, 10(1), 6789 (2020)

12 Dunne, S., Sheffield, D., & Chilcot, J., 'Brief report: Self-compassion, physical health and the mediating role of health-promoting behaviours', *Journal of Health Psychology*, *23*(7), 993–999 (2018)

13 Breines, J. G., & Chen, S., 'Self-Compassion Increases Self-Improvement Motivation', *Personality and Social Psychology Bulletin*, *38*(9), 1133–1143 (2012)

Further reading and sources

van Schie, C. C., Chiu, C.-D., Rombouts, S. A. R. B., Heiser, W. J., & Elzinga, B. M., 'When compliments do not hit but critiques do: an fMRI study into self-esteem and self-knowledge in processing social feedback', *Social Cognitive and Affective Neuroscience*, *13*(4), 404–417 (2018)

Suvilehto, P., & Latomaa, T., 'Writing with horses: poetry with therapeutic art activities supporting self-expression in a case study', *Journal of Poetry Therapy*, *31*(4), 224–243 (2018)

Ackerman, C., 'What Is Self-Efficacy Theory? (Incl 8 Examples & Scales)', positivepsychology.com (2018)

Ohlin, B., '5 Steps to Develop Self-Compassion & Overcome Your Inner Critic', positivepsychology.com (2016)

Robson, D., 'Why self-compassion – not self-esteem – leads to success', bbc.com/worklife (2021)

CHAPTER 13

1 Sirois, F., & Pychyl, T., 'Procrastination and the Priority of Short-Term Mood Regulation: Consequences for Future Self', *Social and Personality Psychology Compass*, *7*(2), 115–127 (2013)

2 Steel, P., & König, C. J., 'Integrating theories of motivation', *The Academy of Management Review*, *31*(4), 889–913 (2006)

3 Zhang, S., Liu, P., & Feng, T., 'To do it now or later: The cognitive mechanisms and neural substrates underlying procrastination', *WIREs Cognitive Science*, *10*(4) (2019)

4 Zhang, W., Wang, X., & Feng, T., 'Identifying the Neural Substrates of Procrastination: a Resting-State fMRI Study', *Scientific Reports*, *6*(1), 33203 (2016)

5 Ibid.

6   Wypych, M., Michałowski, J. M., Droździel, D., Borczykowska, M.,
    Szczepanik, M., & Marchewka, A., 'Attenuated brain activity during
    error processing and punishment anticipation in procrastination – a
    monetary Go/No-go fMRI study', *Scientific Reports*, 9(1), 11492 (2019)

7   Michałowski, J. M., Wiwatowska, E., & Weymar, M., 'Brain potentials
    reveal reduced attention and error-processing during a monetary
    Go/No-Go task in procrastination', *Scientific Reports*, 10(1), 19678
    (2020)

8   Schlüter, C., Arning, L., Fraenz, C., Friedrich, P., Pinnow, M.,
    Güntürkün, O., Beste, C., Ocklenburg, S., & Genc, E., 'Genetic variation
    in dopamine availability modulates the self-reported level of action
    control in a sex-dependent manner', *Social Cognitive and Affective
    Neuroscience*, 14(7), 759–768 (2019)

9   Steel, P., 'The nature of procrastination: A meta-analytic and theoretical
    review of quintessential self-regulatory failure', *Psychological Bulletin*,
    133(1), 65–94 (2007)

10 Lieder, F., Chen, O. X., Krueger, P. M., & Griffiths, T. L., 'Cognitive
    prostheses for goal achievement', *Nature Human Behaviour*, 3(10),
    1096–1106 (2019)

11 Schutte, N. S., & del Pozo de Bolger, A., 'Greater Mindfulness is Linked
    to Less Procrastination', *International Journal of Applied Positive
    Psychology*, 5(1–2), 1–12 (2020)

Further reading and sources

Dietrich, D., 'Overcoming pandemic procrastination', Mayo Clinic
    (2021)

Jamieson, J. P., Black, A. E., Pelaia, L. E., Gravelding, H., Gordils,
    J., & Reis, H. T., 'Reappraising stress arousal improves affective,
    neuroendocrine, and academic performance outcomes in community
    college classrooms', *Journal of Experimental Psychology: General*,
    151(1), 197–212 (2022)

Feng, Z., Nagase, A. M., & Morita, K., 'A Reinforcement Learning
    Approach to Understanding Procrastination: Does Inaccurate Value
    Approximation Cause Irrational Postponing of a Task?', *Frontiers in
    Neuroscience*, 15 (2021)

Ling, T., 'The puzzling psychology of procrastination and how to stop it',
    sciencefocus.com (2021)

Exadaktylos, F., & van den Bergh, J., 'Energy-related behaviour and rebound when rationality, self-interest and willpower are limited', *Nature Energy*, 6(12), 1104–1113 (2021)

CHAPTER 14

1   di Domenico, S. I., & Ryan, R. M., 'The Emerging Neuroscience of Intrinsic Motivation: A New Frontier in Self-Determination Research', *Frontiers in Human Neuroscience*, 11 (2017)

2   Simpson, E. H., Gallo, E. F., Balsam, P. D., Javitch, J. A., & Kellendonk, C., 'How changes in dopamine D2 receptor levels alter striatal circuit function and motivation', *Molecular Psychiatry*, 27(1), 436–444 (2022)

3   Volkow, N. D., Wise, R. A., & Baler, R., 'The dopamine motive system: implications for drug and food addiction', *Nature Reviews Neuroscience*, 18(12), 741–752 (2017)

4   Trifilieff, P., & Martinez, D., 'Imaging addiction: D2 receptors and dopamine signaling in the striatum as biomarkers for impulsivity', *Neuropharmacology*, 76, 498–509 (2014)

5   di Domenico, S. I., & Ryan, R. M., 'The Emerging Neuroscience of Intrinsic Motivation: A New Frontier in Self-Determination Research', *Frontiers in Human Neuroscience*, 11 (2017)

6   Gyurkovics, M., Kotyuk, E., Katonai, E. R., Horvath, E. Z., Vereczkei, A., & Szekely, A., 'Individual differences in flow proneness are linked to a dopamine D2 receptor gene variant', *Consciousness and Cognition*, 42, 1–8 (2016)

7   Alcaro, A., Huber, R., & Panksepp, J., 'Behavioral functions of the mesolimbic dopaminergic system: An affective neuroethological perspective', *Brain Research Reviews*, 56(2), 283–321 (2007)

8   Ulrich, M., Keller, J., Hoenig, K., Waller, C., & Grön, G., 'Neural correlates of experimentally induced flow experiences', *NeuroImage*, 86, 194–202 (2014)

9   di Domenico, S. I., & Ryan, R. M., 'The Emerging Neuroscience of Intrinsic Motivation: A New Frontier in Self-Determination Research', *Frontiers in Human Neuroscience*, 11 (2017)

10 Deng, H., Xiao, X., Yang, T., Ritola, K., Hantman, A., Li, Y., Huang, Z. J., & Li, B., 'A genetically defined insula-brainstem circuit selectively controls motivational vigor', *Cell*, 184(26), 6344-6360.e18 (2021)

11 Müller, T., Klein-Flügge, M. C., Manohar, S. G., Husain, M., & Apps, M. A. J., 'Neural and computational mechanisms of momentary fatigue and persistence in effort-based choice', *Nature Communications*, *12*(1), 4593 (2021)

12 Beshears, J., Dai, H., Milkman, K. L., & Benartzi, S., 'Using fresh starts to nudge increased retirement savings', *Organizational Behavior and Human Decision Processes*, *167*, 72–87 (2021)

13 Valdez, P., 'Circadian Rhythms in Attention', *The Yale Journal of Biology and Medicine*, *92*(1), 81–92 (2019)

Further reading and sources

Ling, T., 'Your motivation is at rock bottom. Here's how neuroscience can help', sciencefocus.com (2021)

Zinchenko, O., Savelo, O., & Klucharev, V., 'Role of the prefrontal cortex in prosocial and self-maximization motivations: an rTMS study', *Scientific Reports*, *11*(1), 22334 (2021)

Zhang, X., Guan, W., Yang, T., Furlan, A., Xiao, X., Yu, K., An, X., Galbavy, W., Ramakrishnan, C., Deisseroth, K., Ritola, K., Hantman, A., He, M., Josh Huang, Z., & Li, B., 'Genetically identified amygdala–striatal circuits for valence-specific behaviors', *Nature Neuroscience*, *24*(11), 1586–1600 (2021)

Hori, Y., Nagai, Y., Mimura, K., Suhara, T., Higuchi, M., Bouret, S., & Minamimoto, T., 'D1- and D2-like receptors differentially mediate the effects of dopaminergic transmission on cost–benefit evaluation and motivation in monkeys', *PLOS Biology*, *19*(7), e3001055 (2021)

Correia, P. A., Lottem, E., Banerjee, D., Machado, A. S., Carey, M. R., & Mainen, Z. F., 'Transient inhibition and long-term facilitation of locomotion by phasic optogenetic activation of serotonin neurons', *ELife*, *6* (2017)

MacInnes, J. J., Dickerson, K. C., Chen, N., & Adcock, R. A., 'Cognitive Neurostimulation: Learning to Volitionally Sustain Ventral Tegmental Area Activation', *Neuron*, *89*(6), 1331–1342 (2016)

Hamid, A. A., Pettibone, J. R., Mabrouk, O. S., Hetrick, V. L., Schmidt, R., vander Weele, C. M., Kennedy, R. T., Aragona, B. J., & Berke, J. D., 'Mesolimbic dopamine signals the value of work', *Nature Neuroscience*, *19*(1), 117–126 (2016)

Berke, J. D., 'What does dopamine mean?', *Nature Neuroscience*, *21*(6), 787–793 (2018)

Lüscher, C., Robbins, T. W., & Everitt, B. J., 'The transition to compulsion in addiction', *Nature Reviews Neuroscience*, *21*(5), 247–263 (2020)

CHAPTER 15

1   Hollands, G. J., Bignardi, G., Johnston, M., Kelly, M. P., Ogilvie, D., Petticrew, M., Prestwich, A., Shemilt, I., Sutton, S., & Marteau, T. M., 'The TIPPME intervention typology for changing environments to change behaviour', *Nature Human Behaviour*, *1*(8), 0140 (2017)

2   Garnett, E. E., Balmford, A., Sandbrook, C., Pilling, M. A., & Marteau, T. M., 'Impact of increasing vegetarian availability on meal selection and sales in cafeterias', *Proceedings of the National Academy of Sciences*, *116*(42), 20923–20929 (2019)

3   Hollands, G. J., Shemilt, I., Marteau, T. M., Jebb, S. A., Lewis, H. B., Wei, Y., Higgins, J. P. T., & Ogilvie, D., 'Portion, package or tableware size for changing selection and consumption of food, alcohol and tobacco', *Cochrane Database of Systematic Reviews*, *2018*(11) (2015)

4   Vohs, K. D., Redden, J. P., & Rahinel, R., 'Physical Order Produces Healthy Choices, Generosity, and Conventionality, Whereas Disorder Produces Creativity', *Psychological Science*, *24*(9), 1860–1867 (2013)

5   Li, Z., Liu, N., & Li, S., 'Environmental Orderliness Affects Self-Control and Creative Thinking: The Moderating Effects of Trait Self-Control', *Frontiers in Psychology*, *11* (2020)

6   Guarana, C. L., Barnes, C. M., & Ong, W. J., 'The effects of blue-light filtration on sleep and work outcomes', *Journal of Applied Psychology*, *106*(5), 784–796 (2021)

7   Keeler, K. R., & Cortina, J. M., 'Working to the Beat: A Self-Regulatory Framework Linking Music Characteristics to Job Performance', *Academy of Management Review*, *45*(2), 447–471 (2020)

8   Emery, L. F., Gardner, W. L., Finkel, E. J., & Carswell, K. L., '"You've Changed": Low Self-Concept Clarity Predicts Lack of Support for Partner Change', *Personality and Social Psychology Bulletin*, *44*(3), 318–331 (2018)

9   Fivecoat, H. C., Tomlinson, J. M., Aron, A., & Caprariello, P. A., 'Partner support for individual self-expansion opportunities', *Journal of Social and Personal Relationships*, *32*(3), 368–385 (2015)

10   Kim, E. J., & Lee, K. R., 'Effects of an examiner's positive and negative feedback on self-assessment of skill performance, emotional response, and self-efficacy in Korea: a quasi-experimental study', *BMC Medical Education*, *19*(1), 142 (2019)

11   Casal, S., DellaValle, N., Mittone, L., & Soraperra, I., 'Feedback and efficient behavior', *PLOS ONE*, *12*(4), e0175738 (2017)

12   Wing, R. R., & Jeffery, R. W., 'Benefits of recruiting participants with friends and increasing social support for weight loss and maintenance', *Journal of Consulting and Clinical Psychology*, *67*(1), 132–138 (1999)

13   Shteynberg, G., & Galinsky, A. D., 'Implicit coordination: Sharing goals with similar others intensifies goal pursuit', *Journal of Experimental Social Psychology*, *47*(6), 1291–1294 (2011)

14   Klein, H. J., Lount, R. B., Park, H. M., & Linford, B. J., 'When goals are known: The effects of audience relative status on goal commitment and performance', *Journal of Applied Psychology*, *105*(4), 372–389 (2020)

15   Lee, D. S., & Ybarra, O., 'Cultivating Effective Social Support Through Abstraction', *Personality and Social Psychology Bulletin*, *43*(4), 453–464 (2017)

16   Huang, S., Lin, S. C., & Zhang, Y., 'When individual goal pursuit turns competitive: How we sabotage and coast', *Journal of Personality and Social Psychology*, *117*(3), 605–620 (2019)

CHAPTER 16

1   Diekelmann, S., & Born, J., 'Slow-wave sleep takes the leading role in memory reorganization', *Nature Reviews Neuroscience*, *11*(3), 218–218 (2010)

2   Li, Z., Sheth, A. B., & Sheth, B. R., 'What drives slow wave activity during early non-REM sleep: Learning during prior wake or effort?', *PLOS ONE*, *12*(10), e0185681 (2017)

3   Marshall, L., Helgadóttir, H., Mölle, M., & Born, J., 'Boosting slow oscillations during sleep potentiates memory', *Nature*, *444*(7119), 610–613 (2006)

4   Aeschbach, D., Cutler, A. J., & Ronda, J. M., 'A Role for Non-Rapid-Eye-Movement Sleep Homeostasis in Perceptual Learning', *Journal of Neuroscience*, *28*(11), 2766–2772 (2008)

5   Lee, Y. F., Gerashchenko, D., Timofeev, I., Bacskai, B. J., & Kastanenka, K. v., 'Slow Wave Sleep Is a Promising Intervention Target for Alzheimer's Disease', *Frontiers in Neuroscience, 14* (2020)

6   Kastanenka, K. v., Calvo-Rodriguez, M., Hou, S. S., Zhou, H., Takeda, S., Arbel-Ornath, M., Lariviere, A., Lee, Y. F., Kim, A., Hawkes, J. M., Logan, R., Feng, D., Chen, X., Gomperts, S. N., & Bacskai, B. J., 'Frequency-dependent exacerbation of Alzheimer's disease neuropathophysiology', *Scientific Reports, 9*(1), 8964 (2019)

7   Bellesi, M., Riedner, B. A., Garcia-Molina, G. N., Cirelli, C., & Tononi, G., 'Enhancement of sleep slow waves: underlying mechanisms and practical consequences', *Frontiers in Systems Neuroscience, 8* (2014)

8   Cabral, J., Kringelbach, M. L., & Deco, G., 'Exploring the network dynamics underlying brain activity during rest', *Progress in Neurobiology, 114*, 102–131 (2014)

9   Kamp, T., Sorger, B., Benjamins, C., Hausfeld, L., & Goebel, R., 'The prestimulus default mode network state predicts cognitive task performance levels on a mental rotation task', *Brain and Behavior, 8*(8), e01034 (2018)

10   Kühn, S., Ritter, S. M., Müller, B. C. N., van Baaren, R. B., Brass, M., & Dijksterhuis, A., 'The Importance of the Default Mode Network in Creativity: A Structural MRI Study', *The Journal of Creative Behavior, 48*(2), 152–163 (2014)

11   Yeshurun, Y., Nguyen, M., & Hasson, U., 'The default mode network: where the idiosyncratic self meets the shared social world', *Nature Reviews Neuroscience, 22*(3), 181–192 (2021)

12   Lee, K. E., Williams, K. J. H., Sargent, L. D., Williams, N. S. G., & Johnson, K. A., '40-second green roof views sustain attention: The role of micro-breaks in attention restoration', *Journal of Environmental Psychology, 42*, 182–189 (2015)

13   Engelmann, C., Schneider, M., Kirschbaum, C., Grote, G., Dingemann, J., Schoof, S., & Ure, B. M., 'Effects of intraoperative breaks on mental and somatic operator fatigue: a randomized clinical trial', *Surgical Endoscopy, 25*(4), 1245–1250 (2011)

14   Zetlin, M., 'For the Most Productive Workday, Science Says Make Sure to Do This', inc.com (2019)

15   Facer-Childs, E. R., Campos, B. M., Middleton, B., Skene, D. J., & Bagshaw, A. P., 'Circadian phenotype impacts the brain's resting-state

functional connectivity, attentional performance, and sleepiness', *Sleep*, *42*(5) (2019)

16 Mandolesi, L., Polverino, A., Montuori, S., Foti, F., Ferraioli, G., Sorrentino, P., & Sorrentino, G., 'Effects of Physical Exercise on Cognitive Functioning and Wellbeing: Biological and Psychological Benefits', *Frontiers in Psychology*, *9* (2018)

17 Tang, Y.-Y., Hölzel, B. K., & Posner, M. I., 'The neuroscience of mindfulness meditation', *Nature Reviews Neuroscience*, *16*(4), 213–225 (2015)

18 Bodas, M., Siman-Tov, M., Peleg, K., & Solomon, Z., 'Anxiety-Inducing Media: The Effect of Constant News Broadcasting on the Well-Being of Israeli Television Viewers', *Psychiatry*, *78*(3), 265–276 (2015)

19 Skylar, J., 'Endless scrolling through social media can literally make you sick', nationalgeographic.com (2021)

INDEX

Page numbers in **bold** refer to illustrations.

brain (*cont.*)
connectivity 21–2, **21**, 24–5, 27–30, **30**, 34–5, 42–4, **43–4**, 49
and control issues 78
and decision-making 161–2, 164–6, **165**
development 33–7, **33**, **34**, 40
electrical impulses of the 15–17, **15–17**, 28–9, **28**
energy supply 52–3, **53**
and evolution 18, 27, 30–3, **31**
and focus 106–8, **107**
functions 18–21
and genetics 36–8
and goal-directed behaviour 59
and gut microbes 22–3, **23**
and habits 140–1
and imposter phenomenon 181
internal wiring 4
and junk proteins 235
language centres 94–5, **95**
and the 'little and often' approach 4–5
lobes 19, **19**
and motivation 209–12, **209**, **211**
as network 20–2, **21**, 29–30, 36, 43
and neural pruning 27–8, 34–5, **35**
as part of a system 22–3
and procrastination 193, 195–7, 204
and pushback 3–4, 6, 219
response storage 41–3
and resting/recharging 231, 234–6
reward systems of the 45, 155–6, 165, 181
and routines 133
and safety-seeking 49
and self-compassion 182
and self-esteem 178–9
and self-identity 121–3, **122**
shaping of 33–7, **33**, **34**, 40
and social prediction errors 178–9, **178**
weight 34
brain damage 20, 92
brain networks 3
brain surgery 94–6, **94**
brain waves 35, 235
brain–body connection 22–3
brain-imaging 20, 166–7, 182, 211
brainstem 18, **18**
Braintenance
maintenance 7, 189–242
mastery 7, 73–130
mechanics 7, 9–71
methods 7, 131–88
breaks, taking 232–3, 236–7, 240–1, **240**
burnout 233

cancer 39
catastrophizing 93–4, **93**
celebration 149–50, 156, 157–8, 247

cell specialization 13
see also neurons
cerebellum 18–19, **18**
cerebral cortex 18, **18**, 19–20
challenges 79, 182
change 3–8, 41–56, 79, 245–6
beliefs preventing 7
and the brain 3–4, 6, 41–56
fulfilling 5–6
'little and often' approach to 4–5
motivation for 212
resistance to 3–4, 6, 48–56, 139, 170–1, 219–30, 229
and self-identity 118–20
and social support 124
see also behavioural change; new behaviours
childhood experience 36, 39
chimpanzees 29, **29**
choice error 164
Clear, James, *Atomic Habits* 127, 152
cognitive behavioural therapy (CBT) 93
cognitive biases 24, 49–50, **49**, 107, 166–7, **166**, 195
cognitive control network 122–3, **122**
cognitive control system 196, **196**
cognitive ease 50
cognitive flexibility 197
comfort zones 1–2, 6, 191, 219
commitment pacts 170
communication 32
commuting 102
competence 210, **211**, 217
completeness, premature feelings of 110
compulsions 45, 210
confidence 179
confirmation bias 107
conscientiousness 37, **37**, 197
conservation 80–1, **80**
consistency 138–9, 144
control issues 78, 151, 180, 195, 221
'core self' network 122, **122**
cravings 140–1, 210
creativity 91, 144, 156, 224, 231
criticism 173–4, 180–2, 184–5, 187
Csikszentmihalyi, Mihaly 217
cybersickness 237

deadlines 170, 194–5, **195**
decision fatigue (ego depletion) 166
decision-making 24, 49, 80, 161–72, 177, 195–6
default mode network 92, 211, 236–7
delta waves 235
dementia 20, 85, 232
see also Alzheimer's disease
dendrites 13, **13**
deoxyribonucleic acid (DNA) 30, **30**, 37–9

goals (*cont.*)
  pushback against 219–23, 225–6, 228–30
  random approaches to 115–16
  and recharging 231–3, 238–40, 242
  and routines 141–2, 144
  and selective attention 107
  and self-awareness 89–91, 97–8, 101
  and self-belief 173–4, 177–9, 182, 185–7
  and self-compassion 182
  and self-identity 117, 119–20, 125–6, 128–30
  setting 1–8, 63–4, 69–71, 114–15
  and skills 112–14, **113**
  SMART 63
  and striving for more 57–71
  visualization 109
gratitude practice 66–7
great apes 58
groups 31–2
gut microbes 23, **23**

habit theory 46
habits
  altering 46–8
  and awareness 90
  breaking unhelpful 138, 140–1, 143, 145–6
  call-and-response model 134, 136–41
  formation 41–8, **42**, 121, 127, 135, 156, 207
  and goal-directed behaviour 59
  and procrastination 193, 194, 203
  recognizing other choices 90
  and self-identity 118, 123–4, **124**, 127
  triggers 134–5
hallucinations 94
happiness 64–6, **65**
healthy living 127
heart 11–12
hedonic treadmill 65–6, **65**
helping behaviours 82, 84–5
hemispherectomy 94–6, **94**
hemispheres 18, 94–5
hippocampus 20, **20**, 29, 178
Homo sapiens, dominance 29, 33
'hustle culture' 232

'ideal days' 5–6, 69–71, 85, 104
ideals 104–5, 110–11
'if–then–and' 184
imagination 32, 58
imposter phenomenon 181
impulsivity 197, 201
indecision 168, 213
information processing 28–30, **28**, **30**, 49–50
inheritance 36–40
inhibition 62–3, **62**
inner critics 180–1

inner voices 94–6, 100–1, 157, 180–2
  negative 173–6, 180–5, 187
  self-compassionate 186–8, **187**
insula 92, **92**
intelligence 32
internal control 18
interpretation 25, 96–7, 102

language 32, 94–5, 129
'last-minute-itis' 194–5
learning 35, 61, 155–6
life events 40, 78–9, 124
'little and often' approach 4–5
'looking inwards' 92

master–model–motivate 184–5
mastery-based goals 153–4, **154**, 156
meaning 77–9, 82
meditation, mindfulness 99–100, 237
memory 20, 61, 62, 107, 178, 235
'mental blinkers' 111
mental contrasting 110–11
mental preparedness 109
'mere-exposure effect' 50
metacognition 92
mice studies 39, 108, 109, 211, 235
microbes, gut 23, **23**
microbreaks 240, **240**
microsleeps 235, **236**
milestones 112–15, **113**, 154–5
Milkman, Katy 140
mindfulness 99–100, 198, 237
mission statements 85–6, 115
mistakes, learning from 61
mobile phones 44, 78, 144–6, 233–4, 237–8, 241
  intentional scrolling 241
  and procrastination 193–5, 199–200, 203
models 92, 122–4, **122**
Molaison, Henry 20
momentum 193
money, attitudes towards 81
monitoring 60–1, **61**, 66
motivation 75–87, 105
  extrinsic (external) 209–10, 217
  and habits 145–6
  'hijack' 210
  and hitting rock bottom 207
  intrinsic (internal) 209–12, 217
  learning not to rely on 205–18
  low 205–9, 213–17
  and 'pain points' 208, **208**
  and reward 140, 217
  and self-efficacy 184–5
  and time of day 212
  and visualization 109
motivators 155

vision boards 109
visual cortex 29, **29**
visualization 109–10, 198
voices
    hallucinatory 94
    see also inner voices
volunteering 114

walking 69–70, 96, 99–100, 133, 138, 142,
    155, 168–9, 213, 234, 236–7, 241
weight training 158
'what if' thinking 93, 184, 244

'what' questions 100–1
'why not me?' thinking 187
'why' questions 100–1
wind-down routines 238–9
wind-up routines 239
working days, 'ideal' average 5–6, 69–71,
    85, 104
working hours, flexible 237, 239–40
working memory 61, 62, 107
worst-case scenario planning 93, 181, 184
writing skills 135–6, 200, 227–8
    see also free writing